JAMES HOLLAND

HEROES

THE GREATEST GENERATION
AND THE SECOND WORLD WAR

HARPER PERENNIAL

London, New York, Toronto and Sydney

For Jimmy P

Harper Perennial
An imprint of HarperCollins*Publishers*
77–85 Fulham Palace Road
Hammersmith
London W6 8JB

www.harperperennial.co.uk

This edition published by Harper Perennial 2007

1

First published in Great Britain in 2006 by
HarperCollins*Entertainment* under the title *Twenty-One*

A catalogue record for this book is
available from the British Library

ISBN-13 978-0-00-721381-8
ISBN-10 0-00-721381-6

Set in Linotype Minion

Printed and bound in Great Britain by Clays Ltd, St Ives plc

Contents

Picture Credits

James Holland and HarperCollins*Publishers* would like to thank the following for providing photographs and for permission to reproduce copyright material.

While every effort has been made to trace the owners of copyright material reproduced herein, both the publishers and the author would like to apologize for any omissions and will be pleased to incorporate missing acknowledgements in any future correspondence.

Photograph Collection, Imperial War Museum
Plate section 1: page 1, middle; page 3, top right, bottom left and bottom right; page 4, top right, middle left and right; page 6, middle and bottom; page 7, all three pictures; page 8, lower middle and bottom left.
Plate section 2: page 5, bottom right.

Still Pictures Unit of the Special Media Archives Service, National Archives and Records Administration, College Park, MD, USA
Plate section 2: page 8, top right, middle and bottom.

ww2images.com
Plate section 2: page 6, middle.

Top Foto
Plate section 2: page 1, bottom.

South African National Museum of Military History, Johannesburg, South Africa
Plate section 2: page 2, bottom right.

Books
No Dishonourable Name: The 2nd and 3rd Battalions Coldstream Guards, 1939–1946, edited by D.C. Quilter (William Clowes & Son, 1947) – *plate section 2:* page 2, middle and bottom left.
German Paratroopers, edited by Chris McNab (MBI Publishing Company, 2000) – *plate section 2:* page 13, lower middle and bottom.
The Fate of the Poles in the USSR, 1939–1989 by Tomasz Piesakowski (Gryf Publications Ltd, 1990) – *plate section 2:* page 5, top left and right.

The remaining photographs are from the personal collection of:
Bill Byers – *plate section 1:* page 1, top and bottom; chapter photograph.
Tom and Dee Bowles – *plate section 1:* page 2, all pictures; chapter photograph.
Bobby Brown – *plate section 1:* page 3, top left; chapter photograph.
Bill Laity – *plate section 1:* page 4, top left and bottom right; chapter photograph.
John Leaver – *plate section 1:* page 5, top left, top right and bottom; chapter photograph.
Warren and Frances Evans – *plate section 1:* page 6, top left and right; chapter photograph.
Sir Ken Adam – *plate section 1:* page 8, top left, top right and upper middle; chapter photograph.
Sir Tom Finney – *plate section 2:* page 1, top; chapter photograph.
Giampietro Lippi – *plate section 2:* page 2, top right.
Lise Graf – *plate section 2:* page 3, all pictures; chapter photograph.
Captain M.L.C. Crawford – *plate section 2:* page 4, both pictures; chapter photograph.
Wladek Rubnikowicz – *plate section 2:* page 5, lower middle; chapter photograph.
Squadron Leader Jimmy James – *plate section 2:* page 6, top and bottom; chapter photograph.
Heinz Puschmann – *plate section 2:* page 7, top left; chapter photograph.
Bill Pierce – *plate section 2:* page 8, top left; chapter photograph.
Sir Carol Mather – chapter photograph of George Jellicoe.
Luigi Tommasini – chapter photograph of Gianni Rossi.

Introduction

When Roland Beamont turned twenty-one, he was already a veteran of the Battle for France and the Battle of Britain, had shot down a dozen enemy aircraft, and won a Distinguished Flying Cross. A year later he was a squadron leader with over sixty pilots and groundcrew under his command; before he was twenty-four, he was in charge of an entire wing of three squadrons, operating a brand-new aircraft that he personally had played a significant role in developing.

Today in the Western world none of us is forced to spend the best years of our life fighting and living through a global war. International terrorism may be a cause for worry, but it has directly touched few of our lives so far. For the generation who were born from the embers of the First World War, however, coming of age offered little cause for celebration. Youth was sapped as the young men – and women – were forced to grow old before their time. Mere boys found themselves facing life-threatening danger and the kind of responsibility few would be prepared to shoulder today.

These people were an extraordinary generation. The majority of those who fought were not professionals, but civilians who either volunteered or were conscripted as part of a conflict that touched the lives of every person in every country involved; ordinary, everyday people. One of the fascinations of the Second World War is wondering what we would have done were we in their shoes. Would we have

willingly answered the call? Which of the services would we have
joined? And would we have been able to control our fear and keep ourselves together amidst the chaos and carnage? Or would we have
crumbled under the weight of terror and grief? 'How did you deal with
seeing friends killed in front of your eyes?' is a question I have asked
veterans over and over again. 'You simply had to put it out of mind and
keep going,' is the usual reply. Would we have been able to do that in
an age when we like to demonstrate mass expressions of grief and to
turn to counselling as the panacea for any trauma? One veteran who
had survived much of the war in North Africa and then the bloody
slog up through Italy told me how when his house was recently broken
into, someone offered him victim-support counselling. 'I told her to
bugger off,' he said.

Nonetheless, most veterans believe we would behave exactly as
they did. I would like to think so, but am not so sure. It was hard
growing up in the 1920s and 30s. In Britain and the Commonwealth
countries, communities had been devastated by the losses on the
Western Front or at Gallipoli. In the United States, the Great
Depression touched the entire nation; appalling poverty was rife.
Healthcare was in its infancy and the standard of living – both in the
USA and Europe – was way, way lower than it is now. Of the many I
have interviewed, over fifty per cent had lost at least one parent by
the time they were fifteen. Corporal punishment was a part of every
child's life. For the privileged, nannies and household staff ensured
that parents often remained distant figures, while among the poor, a
child might share a bed with his siblings and a bedroom with his
mother and father. This is not to suggest that the twenty-one-year-
olds of the war generation loved any less than we do today, or had
fewer feelings; of course they did not. But perhaps their expectations
were lower. Perhaps they were used to hardship in a way that is unfa-
miliar to us today. For those in Britain and her Dominions, the post-
Great War generation also grew up during a time when wars and
conflict were a part of British life. Even after the slaughter of the First
World War, there were still plenty of Empire spats: in Ireland,

Afghanistan, and along the North-West Frontier. Iraq. And while during the inter-war years, the United States largely stuck to her iso-lationist policy, life was every bit as hard in America, if not more so, than in Britain.

Perhaps we are too soft in this age of Health and Safety, when the threat of litigation means we are mollycoddled and protected more than ever before. Certainly we are less interesting. For all its horrors, no one can deny that the Second World War provided human drama on an enormous scale. The First World War, despite the terrifying ordeal of the trenches, did not touch as many lives as the war of 1939–45, where in Europe, certainly, the majority of civilians, as well as combatants, found themselves in the front line. Britain suffered considerable aerial bombardment, severe rationing, displacement of many thousands of men, women and children and dispatched its young men all around the globe to fight for a better world. By 1945, the United Kingdom had sent off so many men to war that there were almost no reserves of manpower left. Yet compared to Germany, Italy, Russia or Eastern Europe, Britain got off lightly. So, too, did the United States, but this is not to demean their huge losses. Of the front-line formations in northwest Europe and Italy, America suffered 120 per cent casualties between D-Day and VE Day. In the Pacific, the trauma for US troops was even worse, where they suffered unimaginable horror as they battered their way from one tiny dot in the ocean to another. The Battle for Okinawa, raging while in Europe the Allied armies were enjoying the fruits of victory, was one of the bloodiest, if not *the* bloodiest, battle of the entire war.

No one in their right mind would wish another world war, but no matter how terrible it may have been, many who lived through it will also admit that when facing death every day, they never felt more intensely alive. When one said goodbye to friends or family, one might well be doing so for the last time, so worrying over trivialities was pointless, and petty disagreements and squabbles were often cast aside. *Carpe diem* was not a catchphrase but a state of mind, and this meant that most people were far better at living back then than we are today. Communities were drawn together by the war. Britain as a whole was more united than it has been since; the same can be said of the United States. There was a collective understanding that the burden of war needed to be shared. This has long gone. As every year takes us further away from the war, so we become more selfish, more materialistic, more interested in the minutiae of life.

For those in the firing line, the war also provided extraordinary bonds of comradeship, that special link between brothers in arms that can only be forged in wartime; it is something that cannot be experienced or truly understood by those who have never seen active service, as any combat veteran will tell you. For all the death and destruction that surrounded them, this bond was a positive, something they have experienced that has enriched their lives; something they keep for ever.

This is not to glorify war, however. One can appreciate some of the human qualities and priorities of wartime without feeling nostalgic for a time when millions of people were being killed, wounded and severed from their homes and families. Nonetheless, it is the positive aspects of war that, understandably, many veterans like to think about in their twilight years: this is basic human instinct. There is also no question that only in the last fifteen or twenty years have many of the veterans begun talking and writing about their experiences.

After the war, most wanted to get home and get on with their lives. Find a job, marry, have kids and settle into 'normal' life once more. They never thought of themselves as special because everyone had been in the same boat. Only once they had retired, with their children flown the nest, did they have the time to really analyse what had happened to them. Most veterans tell me the same: 'I never really talked about it until I was in my seventies when I started going to reunions.' Perspective takes time. A period of quarantine is needed. Most veterans need maturity, not the callowness of youth, to be able to properly weigh up the experience of what happened to them.

There is also a sense that time is marching on. Most veterans are now over eighty and many feel the need to tell their stories before they are gone for ever. And as their numbers dwindle, their experiences cease to be commonplace, but rather special instead. 'Only now am I beginning to realize that what I did back then was pretty incredible,' one former fighter pilot told me.

The wheel of change has been swift in recent years, which often makes the sixty years since the end of the Second World War seem longer than it really is. Yet talking to many of those who lived through those times soon draws the war closer again. Sixty years is not *that* long really – we can still touch it through these survivors, and still find inspiration from their heroism.

Those that survive, are, of course, the lucky ones. They have had a chance to live full lives and to grow old. A former German paratrooper visited Cassino in Italy for the sixtieth anniversary of that most terrible battle. He toured all the cemeteries, hugged his former comrades and enemies, and told me the story of his friend who had died slowly in his arms. 'And here we all are now,' he said, 'so what was the point?' We are fortunate today that we can make the most of our youth. Europe is now united and the United States our ally still. The generation who fought in the war should not be forgotten, not now, while many still live, nor in the future when they are gone. We should learn their lessons and remember and recognize the enormous sacrifices they made.

TWINS

Bill & George Byers

Shortly after 10 a.m. on Wednesday, 3 November 1943, a cipher clerk at RAF Leeming in Yorkshire received a signal from Bomber Command Headquarters that there would be an operation that night. There was nothing unusual about this – they often came in about this time, after the morning meeting at High Wycombe. A WAAF immediately put a call through to Wing Commander Jack Pattison, CO of 429 'Bison' Squadron, Royal Canadian Air Force. 'There's a "war" on tonight, sir,' she told him. A few minutes later, he was in the operations room himself.

Pattison was handed the fully decoded message in silence. Another maximum effort was being called for; it was ever thus. The target: Düsseldorf, an industrial city that had been designated a 'Primary Industrial Area' in the Air Ministry's directive to Bomber Command early the previous year. Even so, and despite being in the heart of the Ruhr industrial area, the city had been attacked only four times, and not since June. But that night, Bomber Command wanted six hundred aircraft to take part, a large raid indeed. A glance at the board showed that fifteen of their sixteen Halifaxes were fit to fly. Almost maximum strength – and that included the CO and his crew flying as well.

Flight Sergeant Bill Byers wandered over to the Flight Room at around 10.30 a.m., and there learnt that he would be going out that night. A notice on the board merely warned them that they were under battle orders, but nothing more – no clue to the destination or size of the raid was given. He immediately went to see the meteorological officer to try and find out what the weather was due to be like over Europe, then called his crew together. Once assembled, they took a truck – or a blood wagon, as they were known – over to their aircraft, 'Z' for Zebra, so they could run up the engine and go through the pre-flight tests. It was a grey, damp, cold day – the kind of day that never really grew light – and drizzling slightly. Mist shrouded the airfield. The Halifaxes around the perimeter loomed like spectres. Most of the other crews had followed suit, and despite the chill stillness of the day, RAF Leeming was now a hive of activity. As well as the jeeps and trucks rumbling by, trolleys of bombs, fuel bowsers and ammunition carts were all hurrying to the dispersal areas.

Not far away, Bill's twin brother George was going through the same process with his crew. The brothers had only been with the squadron a month but were already considered quite a unique pair at Leeming – after all, there'd not been identical twins at the station before. Moreover, not only did they look exactly the same, they were also practically inseparable, apart only when with their respective crews and in the air. They even shared a house together. On their arrival they'd been allocated a married quarters house in Leeming. Dick Meredith, Bill's wireless operator, shared the house with Bill and George. The twins took a room upstairs, while Dick and several other crew members took rooms downstairs. 'They were so much alike, you could barely tell them apart,' recalled Dick when I spoke to him some time later. 'And so close. They never said, "Where's *my* shirt or socks?" but "Where's *our* shirt?"'

Shortly after the pre-flight tests, it was time for lunch – a simple but nutritious hot meal, followed by chocolate or biscuits. Bill would always take a bar of chocolate and a tin of apple juice with him on the mission, but it was important to make sure the crews were well fed before they took off. The food was a perk of the job – and there needed to be some – for while most in Britain struggled with the stringent rationing, there were fewer shortages for the bomber boys. Bill and George ate their meal with Dick Meredith and some of their other crew members in the sergeants' mess. Strangely, although the twins were the captains of their aircraft, they were not officers, even though two members of their respective crews were, and messed separately; the social divide between officers and non-commissioned officers might have been put to one side in some theatres of the war, but not so in Britain. Not everyone felt like eating a heavy meal – nerves and apprehension gave people a nauseous sensation in their stomachs. The key was to try not to think about it too much, and to keep the conversation going. Distraction was everything.

Between the end of lunch and the final briefing there was not much time – the chance for a quick game of cards, or to write a letter, but not much more. In the Flight Rooms, they would put on silk underwear, thick pullovers and flying boots, then head to the Briefing Room. There, all the crews came together, not just from 429 Squadron, but 427 'Lion' Squadron as well, also based at Leeming: pilots, navigators, flight engineers, air bombers, wireless operators and the air gunners, piling in and scraping back chairs as they sat down. Since that first message earlier in the day, more information had reached Leeming about the route, the bomb loads required, timings, and, crucially, frequent weather updates. In the Briefing Room, there were rows of desks on which pilots and crews could make notes, while on the end wall was a large map, covered over with a cloth until the Station Commander came in and announced the destination. This could be an anxious moment: the further away, and the deeper into Germany the raid, the more dangerous it was. Then the Navigation Officer spoke, explaining the forming-up procedure and the route to Düsseldorf, marked on the map with lines of white tape. The Met Officer was next. Despite the low cloud over northern England, the target area was, he assured them, expected to be clear. Bill listened carefully, jotting down a few notes on a scrap of paper. This was only his second mission as skipper and he felt his stomach tighten.

The briefing over, the crews collected the rest of their kit – flight suits and Irvins, flak jackets, Mae West lifejackets, as well as chocolate and apple juice, then clambered once more into the blood wagons and set off for their aircraft. It was nearly four o'clock by the time they reached their Halifaxes, and the light was already beginning to fade. Once aboard their aircraft they waited for nearly half an hour. In the cockpit, some twenty-two feet off the ground, Bill went through final checks. It was cold in there, without the heat from the engines to warm it up. It smelled of metal, dust and oil. And it was quiet; there was no more joking, no laughter. The mood amongst all the crew was now serious, their thoughts directed to the job in hand. Christian names and nicknames were replaced with their proper titles: Navigator, Mid Upper Gunner, Skipper – with communication through the aircraft's intercom. The minutes seemed to have slowed. As Bill was discovering, this half-hour before they took off was the worst part of the whole trip. He felt scared – of course he did. Anyone who said they weren't was a liar as far as he was concerned.

At last the signal came and Bill started the four Rolls-Royce engines, licks of flame flicking from the exhaust outlet brightly against the darkening sky. The great aircraft shook and they moved into line, taxiing onto the perimeter track running around the left side of the airfield. Further away, 427 Squadron were lining up on the right. The first Halifax from 429 thundered down the runway at 4.25 p.m., then off went a plane from 427, the two squadrons feeding in turns from their respective sides of the main runway. Bill inched his aircraft forward. George was two ahead. At a quarter-to-five, he watched his brother reach the top of the runway, pause, then accelerate and lumber into the air. Three minutes later, it was his turn. As he taxied round, he saw the usual groups of groundcrew and WAAFs along the edge of the airfield. As Bill pushed open the throttle and felt the Halifax clatter and surge forward he could see them waving and holding their thumbs up in a sign that meant good luck. With both hands, he gently pulled back the control column and felt the Halifax lift from the ground, the perimeter hedge disappearing beneath them. Trees, roads, villages rushed by and then they were in cloud and climbing high into a dark and uncertain sky.

The first time I met Bill Byers was on a warm but blustery day in May 2002 at Croft Racing Circuit in North Yorkshire, England. He was there with a number of veterans and their families for the unveiling of a plaque dedicated to the men of the Royal Canadian Air Force who had flown from there during the war. I noticed Bill because he stood out so obviously from the other veterans. Wearing a baseball jacket and cap, he moved about easily and when he talked it was with a quiet but animated Canadian accent that sounded many years younger than his eighty-two years. Wandering over, I introduced myself and we soon got chatting. He'd only been at Croft a short while during the war. It was not long after his arrival in Britain in the summer of 1943. He and his identical twin brother George had been sent there to convert from twin- to four-engine bombers. After that they'd both joined 429 'Bison' Squadron, RCAF, based down the road at Leeming, flying Halifaxes. He told me about the weather that winter. 'Boy, it was cold,' he said. When it wasn't snowing it was raining. Because they always flew their bombing missions at night, the lack of sunshine started to really get him down. At one point, he realized he'd not seen a hint of sunlight in over two weeks, so with no ops that evening, told his crew they were going for a practice flight and took them high above the clouds. 'I just needed to see some sunlight,' he told me. 'We flew up and down the country, and felt much better after that.'

We were still talking when someone started pointing to a dot in the sky beyond the trees at the end of the circuit. Then we heard the faint thrum of engines and in what seemed like no time at all, the Battle of Britain Memorial Flight's Lancaster was humming past. After one flypast we began to talk again, but then the Lancaster slowly banked and turned in for another sweep over our heads. Everyone gazed skywards, mesmerized, as it then circled again and came back for a third pass. Once it had disappeared over the horizon, I turned back to Bill who introduced me to his wife, Lil. They'd met during the war. She had been a young girl from nearby Northallerton, and when Bill finished his combat tour they'd got married and after the war she'd journeyed with him back to his native Vancouver.

'We've made the trip back to England about twenty times since the war,' Bill grinned. 'I love it here. And you see, my mother was English too. She met my dad during the First World War, so I've always felt attached to the place.'

We met again some eighteen months later at their home in Redwood City, a few miles south of San Francisco in California. It was a couple of weeks before Christmas, but in Carmel Drive it was warm and, for the most part, sunny. They'd moved there over forty years ago – his job with the Post Office had been 'boring as anything', and his cousin, Hal, had always wanted him to come on down to California. So finally that's what they did, with Bill buying into Hal's masonry business in November 1959. It turned out to be a good move. 'We did reasonably well,' Bill told me, 'and we're secure financially. We've been able to do what we wanted to.'

He suddenly leant forward, his fingers together. There was still a lot of energy there; he never seemed to sit still for long. 'But you want to hear about the war,' he said. 'What do you want to know?'

Let's go back to the beginning, I suggested. I was interested to know about his background, about what shaped him, and what led him to fly bombers from an icy airfield in northern England.

There were no other brothers or sisters, just Bill and George. 'My mother's first husband was killed during the First World War,' said Bill. 'Then she met my dad and followed him back to Canada. Then my brother and I were born.' His dad was in lumber mills, for most of the time working around Vancouver, although when the twins were six, they moved to Burbank in southern California for a few years before returning to Canada. Their childhood was, he admitted, pretty happy. He and his brother did most things together and although they had occasional spats, were very close most of the time. 'Our thoughts were often identical,' said Bill. 'Whether it was some kind of telepathy I don't know, but if we thought about some problem, we'd be sitting there looking at each other and both get the same idea at the same time. That would happen loads of times.' Neither was particularly keen on class work and they took far greater interest in woodwork and the more practical subjects. 'I hated Shakespeare until I got to England,' said Bill. 'Now I think he's the greatest.' They left school and both went straight into a course in aeronautics, part of the Dominion Provincial Youth Training Scheme. They'd been there about six months when war broke out. The RCAF was soon recruiting hard and both Bill and George were accepted, although as groundcrew rather than pilots. Their training took them to bases all around the country, but they were at Saskatchewan when they turned twenty-one. 'It wasn't a big deal at all,' said Bill. 'In wartime they don't give you a day off for your birthday.'

Shortly after, George heard that he was to be posted to another air base in Manitoba. When Bill discovered this, he wanted to be posted with him. Luckily for them there was a new warrant officer at Saskatoon who knew there was a section in the King's Rules that said brothers could stay together if they so desired. 'From then on,' said Bill, 'we pretty much stayed together all the way through.'

Around that time, it was decided that groundcrew should some-times fly in the aircraft they were working on – this was seen as a means of ensuring their work was up to scratch. Bill enjoyed this aspect of the job and could soon tell when the pilots were making mistakes. He began thinking it would be more fun to be flying and so suggested to George that they re-muster as aircrew. To get in, they had to pass an IQ test, but they'd done several of these back at school and knew the form. Both of them finished their exam in half the time allowed and both passed, and so they were sent to Ground School at Edmonton in Alberta. Their subsequent medicals revealed them to have perfect 20:20 eyesight, and so having scraped through their algebra and geometry tests, they were sent to High River, Alberta, to begin training as pilots.

Initially, they flew Tiger Moths, open cockpit biplanes, before progressing to twin-engined Cessnas. As long as there wasn't too much snow about – and for the most part they were training during the summer months – Canada was an ideal place to learn, with its vast open expanse of country. In December they both passed their wings examination and were told they'd been earmarked to become instructors. The brothers had both been hoping they would be going to England and so were disappointed. 'We were gung-ho,' Bill admitted. They were saved, however, by a couple of Australians who'd been training with them, and who had fallen in love with Canadian girls and were desperate to stay in Canada. 'I don't know whether it was the girls or they just didn't want to go into combat,' said Bill, 'but we told them that if they could arrange it, we were happy to switch. They did, and so we went overseas.'

That was in January 1943, but before they left for war, they were given a couple of weeks' leave and were able to spend one last Christmas with their family. Their mother was worried about them going, but Bill was not especially apprehensive. 'We had no idea what war was about,' he said. They crossed the Atlantic on board the former liner, *Queen Elizabeth,* zigzagging all the way to avoid the Wolf Packs. By the time they reached Scotland, however, Bill was starting to feel pretty ill. Before he knew it, he was in hospital in Glasgow with acute appendicitis. Worse, he'd been separated from his brother again, who had been sent with the others to a holding camp in Bournemouth while they waited to be posted elsewhere. Bill got out of hospital as quickly as he could – a few days after his operation he told the civilian doctor that he was discharging himself. 'You can't,' the doctor told him, but Bill insisted, so the doctor sent him to the RAF for a medical. 'What's all the bother about?' asked the Medical Officer.

'I want to get to my brother,' Bill told him.

'Where is he?'

'In Bournemouth.'

'I don't blame you,' the MO told him. 'I'm going down there myself in three weeks,' and with that, he let Bill go. He wasn't really up to it though. Having had his stomach muscles cut to reach his appendix, Bill was suffering from the undue stress this was placing on his back. 'It was at least a month before I was really fit to fly,' he confessed. But he did find his brother – eventually. Unbeknown to him, George had moved into a private boarding-house. Nonetheless, Bill worked out that most of the airmen had to walk past the park on their way to the mess, so he went there and sat on a bench and waited. Eventually he saw two WAAFs walking with a familiar-looking Canadian pilot – about five-foot-eight, and with his dark brown hair combed back into a neat quiff.

'Hi George,' said Bill as they walked up.

'Bill, you're here!' exclaimed George.

Bill recalled the WAAFs' surprised faces. 'They looked at him and then they looked back at me,' he told me. 'It was funny – they were thunderstruck.'

Bill liked Bournemouth. They were just kicking their heels but they played a little golf and went to shows and he soon began to build his strength back. The life of leisure soon came to an end, however. Since their arrival they'd hoped they would be sent to fly fighters, but it was not to be. Both Bill and George were to be trained as bomber pilots. It was at RAF Pershore that they were allocated their crews. Bill Morison, Bill's navigator, remembers how hard it was to tell the brothers apart. 'They really *were* identical,' he said, when I spoke to him on the phone. 'It caused quite a bit of confusion to start with.' After a further three months flying Oxfords and Wellingtons, they were then sent to Croft, for conversion onto Halifaxes. This was quite a jump. Four engines were a lot more to handle than two. Furthermore, the aircraft was that much bigger. 'The Halifax was a pretty fair-sized airplane,' pointed out Bill, 'and you had to get used to the different attitudes. On take-off, for example, there was slight swing, and you needed more speed to get airborne. There were all kinds of different settings. And when you landed, because the Halifax was so much taller, you hit the ground sooner.'

Bill and George joined 429 Squadron at the very end of September 1943. The squadron had been formed in November the previous year at East Moor, some ten miles north of York, then flew its first operational mission over the Ruhr two months later. In August the squadron had moved to Leeming, further north between Richmond and Northallerton, and by then the operational centre of the all-Canadian 6 Group of Bomber Command. The twins arrived at a time when the American Eighth Air Force and British Bomber Command were bombing enemy targets round the clock, the Americans by day and the British by night. The bomber war would prove fearsomely dangerous for every man that took part until the very end of the war, but in the autumn of 1943, Nazi Europe was still heavily defended by an enormous array of over 50,000 anti-aircraft guns, many of which operated in conjunction with tracking radar. In the German industrial area of the Ruhr, some anti-aircraft guns were even mounted on railway cars, which followed incoming bomber streams and kept them under continuous attack. And the skies were still held by the Luftwaffe. Particularly perilous for the night-time bomber crews were the German night-fighters, guided by increasingly sophisticated radar systems. By the autumn of 1943, forward German radar units on the Atlantic and North Sea coast were tracking the radio traffic of squadrons as they took off, with individual aircraft selected for interception. Unbeknown to a bomber crew, its fate might already have been marked before it had barely heaved itself into the sky. German night-fighters were fast, agile and ferociously armed; skilled bomber pilots could and did successfully evade them but the odds were not good, to put it mildly.

Bill and George knew little about any of this. Like most new crew, they were hopelessly ignorant and naïve with regard to what lay in store for them. They had no access to the kind of information enjoyed by those higher up the chain, and although they were aware of the basic aims of the bomber war, they did not think about any wider issues such as the relationship between the British and the Americans, or the overall strategy, or whether these endless bombing raids were actually achieving very much. Rather, they arrived eager to get on and do their bit and excited to be finally part of a real, active, front-line squadron.

Unlike the Americans, Bomber Command sent its aircraft up over Europe with only one pilot, but new arrivals were not given the controls straightaway; rather, they spent a couple of missions as a '2nd Pilot' in order to give them an idea of what to expect. Bill and George went on their first combat missions over Europe as 2nd Pilots on 3 October 1943, George getting airborne at 6.45 p.m., Bill, the next in line, just three minutes later. The target was Kassel, an industrial centre to the east of the Ruhr. It was a good day for the squadron. Two aircraft returned early because of mechanical failure, but the rest reached their intended destination, dropped their bombs and returned home safely, just under six hours after they'd set off.

Bill and George were sent out as 2nd Pilots the following night as well. This time the target was Frankfurt and 429 Squadron were part of a four-hundred-strong raid that would be the first serious attack on the medieval city. Visibility was good, and the red flares of the bomb markers were clearly visible. Just as Bill's aircraft began its run in to the target a massive explosion erupted from the ground, and a huge spout of flame burst into the sky. After they had dropped their own bombs and turned for home, Bill could still see the flames of the burning city glowing from as far as fifty miles away.

George, meanwhile, was suffering a far more alarming mission. Before they reached Frankfurt, they came under repeated attack by a night-fighter, and although they managed to escape as they came into reach of the enemy anti-aircraft guns, it was not before they'd lost one of their engines and suffered a succession of hits. There were fires on board and as they began their bomb run, they realized the electrics for the bomb doors had been damaged. This meant they had to open them manually, which was time-consuming and so they were delayed in releasing their bombs until after they'd left the target. Fortunately, they were not attacked again on their return trip and managed to make it to England with just three engines. But the situation was still perilous. Before reaching Leeming, it became clear they did not have enough fuel left to get them home. Furthermore, their landing gear had also been shot up and was now inoperable. There was only one option: they would have to bail out. Six managed it safely. Two did not: the Air Bomber and the Flight Engineer both crashed to their deaths along with the aircraft, exploding on impact in a field just short of Leeming.

A fortnight later, both brothers had been given crews and their own aircraft. On 22 October, the target was once again Kassel. George had technical problems opening his bomb doors, so once again missed the target and was forced to jettison his bomb load later. Both, however, made it back safely. As Bill recorded, 'Appeared to be a good raid.' Even so, of the eleven crews that took off that night, only nine returned home. As the twins were discovering, bombing missions over Germany were hazardous in the extreme.

Bill and George were settling in well, however. As a pre-war station, Leeming had more extensive facilities than many of the other airfields, such as Croft. Even better, the twins were delighted to be able to share a room in their house in the town, a house that had a coal fire and a bathroom. The coal store was outside and was guarded, but they would raid it anyway. The guards never troubled them. 'It was a great joke,' said Bill.

It was about half-past-five on the night of 3 November 1943, and the bombers of 6 Group were now crossing over the Channel and beginning to meet up with the rest of the raiding party. The bombers – a mixed force of mostly Halifaxes and Lancasters, but with Mosquitoes leading the way – did not fly in formation as such, but kept roughly close together in what was known as a bomber stream. There were dangers all along the way. German night-fighters lurked over the Channel. Gunners strained into the darkness, but very often the first they knew about coming under attack was when cannon fire started clattering around them. Then came the coastline anti-aircraft fire and more night-fighters, and finally an intense flak barrage over the target itself.

Bill glanced out of his side window and saw that some of their aircraft were under attack from night-fighters. One Halifax he saw plummet in flames. He pushed on, through the flak of the Dutch coast, until he was well into Germany. The anti-aircraft fire was pretty heavy over the target, but although the Halifax rattled and shook as shells exploded all around them, they dropped their bombs over the marker flares and climbed out of the fray without so much as a scratch. Their bombs, like those of most of the bomber force, landed to the centre and south of the city, destroying a number of industrial buildings as well as homes in the area.

Nearly four hours after they had taken off they were approaching Leeming once more, along with the rest of the bomber stream. Three had already returned home early with technical problems, but of those who had made it to Düsseldorf, the first landed back just before ten o'clock. Wing Commander Pattison and his crew touched down at 10.04 p.m. Bill called up Leeming flying control and told them they would shortly be joining the planes circling the airfield waiting their turn to land.

Most had landed by half-past-ten, but Bill had continued circling, waiting to hear George's voice crackle through his headset. But there was no sound of his brother. 'Skipper, I think you'd better land,' said Jim Moore, the Flight Engineer, eventually, 'we're getting low on fuel.' Reluctantly, Bill did so, the sixteen-ton bomber touching down with a lurch and a screech of rubber. Z for Zebra was the fourteenth aircraft from 429 Squadron to make it safely back. Bill hung around for as long as he could, and then made his report to the Intelligence Officer. Tots of rum and cups of tea were handed out to the exhausted crews, but as soon as Bill had changed out of his flying kit, he made his way over to the control tower, and waited. Minutes passed. Eleven o'clock came and went, then midnight; but there was nothing. No distant beat of engines, just a dark and empty sky.

He waited up all night for his brother, but in his heart of hearts, Bill knew that night that George wasn't coming back. The following morning, Wing Commander Pattison offered him some compassionate leave – everyone knew how close the twins had been – but Bill turned the offer down. The CO accepted his decision, but insisted on accompanying him on a twenty-minute flight to see how he was holding up. All right it seemed – but even so, Pattison did not send the crew out again for a fortnight.

His crew did their best to help him, but it was difficult. 'There was little I could say,' said Dick Meredith, who moved into George's old bed to keep Bill company. 'We did do a bit of praying back then, and secretly I couldn't help thinking that the Lord could not possibly be cruel enough to take both George and Bill. I thought Bill had to come through, and that gave me a sense of reassurance really. It was probably the wrong thing to think, but I couldn't help it.'

Somehow, Bill kept going. On 18 November, they were on another mission, this time part of a raid on Mannheim. Strong winds of over a hundred knots pushed them way off course and so they hit Frankfurt instead. The following night, unusually, they were out again, this time to Leverkusen. 'I think that if I had stopped I might have broke down,' Bill told me. He also wanted to be there in case any news did come through. There was a chance George and his crew had been made prisoners of war – lots of them had, and it usually took about four to six weeks for word of POWs to filter through to the Red Cross. Six weeks came and went, but still Bill refused to give up all hope.

The rest of the crew never mentioned it. Some had lost good friends. Everyone lost someone. The statistics of the Allied bomber offensive are chilling: just over 110,000 men flew with the RAF's Bomber Command; 55,000, almost exactly half, lost their lives. The US Eighth Air Force, joining the battle in 1942, lost 26,000 young men. Over 15,000 Allied bombers never came back – a staggering number, and a figure that equates to three-quarters of the numbers of Spitfires that were ever made. That Bill survived and George did not was simply conforming to the law of averages. 'I don't know what makes you press on,' Bill sighed, 'but you just do. There's something in us . . . you know it's crazy, but you still do it. It's life itself. You know it's dumb and stupid but you press on.'

By the end of November, the Battle of Berlin had begun. Bill's fifth mission was what was labelled the 'the first thousand-bomber raid' on the German capital. In fact, only 764 aircraft took part, but the British press was happy to help with the propaganda. With the enemy capital deep in Germany, they could only get there by adding auxiliary fuel tanks at the expense of some of their bomb load. When they finally arrived, after nearly four hours in the air, Berlin was covered. The flak was intense, but despite the poor visibility, they could just about make out the red target indicator markers and the thousands of explosions pulsing orange and crimson through the cloud.

The bitingly cold winter and endless cloud and rain did not help Bill's sense of gloom. 'Boy, it was cold,' he said. It was early in the New Year that he took his crew out on a flight above the clouds, just so they could see some sunlight.

And he also tried to keep his days busy, and to keep his mind on the job in hand. Routine helped. He'd be out of bed some time around seven or eight in the morning, then he'd shower, get dressed and head over to the mess for a breakfast of porridge and perhaps some toast. Then he would wander over to the Flight Room, where he would chat and wait with the rest of the crews, wondering whether they'd be sent out on a 'war' that night. There could be days without a mission, but they still made sure they looked at the daily routine orders. They might have to take their aircraft to the maintenance hangars or any number of tasks. After he was commissioned in December 1943, Bill ran the station post office for a while. 'I didn't know a damn thing about it,' he said, 'and it was in a hell of a mess when I took it over.' It was another thing that kept his mind busy.

But he was rarely leaving the base. Just before Christmas, he decided it was time he tried to get out a bit, and so with a few of the others, went to a dance at the Catholic Hall in Northallerton. It was there that he first saw Lil.

Lil had been listening on and off to our conversation, sometimes sitting down with us in the lounge, sometimes attending to something in the adjoining kitchen. She now brought through some tea. 'Tea,' said Bill, his face brightening. 'We always drink plenty of tea here!' Then he got up and disappeared – he had some pictures and other bits and pieces to show me, but had to dig them out from the study next door. I asked Lil about this first meeting. 'It wasn't that night. He saw me, but I didn't see him. I remember it was so crowded you could hardly move,' she told me. She'd been taken by a young sailor friend and they began dancing. 'But he was all over me and I thought, "This is no good," so we left.'

Soon after, Bill was back, jiggling his leg up and down and sipping his tea, so I asked him about his side of the story. He grinned. 'She walked in with her head held high,' Bill said, 'and she had nice long blonde hair.' He immediately decided he had to dance with her, but he couldn't reach her – by the time he got to her side of the dance-floor, she was gone. Still, it gave him an incentive to go again, and sure enough, a couple of weeks later she was there once more – and this time there was no sign of the sailor. Plucking up his courage, he went over to her and asked her to dance.

Afterwards, he walked her home. She, too, had lost a brother – a Flight Engineer and also on bombers – and in the weeks that followed, they began to see more and more of each other. Every fifth week, the crew would be given seven days' leave. Some went to London, while others, like Bill Morison, would play golf, sometimes at Ferndown near Bournemouth, sometimes even at St Andrews, in Scotland. Bill, however, spent his leave with Lil, at her parents' house in Northallerton. Then, in the spring, he asked her to marry him, although he told her they should wait until after he had finished his combat tour. 'We were losing a lot of guys,' said Bill, 'and I was still operational.' Did Lil worry about Bill? 'No,' she said quite firmly. 'You have faith. It was a way of life; you took one thing at a time.'

Bill was also extremely lucky to have the crew he had. Crews tended to find each other on arrival at their Operational Training Units. There had been five of them at first, then at Croft, when they converted to four-engined bombers, two more had joined them. The same seven men had stayed together ever since. Close friends on the ground, they discovered a perfect working relationship that depended on mutual respect and complete trust. 'All of them were brilliant,' Bill admitted. Once the war was over, they all kept in touch, despite going their separate ways. The sense of camaraderie they had felt had been intense. Bill freely admits they were the closest friendships he ever made. Sixty years on, only Bill, Bud Holdgate (the mid upper gunner), and Bill Morison are still alive; Dick Meredith died in November 2005. They don't see each other so often now – Bill Morison is in North York, Ontario, although Bud is from Vancouver – but they do speak regularly. Bill gave me Bill Morison's and Dick Meredith's numbers and when I was back in England, I called them. Both were anxious to help and equally quick to heap praise on Bill and their other friends in the crew. 'Once the engines were running, we became a real team in every sense,' said Bill Morison, in his gentle and measured voice. 'We welded perfectly.' Dick Meredith had been a farmer before the war, a reserved occupation, and could have avoided active service, but admits that he would not have missed the experience for anything. 'They were all great guys,' he told me, 'and we were a dedicated bunch. We were a very good crew, all of us, and we never stopped learning.'

As the weeks and then months passed, so the crew's number of missions began to steadily mount – ten were chalked up, then fifteen, then twenty. They went from being the new boys to the most senior and experienced crew in the squadron. Bill was commissioned in December, while at around the same time Bill Morison became the squadron's navigation leader: it was now up to him to not only help plan their routes to the target, but also improve the standard of the less experienced navigators.

Casualties during the Battle of Berlin, which lasted from November to the end of March 1944, were particularly high – 1,128 Allied bombers were shot down during this period, a staggering number. Yet every time they went out on a 'war', Bill and his crew miraculously seemed to make it back in one piece. 'Once you'd done five or six,' said Bill Morison, 'your chances were improved, but you could still get shot down at any time. The fact that you were a very experienced crew didn't guarantee anything.' On 24 May 1944, the squadron took part in an attack on the German town of Aachen. Fifteen aircraft took off, Z for Zebra included, and made it safely to the target. There was little flak – the raid appeared to be one of their more straightforward missions, but on the return home, they came under repeated attack by night-fighters, and three of the squadron's Halifaxes were shot down. All those lost had been experienced crews, the backbone of the squadron for many months. One had even been on their last mission – had they made it back to Leeming, their tour of duty would have been over.

Yet although Z for Zebra continued to make it back almost unscathed, these missions were not without incident for the crew. On one occasion Bill had thought they would never even manage to get airborne. There had been a strong crosswind and the aircraft had started to swing so badly as they hurtled down the runway that he'd thought he would lose control and flip the plane. Another time one of his port engines caught fire almost as soon as they'd left the ground. It was 30 March 1944, and they were due to bomb Nuremberg.

'That was scary,' he admitted. 'Fire in the air like that is scary. You can't just land again – not with all those bombs and full tanks of fuel.' A pipe had burst and petrol was spewing everywhere. Bill had to cut the engine immediately, but ahead was a small hill and with a quarter of their power gone, it looked as though they were not going to get enough lift and so fly straight into it. Somehow, though, he managed to clear it, and was able to get to the North Sea and discard his bomb load. He still had to burn off much of the fuel, so circled for a couple of hours before finally turning back to Leeming. They'd had a lucky escape. The girls in the control tower thought they must have crashed and so when he called up and gave his call-sign, 'Must We', they thought they were talking to a ghost.

Landing was potentially more dangerous than taking off. Although they never flew in formation, aircraft could frequently land within minutes of each other. Often the Halifaxes would be damaged, and were nearly always low on fuel. 'One night my hydraulics were shot away and I couldn't use the flaps and even the undercarriage didn't want to come down.' This was where experience came in. Bill eventually got the wheels down by diving the aircraft and then pulling back up; the force of gravity eventually locked them into place. Even so, without flaps, he hit the ground at 170 knots rather than 130. 'I went off the end of the runway,' he said.

Having finally landed and switched off the engines, a van would arrive and take them off for debriefing. There was coffee and a slug of rum, but Bill never touched either. Back then, he was not a great drinker. 'I can make an ass of myself without drinking,' he says, 'that's the way I look at it.' The Intelligence Officer would ask them about the mission. What did they see? Were they attacked? What was their view over the target? Each of the Halifaxes had a camera. As soon as the bombs were released they would take pictures, with the fourth snapping as the bombs hit the ground. 'You couldn't come back and say, "We definitely hit the target." You had to wait for the pictures to be developed for that.' Bill tells me about the time one aircraft went out on a mission then flew up and down the North Sea. Unbeknown to the pilot, he was being tracked by British radar and when he returned had not taken any pictures either. 'He was scared. There were people . . . sometimes people broke down.' Not that Bill ever saw anyone really fall to pieces. Those suffering from shattered nerves were whisked away off the station immediately, before the other men could see. 'LMF,' said Bill. 'That's what they called it. Lack of Moral Fibre. But you could only take so much; everyone will break down after a while.'

But not Bill, despite chalking up over thirty missions in ten months of front-line duty. 'I was lucky. A very lucky pilot,' he told me. One time, they were flying over Germany. It was quite dark – they were nowhere near their target – when tracer started streaming past and cannon shell bursts exploded in front of them. They'd been picked up by radar and now had a night-fighter attacking them. Bill immediately changed course, weaving back and forth as shells continued to explode either side of him. In the end he was forced to 'corkscrew' and eventually managed to shake off the enemy fighter. Another time they were flying over a city and flak – anti-aircraft shell bursts – began exploding all around. A near explosion could severely jolt the aircraft, but on this occasion Bill had just dropped his bombs and had selected the bomb doors to close, when the flak burst beneath them and flipped the Halifax onto its back. 'The gyro was telling me I was upside-down, and we were falling fast, so I immediately rolled out of it.' But they were still in a dive, with the airspeed indicator pointing at over 300 miles per hour, far in excess of the Halifax's maximum speed. 'I thought, "I'd better not pull out too fast or I'll pull the wings off," so I kept the throttle back and let her slow down a bit.' Eventually they levelled out and began climbing once more. But in that short space of time, they'd dropped around 5,000 feet. 'I heard a hell of a noise from the airplane, but the strangest thing was we suffered no damage at all. We checked everything. The crew had been holding their breath and I heard a loud "Pheww!" once everything had been ticked off.' Bill chuckles. Another time they came back and there were 173 holes in the plane. But they'd still made it home.

They could often be in the air for long periods of time, especially if flying to Germany and back. Not only did he have to concentrate on piloting and be ready to take evasive action at any moment, he had to do so in freezing temperatures. At the kind of height they were operating from – and the higher they flew the safer they were and the better the engines ran – temperatures could drop to fifty below. 'There was heat coming off the engine,' said Bill, 'but no insulation. When it's that cold, you soon feel it.' He always wore silk underwear, silk gloves and a long white silk scarf under his flying jacket, so managed to keep his upper body warm enough. The problem was his feet, with which he operated the rudder. 'Most of the time, I couldn't really feel them.' Despite the length of some journeys and the mental and physical exhaustion these missions entailed, he rarely felt too tired to fly. 'If I did, I'd open the side window and that cold air would slap me round the face.'

As well as relieving himself before he got into the plane, he also always needed to go as they began the bomb run. 'It was strange. I've never had the strongest kidneys, but I'd have to pull out and pee into this pipe. It led straight out and would just suck out the moisture. So I peed on every German city I flew over . . . '

What about dropping bombs on civilians? I ask him. 'You don't think about the people getting hit,' he said. 'I didn't build the airplanes; I didn't build the bombs; I didn't gas them – I just went there and back – the guilt was shared by all of us, you know.' He paused again, then said, 'You can't help but feel a certain amount – well, you wished it never happened, at any rate. You can't divorce yourself from it because you had something to do with it, but I don't feel responsible for the whole thing.'

On D-Day, he and his crew took part in their first-ever daylight mission. Nearly a thousand of Bomber Command's aircraft were directed against the Normandy coastal batteries. Crossing the Channel as dawn was breaking, navigator Bill Morison suddenly noticed hundreds of white blips on his H2S radar set. Informing his skipper, they soon after saw the sea full of ships from one end of the horizon to the other. Like everyone else, they had been kept in the dark about exactly when the landings would be. Despite this exciting bird's eye view of the invasion, they found the experience unsettling. In order to improve their accuracy, they flew over the target at 10,000 feet, far lower than they were used to. 'There were not many enemy fighters,' recalled Bill Morison, 'but the flak was definitely a problem.'

They flew a number of other missions over Normandy, until, on 18 July 1944, they chalked up their final and thirty-fourth mission as a crew – Bill had flown two more than the rest. It was an attack on German flying-bomb sites near Caen, and was largely uneventful – they found their markers, dropped the bombs, then Bill banked the plane, pulled back on the control column, climbed the Halifax to safety, and turned for home. Afterwards, there was a little bit of rejoicing, but not too much. Their relief at surviving was marred by the knowledge that they would now be split up and sent to different parts of the country. Their services were now needed as instructors to train the final batches of crews in the endgame to the bomber war. They were briefly reunited a few weeks later, however. Although the war still had ten months to run, Bill's combat flying career was now over so he and Lil decided to marry right away. 'It was a very happy occasion,' said Bill Morison, who, in the absence of George, was the best man.

Bill still hadn't given up complete hope for his brother, and when the war was finally over, he went back down to the south coast to meet the POWs coming back. 'I talked to lots of them – some I even knew. I wanted to check whether anyone had heard anything about my brother's crew.' They hadn't. By the time he finally returned home to Vancouver, he had become '300 per cent certain' his brother had gone down into the sea that night. 'You've got to have hope and your mind rolls over all kinds of possibilities, but eventually . . . ' George's navigator came from British Columbia too. He'd been married with a couple of kids and his father came down to see Bill. He wanted to know whether there was any chance that his son was still alive. 'And even though you want to give them hope, I said no. No way.'

It was, he admitted, a hard thing to say, but added, 'Well, wars make you hard. I used to take care of the chart that listed the crews. When the guys got shot down it was my job to take them off and put a new name on there. The first time I rubbed a guy's name off – gee whiz, it hurt me. He's gone. Shot down. No more. But after a while I was just going through the motions. I'm telling you: people get hard.'

We looked through Bill's old photographs. There were a number of him and George together from their flying training days. It's uncanny, but they really *did* look identical. Same smile, same eyes, same hair. You could see why any girl would have fallen for them. There was his citation for his DFC, and old newspaper cuttings, too. Local news-papers often proudly reported the progress of their gallant sons and the Byers's corner of Vancouver was no exception. One piece was about them joining 429 Squadron together. *'When they arrived on the squadron, the boys craved action. They got it. Within 24 hours they were off on their first operation. "We sure are glad we have been able to stay together," said Bill.'*

Bill still thinks a lot about George. 'I wonder what kind of life I would've had if he'd been here. He was the only brother I had and we were so close, you know.' And what about the war? Do you still think about it a lot? I asked. He paused a moment and said, 'The war seems like a dream now. After the war, nobody talked about anything – it wasn't until about ten years after that you started to get some books on it, but it takes thirty or forty years before a person wants to tell his experiences or say anything about it and then it relieves him somewhat.' He paused again. 'It makes it easier as time goes on; your mind gets a little more reasonable with it. I don't mind talking about it now. Time heals. In a way it's better to share it with somebody. It helps you.' Another pause and Bill looked at some distant spot on the wall. 'I think it does anyway.'

Tom & Dee Bowles

May 1944, with the Allied invasion of northern France just a few weeks away. For the past six months, the US 18th Infantry Regiment has been based in a large camp between the villages of Broadmayne and West Knighton, outside the county market town of Dorchester. It's rolling, green countryside, at the heart of Wessex, in the southwest of England. And on this particular May evening, Privates Tom and Dee Bowles and several of their friends from Battalion Headquarters Company have been given a pass out of camp, and so have headed to one of their favourite haunts, the New Inn at West Knighton. It is a traditional English country pub, quite different from the bars back home in America, but the GIs of the 18th Infantry have always been made welcome there. They've even developed a taste for the beer . . .

It's Tom Bowles who is the photographer: all through their training in the United States and in Britain, and through the campaigns in North Africa and Sicily, he has taken pictures – often surreptitiously – and he has brought his camera with him this evening. Having bought their pints, the young men step outside once more; after all, it's warm enough. There are some old beer barrels outside – it's the perfect picture opportunity, and so Tom gets out his camera and they begin taking snapshots of each other. In one, the Bowles brothers stand around the barrels, clutching their pints, alongside their buddies Dotson and John R. Lamm. In another, the two brothers perch on the broken brick wall at the entrance to the pub. They make a handsome pair in their dress uniforms: square-jawed, with high cheekbones and dark, serious eyes and just a hint of swagger – each has an arm casually draped over a leg; they're adopting matching poses. It's hard to tell them apart. There's confidence there, too, on the faces of these twenty-two-year-olds; it's not just the row of medal ribbons across their chests, or the way they brandish the shoulder badge of the First Infantry Division – the Big Red One. If they're worried about the forthcoming invasion – an operation they know will be happening some day soon – they certainly aren't showing it.

Many years later, the film will be rediscovered, and in perfect condition. When it is developed, the pictures that emerge are so fresh and clear, it's as though they'd been taken the day before. It is hard to believe the reality – that they were snapped on a warm evening in May more than fifty years earlier, just a couple of weeks before one of the most momentous moments in history.

Only a few days after their trip to the New Inn, Tom and Dee (as in Henry D. Bowles) were handing in their ties and dress uniforms and being given their kit for the invasion: new gas masks, gas-proof clothing, and even anti-gas ointment to put on their shoes. It was unusually warm that May and as they began wearing these new gas-proof clothes they all began to sweat badly: the new kit was almost totally air-tight. New canvas assault jackets with extra pockets on the front, sides and back, were also issued. So too were plastic covers for their rifles and weapons. Each man was given a fuse, lighter and a block of TNT – just large enough to blow a hole in the ground that could be then made into a foxhole; these would have been handy back in North Africa where the soil had been thin and the rocky ground hard as iron. Further instruction in first aid was given to every man, and extra sulfabromide tablets handed out. Each man would be carrying nearly eighty pounds of kit: clothing, first aid, weapons, ammunition, canteens, rations, and even candy, cigarettes and toilet paper.

Despite this increasingly frenetic activity, neither Tom nor Dee was unduly worried. During the past few months they had practised amphibious assaults, trained in bomb-damaged houses in nearby Weymouth and listened to the generals who had visited them and given them pep-talks. Large numbers of fresh-faced GIs had arrived from the United States to bring the companies, decimated from campaigns in Tunisia and Sicily, back up to full strength and beyond, but for the old hands like Tom and Dee, who had already been through two amphibious invasions, it was hard to get terribly excited about practising an assault on a concrete pillbox somewhere in southern England.

Then one day, at the very end of May, Tom and Dee came back from a visit to the nearby resort of Bournemouth to discover that they were now restricted to quarters, with British troops patrolling the wire perimeter. No one could get in or out without a special pass. 'I hadn't really given the invasion that much thought until then,' admits Dee. The following morning, they watched as the battalion's officers were marched to the former staff officers' quarters. The doors were then locked and guards placed outside.

When the officers reappeared and rejoined their companies, the rest of the battalion were finally given their briefing. Tom and Dee were both in the same company; Tom had been in Company G throughout North Africa and Sicily, but had joined his brother in Battalion Headquarters Company since arriving back in England the previous November. He'd been part of a mortar team up until then, but he wanted to be closer to his brother and figured that since he'd lost a lot of his buddies whilst on mortars, becoming a wire-man like Dee was a safer bet. Brothers were not supposed to serve in the same regiment, let alone the same company, and especially not if they were identical twins, but somehow Tom and Dee managed to get round that one. They'd been together almost since the day they joined the Army and they weren't going to be split up now. And so it was that they heard about their upcoming role in the invasion of France together.

The Big Red One was going to land in Normandy, east of the Cotentin Peninsula, along a four-and-a-half-mile stretch of coast to be known as Omaha. The beach was overlooked by 150-feet-high sandy bluffs, impassable to any vehicles except at four points – or exit draws – where roads ran down to the sand. The first wave of assault troops was to land early in the morning of D-Day, clear the beaches of mines and other obstacles, secure these four exits and then a few hours later, the next wave would arrive and, passing through the first wave, break out beyond the beachhead. Simple. The 2nd Battalion was to spearhead the second wave, coming in behind the Sixteenth Infantry on a sector of the beach to be known as 'Easy Red', smack in the middle of Omaha, and covering the 'E-1' exit draw. This at least was something: in their previous two invasions, Tom and Dee had been among the first to land. Now they would be three and a half hours behind.

Several days went by. They felt restless in their camp, but there were some perks. At one end of the camp there was a large store full of candy and cigarettes. 'They had cigarettes of all kinds down there,' says Dee, 'and you could take what you wanted.' He didn't smoke, but he took a whole load anyway. 'I figured I could trade with them later,' he admits. They also had some drink to take with them. On their trip to Bournemouth they had bought a bottle of whisky and a bottle of gin. Each man was to take two water bottles, so Dee filled one of his with whisky and Tom filled one of his with gin. 'I don't know whether we thought we were going to celebrate or what, but it seemed like a good idea at the time,' says Tom.

Then on Sunday, 4 June, they were told to get ready to ship out. The men were given one last hot meal, then at dusk clambered into trucks and were taken down in convoy to Weymouth harbour and loaded onto waiting troopships. By the time Tom made it aboard the ship, it was almost bursting at the seams with men. 'I found myself a tiny cubby hole,' he says, 'then curled up and went to sleep.' When he awoke the following morning it was to discover that the invasion had been postponed for twenty-four hours. Tom was struck by the huge queues waiting outside the chaplain's quarters. 'The line was completely up and round the ship,' he says.

Even when the invasion fleet finally began to inch out of harbour on the night of 5 June, Dee and Tom still remained calm. They'd always been pretty easy-going people, about as laid back as it is possible to be in a time of war. 'Being a soldier was our life at that time,' says Dee. 'I know some guys that worried about getting home to their wives and all, but we didn't have that. We really just had each other and the battalion, and we knew we weren't going to get back to the States until the war was over.' He pauses, then adds, 'So to me the invasion was just another job. Neither of us worried too much about it.'

By May 1944, Tom and Dee really were on their own. They had lost both parents, and although there was a kid sister and five much older half-sisters from their father's first marriage, from the moment they joined the Army they considered it as home. Identical twins, they were from America's Deep South, in northwest Alabama. Life was tough, very tough, during the Depression-hit 1930s. The family was poor, although both Dee and Tom claim they were happy enough, with always plenty to eat and enough going on to amuse themselves. There was sadness, however. Tom and Dee were no exception, losing first a brother and then their mother when they were just twelve years old. Their father was a farmer, growing fruit and vegetables that he would then load onto a cart and sell in town, but being a smallholder at that time was hardly lucrative in the Depression-era Deep South and so soon after their mother died, the family moved to the cotton-mill town of Russellville. The twins left school and went out to work – the extra bucks they brought home made all the difference.

By 1940, however, the cotton-mill in Russellville was already in terminal decline, even though the rest of the country was lifting itself out of the Depression. 'We wanted to go to work,' says Tom, 'but there wasn't no work around.' They'd applied for places in the Civil

Conservation Corps – a scheme set up by President Roosevelt to try to combat massive soil erosion and declining timber resources by using the large numbers of young unemployed. But they were turned down. Instead, in March 1940, two months after their eighteenth birthdays, they decided to enlist into the Army. Of the two, Tom tended to be the decision-maker, so he was the first to hitch a ride to Birmingham in order to find out about joining up. Since they were only eighteen, their father had to give his consent. 'I remember his hand was pretty shaky when he signed that,' says Tom. Four days later, on 9 March, Dee followed. 'We hadn't heard from Tom,' says Dee, 'so I told Dad I was going too. He said, "Son, make good soldiers," and we always tried to remember that.' After being given three meal tickets in Birmingham and a promise of eventual service in Hawaii, Dee was sent to Fort Benning in Georgia, one of the country's largest training camps. He still wasn't sure where his brother was – or even if he had actually enlisted – until eventually he got a letter from his father with Tom's address. It turned out they were only a quarter of a mile apart, and that both were in the First Infantry Division, even though Tom was in the 18th Infantry Regiment and Dee the 26th.

In 1940, the US Army was still a long way from being the huge machine it would become just a few years later. There may have been some thirteen million Americans in uniform by June 1944, but less than ten years before, there were just over 100,000, and by the time Tom and Dee joined, the US Army was still languishing as the nineteenth-largest in the world – behind Paraguay and Portugal – and much of its cavalry was exactly that: men on horseback. Tom even has a photo of the cavalry's horses massed in a large pasture at Fort Benning.

Unsurprisingly, their basic training *was* pretty basic. On arrival at Benning they were told to read the Articles of War, then were given a serial number and told to make sure they never forgot it. After eight weeks training – drill, route marches, occasional rifle practice, and plenty of tough discipline – they were considered to be soldiers. They were living in pup tents, but eating more than enough food and surrounded by young lads of a similar age, so as far as the Bowles twins were concerned life in the regular Army seemed pretty good, and a lot more fun than back home in Russellville, Alabama.

Training continued. More marching – three-mile hikes, then ten miles, then twenty-five miles with a light pack and eventually thirty-five miles with a heavy pack. A mile from home, they were greeted by the drum and bugle corps who played them the last stretch back into camp. But while this was doing wonders for their stamina and levels of fitness, they had little opportunity to train with weapons. Their kit was largely out of date too: World War One-era leggings, old campaign hats, and Tommy helmets, and although most in the First Division had now been issued with the new M-1 rifle, they rarely saw any tanks and the field guns mostly dated from the First World War. In July 1941, they were carrying out amphibious training in North Carolina when they received telegrams that their father was critically ill. Given compassionate leave, they were put ashore and hitch-hiked back home to Alabama. 'Daddy died on July 31st, 1941,' says Dee. He was just fifty-four; he had suffered his third stroke.

Soon after, their younger sister joined the Air Force, and Tom and Dee rejoined their units – in time for the Big Red One's participation in the Louisiana Maneuvers of August 1941, the largest military exercise ever undertaken in the US, in which two 'armies' were pitched against one another. They were designed to test staffs and the logistical system as much as anything, but having seen the National Guard divisions still carrying wooden rifles and lorries with logs on that were supposed to simulate tanks, both Dee and Tom began to realize just how unprepared America was for war.

They were both on leave when Pearl Harbor was attacked by the Japanese. There had been talk of war for some months, but now they were in it for sure. They also knew that since the First Division was one of the few pre-war regular army units, they were likely to be among the first in action – although they didn't have the faintest idea when or where that might be. And for the first half of 1942, they

remained in the US, moving from camp to camp, practising amphibious landings, carrying out more marches and exercises, sometimes on
sand, sometimes in the snow. 'All we were doing was moving from
one location to another and getting ready to fight,' says Dee.

Not until 2 August 1942 did the twins finally find themselves
steaming out of New York *en route* to Britain. Like most young men
heading off to war, it was the first time they had ever left home
shores. The entire First Division was crammed onto the *Queen Mary,*
one of the great pre-war transatlantic liners, but as Tom and Dee
discovered, there was little that was luxurious about the great ship
now. It had been designed to carry two thousand passengers, but on
2 August 1942, the *Queen Mary* was carrying 15,125 troops and 863
mostly British crew. 'It sure was crowded,' admits Tom. They were
given hammocks, four banked on top of each other along each wall
of a cabin. Although still in different regiments and in different
cabins, they managed to see plenty of each other, and despite being
packed like sardines, they didn't find it too much of a hardship. 'Well,
to us it was rather like being on a vacation,' says Dee. They were given
plenty of hot meals, each eaten at a table and served by waiters. The
threat of U-boats was ever-present, and there were not nearly
enough lifeboats for the number on board, but it didn't worry the
Bowles twins too much: the ship was fast, and it continually zigzagged all the way to avoid the German submarines. As they
approached the British Isles, aircraft arrived to escort them over the
final part of the journey into Gourock in Scotland.

They docked on the morning of 7 August, beneath the dull-grey
barrage balloons that floated above the harbour. The division was
quickly ushered off the ship past a line of women handing out cups
of tea and then led straight onto waiting trains. The Bowles twins,
separated once more into their respective regiments, still had no idea
where they were heading, but it soon became clear the final leg of
their journey was not a short ride. British officers appeared, demon-
strating in each compartment how to pull down the blinds; the
blackout was something new to the American troops. The train

chugged on through the night, past nameless towns and villages, until at around seven the following morning they finally reached their destination. Tidworth Barracks, some ten miles north of Salisbury in southern England, was shrouded in early morning mist as the soldiers stepped down onto English soil for the first time. On Salisbury Plain, one of the British Army's largest training areas, the Bowles twins and the rest of the division would begin preparing for the largest seaborne invasion the world had ever known – not D-Day, but the Allied landing in Northwest Africa.

Shortly before the TORCH operations in Africa, Dee had managed to transfer regiments and was now with his brother Tom in the 2nd Battalion of the 18th Infantry, although he had joined Headquarters Company, while Tom remained with his mortar crew in Company G. As a result they both landed on African soil at around the same time, on a sandy beach just east of the port of Arzew in Algeria, on 8 November 1942. They would find themselves up against stiffer opposition in the months and years to come, but in fighting the Vichy French – at that time still collaborating with the Axis powers – they faced their first time in action. It was on that first day, whilst taking cover in a cemetery near the town of St Cloud, seven miles inland, that Tom saw his first dead body. 'I saw him lying there,' he says, 'and that made a big impression on me. I thought, this is for real now.' Of all the horrors they would witness before the war was over, this first corpse affected Tom the most.

Both agree that war makes a man harden up pretty quickly. French resistance quickly crumbled and French North Africa – all those troops in Algeria, French Morocco and Tunisia – joined the Allies. While the British Eighth Army advanced from the east after their victory at El Alamein, the joint US and British force that had landed in Northwest Africa advanced from the west. The joint German and Italian Armies were slowly being caught in the vice of Tunisia.

But North Africa was no Axis sideshow. Hitler insisted on pouring hundreds of thousands of troops into Tunisia, as well as equipment:

in Tunisia, the Allies came face-to-face with the superb Focke-Wulf 190 fighter and also the monstrous Tiger Tank. So well protected was the Tiger, there was nothing in the Allied armament at that time that could penetrate its body armour. Furthermore, Tunisia was extremely mountainous and hilly, difficult terrain in which to fight. And to make matters worse, it was now winter and there was so much rain, the battleground soon resembled something out of the Western Front of the First World War. Everyone and everything became bogged down in the mud.

It was also the first time American and British forces had fought side by side, shoulder to shoulder, under one unified command. The British were the old enemy, but now the differences of the colonial era were behind them and they were allies as never before. The 18th Infantry spent forty-seven days detached from the Big Red One, fighting alongside the British Guards Division. 'We wore their uniforms,' says Dee, 'and ate their food, and drank tea instead of coffee. That tea they had was beautiful.' He even preferred British rations to the C-rations they had been eating.

The front line was fairly static during this period, but it taught the 18th a lot. Tom learnt how to dig in with his mortar team and how to get the best from the lie of the land. Dee, on the other hand, was a wire-man. He and a buddy had the task of setting up and maintaining the field telephone system. This meant running lines of wire from battalion headquarters to the various companies, and then making any repairs if the wire was broken by enemy fire. It could be pretty dangerous work, and during this time in the front line, both brothers gained valuable experience of what it was like to operate under enemy shellfire, and what it was like to be dive-bombed by the dreaded Stukas, and strafed by the Messerschmitts and Focke-Wulfs. And what they learnt was that there was still of a lot of ground and air all around them, and that it was the unlucky or careless who got themselves killed.

In February, Field Marshal Rommel launched his last offensive in North Africa, and although the Allied forces were initially heavily defeated and pushed back almost into Algeria, reinforcements from northern Tunisia were hurried south, including the 18th Infantry. Hastily digging in alongside their British Guardsman comrades, they found themselves coming under attack from the full force of the veteran 21st Panzer Division, one of the most experienced German units in North Africa. 'We saw those tanks coming across the valley straight at us,' says Dee, 'and all hell let loose.' The 18th held their line, however, and with a number of German tanks left in flames, the Panzers were forced to retreat. 'It was several days before I could hear good again,' adds Dee.

A month later, with the Allies back on the offensive, the 18th Infantry had rejoined US II Corps along with the rest of the Big Red One, and under the command of General George S. Patton, Tom and Dee found themselves dug in along the El Guettar massif, a long and imposingly jagged range of red mountains in southern Tunisia. But it was here that German forces counter-attacked, and Tom's Company G found themselves isolated on a rocky outcrop on a mountain known as the Djebel Berda. 'We were on a peak about a quarter of a mile ahead of everyone else,' says Tom. From his position he could see German tanks in the valley beneath him. 'We couldn't go nowhere,' he says, and they were beginning to run short of supplies. It was now afternoon on 24 March 1943. The enemy had been mortaring them ever since their counter-attack had begun earlier in the day, but German troops were now moving into positions to the right of them on the Djebel Berda. The Company's situation was becoming more and more precarious. 'They were looking down on us,' says Tom, 'picking us off one at a time.'

His sergeant, Nels de Jarlais, was wounded, so Tom and his friend Giacomo Patti, an Italian from Brooklyn, decided they needed to try and get him out of there. It was evening, and the light was fading. Mortars and machinegun fire continued to burst and chatter nearby. They picked their way carefully down to the aid station and collected a stretcher, then clambered back around the front of the hill. 'Probably the only reason we weren't shot was because we were carrying the stretcher,' says Tom. Having made it safely back to their positions, they were just putting the sergeant on the stretcher when word arrived from their listening post that the Germans had all but surrounded them and were about to attack.

By now it was almost dark, but suddenly flares were whooshing into the sky, lighting up their positions, and German troops were clambering up the slopes beneath them yelling at the tops of their voices. There was now no question of getting the sergeant out. Taking off the scarf he had round his neck, Tom rolled it up and put it under Sergeant de Jarlais's head to make him more comfortable. 'D'you think we can hold 'em?' the sergeant asked him.

'Yeah, we can hold 'em,' Tom replied, then hurried back to his mortar. He never saw his sergeant again. Tom quickly began firing, but he had just thirty-six mortar bombs left. Enemy mortars were landing all about him, exploding with an ear-splitting din followed by the whiz and hiss of flying rock and shrapnel. The enemy was closing in on their positions. Tom saw one mortar land in a foxhole. Sergeant Bobby Dees clambered out of his dug-out to help the wounded man. Tom yelled at him to come back, but it was too late – moments later another shell hurtled down, just twenty yards in front of Tom, killing both the sergeant and the wounded GI instantly. Soon after Patti hurried over. 'The lieutenant says we're going to surrender,' he told Tom. 'Let's get out of here.'

'When one of the officers says that,' says Tom, 'you're on your own. You can do as you please.' They scrambled over the rocks, slid down a small cliff and fell into a pool of water, but got themselves out and away to the comparative safety of Battalion HQ. 'I never hated anything so much in all my life as leaving those guys up there,' admits Tom. 'My squad leader, Arthur Winters, was wounded twice that night and captured by the Germans. And we had to leave the sergeant up there too.' Sergeant de Jarlais did not survive.

Dee had been at Battalion Headquarters all day, but heard that Company G was in big trouble, so he and two of his colleagues set out to try and find Tom. In the dark and with the rain pouring down, they scrambled up through the rocks towards Company G's position, then suddenly heard German voices. One of Dee's friends said, 'Looks like we're caught here. Shall we give up?'

But it was dark and all three were wearing captured German ponchos, so Dee said, 'No. Let's just turn around and head back the way we came.' The ploy worked. Not a single German so much as spoke to them.

In the morning on that same day, Dee had a close shave of his own. Back at Battalion HQ, he and his wiring buddy, Blake C. Owens, were told to get a wire to Company E, so having gathered a spool and armed with a field telephone, they began to lay their line towards the Company E command post. The firing of the previous night had, by now, quietened down, but desultory shell and mortar fire continued to explode among the battalion positions. Dee and Blake were trying to cover as much ground as they could by scrambling along a small wadi, when suddenly they found themselves being shot at from the rough direction of Company E's positions. To begin with Dee thought they must have been mistaken for Germans. 'So I waved at them and they stopped,' he says. On they went a bit further, but then the firing began again, bullets pinging and ricocheting uncomfortably close by. Dee waved again, and once more they stopped. They scurried on a bit further, but sure enough, the firing started up once more. They could see the shots were coming from some rocks just ahead of them, so they ran and dropped behind the safety of a large boulder, bullets whistling over their heads and pinging into the other side of the rock. Frantically, Dee wired up his phone and put a call in to Headquarters. 'We're trying to get to E Company up here,' Dee told them, 'but there's somebody shooting at us.'

'E Company?' came the reply. 'They've already left that position.' Unbeknown to Dee and Blake, 'E' had been moved to higher ground in the early hours of the morning. 'You better get out of there quick,' they were told.

'We can't,' Dee told him. 'We're out in the open here.'

'Just wait a minute kid,' said the man on the other end. 'The artillery liaison officer's right here. You can talk to him.'

The LO came on the phone and asked Dee whether he thought he could direct their fire onto the enemy position. Dee told him he would try. Shortly after two shells whistled over, but landed short. 'Raise up two hundred yards,' Dee told him from his crouched position behind the rock.

'All right,' said the LO, then added, 'now when you hear those shells coming in, you get out of there.'

'And boy when we heard that whistling we took off,' says Dee. 'The Germans still shot at us a couple of times, but we zigzagged down and managed to get away.' Both men were later awarded the Silver Star for this action. 'For escaping, I guess,' says Dee.

Shortly after this, the Germans retreated for good, and with the two Allied Armies having finally linked up, the whole of US II Corps, including the Big Red One, were moved north for the endgame of the Tunisian campaign. Company G, all but wiped out during the battle on the Djebel Berda, was hastily reinforced. They had one last bitter battle for Hill 350 in the closing stages of the campaign, but when the Axis forces in North Africa finally surrendered on 13 May 1943, the men of the Big Red One were already out of the line and back in Algiers, training for their next invasion: Sicily. They had come a long way during those six months of bitter fighting, and with victory in Tunisia came the surrender of over 250,000 enemy troops, more than at Stalingrad a few months before.

They made their second seaborne invasion on 10 July 1943, when the Allies landed in Sicily. The 18th did not come ashore until the evening, by which time the beaches at Gela had already been taken. Even so, a number of their landing craft ran into a submerged sandbar some way from the shore, and when Tom jumped into the sea, he promptly sank until the water was over his head. It was also now dark, but he still had the wherewithal not to panic, and to calmly walk forward. Soon his head was clear of the waves, and he was able to make his way safely to the shore.

The fighting was over in little more than a month, but although the Big Red One was almost constantly moving forward, Dee remembers Sicily as a tough campaign. 'It was hard fighting across every town,' he says. 'Most of it we walked.' At Troina, at the foot of Mount Etna, the giant volcano that dominates the island, they fought their last battle before being withdrawn from the front. The Big Red One would not be going on to Italy – instead they were to head back to England to begin training for their third and final seaborne invasion: Operation OVERLORD, the assault on Nazi-occupied France.

They landed at Liverpool in northern England in early November 1943, almost exactly a year after they had left for North Africa. 'It was great to be back,' says Dee. They felt as though they'd come home. The twins enjoyed their times in England – the pubs, the hospitality of the people, the trips to London and other English cities. Inevitably, many American troops soon got themselves British sweethearts and Dee was no exception. Just before leaving for North Africa, the Big Red One had been sent up to Scotland for training and Dee had started going out with a Scottish girl. 'She was singing down the street,' he says, 'and we got talking. We never got up to much – we'd just ride a tram up to the park and talk and so on.'

So for a few precious months, the brothers had a good time. They trained hard, but there were plenty of opportunities for rest and recreation – R&R – as well. Dee even managed to get back to Glasgow and see his girlfriend. 'The war was forgotten for a while,' he adds. 'I wasn't too worried.'

But by early morning on 6 June 1944, it was time to start the fighting again. Tom's and Dee's troopship was now some twelve miles off the Normandy coast, just out of range of enemy shellfire. Everyone was told to get up, put on their packs, helmets and other gear, and form into their assault teams ready to clamber down the side nets and into the landing craft that would take them to the beaches.

Before first light, the men of the 18th were doing their best to climb down into their Higgins boats landing craft. The sea was far from calm, and even the troopship was rolling. The flat-bottomed Higgins boats alongside were lurching up and down dramatically. Clambering down the nets was no easy task – it was still quite dark, they were carrying a heavy pack and equipment, and Tom and Dee also had two rolls of wire and a field telephone each – and because the men had to time their jump into the boat, the nets soon became congested. Tom's hands were constantly being trodden on by men above him. Even so, both brothers, who had been placed in the same squad, managed to successfully judge their leaps into the boat without injuring themselves. Then began a long and deeply uncomfortable wait. The brothers had lost track of one another and neither knew if they were on the same landing craft.

The first wave of troops was due to hit the beaches at 6.30 a.m., but the battle for Normandy began some forty minutes earlier. As Tom and Dee circled round and round in their landing craft, pummelled and flung against the sides as the boat crashed up and down on the rising swell, the huge naval armada opened fire, followed soon after by wave after wave of Allied bombers. The noise was incredible: the report of the guns, the sound of shells whistling overhead, and the eventual explosions along the coast.

The first wave, meanwhile, was already heading towards the beaches but things were not going well. The enemy bunkers and gun emplacements had not been knocked out as planned and many of the 16th Infantry's Higgins boats were landing in completely the wrong place. Those that did reach Easy Red came under heavy fire, with appalling losses of men. It was a similar story elsewhere along Omaha, and soon the whole operation was behind schedule. In the hold of their boat, Tom and Dee could not see what was going on, but the men manning the craft were watching through field glasses and radio messages were coming through continually, and it quickly became clear the landings were not going to plan. To make matters worse, over half the men on the boat were being violently seasick, the acid stench of vomit filling the close space of the boat. Dee and Tom were not sick themselves, but Tom admits he felt 'kind of nauseated'.

Just after 9 a.m., having been in their landing craft for over three hours, the 2nd Battalion of the 18th were ordered to land immediately to help the struggling 16th. But at the time, they were still circling some twelve miles out and it would take them the best part of two hours to reach the shore. At least they were now on their way, however. 'By that time, all I wanted to do was get on land and get on with it,' says Dee. The deafening sound of battle accompanied them all the way to the beach. 'You could actually see those shells flying over,' says Tom. 'Them things looked like a fifteen-gallon barrel hurtling through the sky.'

Before they landed they were warned they should get off the beach as quickly as they could, and not to stop for anyone. Fifty yards from Easy Red, the ramp on their Higgins boat was lowered and Tom and Dee jumped out into the sea. The beach was already a scene of carnage. 'You could see bullets hitting the sand, and the sand flying up all over the place,' says Tom, 'and mortar shells bursting all around. And in the water were bodies floating everywhere and lying all over the beach.' There was also plenty of barbed wire, countless German obstacles, and radios and other equipment littered all over the place. The water was only knee-deep now, but Dee remembers seeing bullets hitting the water all around him as he hurriedly waded to the shore. Explosions continued bursting, but Dee could only think of one thing: to get off that beach as quickly as possible.

While Dee was running as fast as he could, past the dead and dying, Tom had reached the beach and had thrown himself down in a shallow washout in the sand. 'It was a natural thing to do, I guess,' he says, 'but it wasn't no shelter at all.' He lay there a moment then realized that if he stayed there he was going to get himself killed, and so he jumped up and took off across the beach, hoping to God that he wouldn't get hit.

Both of them made it to the shelter of the beach wall without so much as a scratch, and shortly after a US Navy destroyer, USS *Frankford,* came close to the shore – within a thousand yards – and managed to knock out several machinegun nests and a pillbox overlooking Easy Red. 'That pillbox stopped firing just as we were running across the beach,' says Dee. 'I tell you, that destroyer saved a lot of lives.'

Soon after eleven in the morning, the battalion managed to move off away from the shelter of the cliff, and capture the E-1 exit from the beach. As Dee was moving up along the draw, he saw an American soldier lying to one side. 'He's laying there with one leg blown off,' says Dee, 'and telling everyone to be careful because there was a minefield up ahead.' Although Tom and Dee had become separated during the landing, Tom saw the same man. 'He was shouting, "Follow the others! Stick to the cleared path!"' recalls Tom. 'Those medics must have given him plenty of morphine. I don't know whether he made it or not . . . '

As they moved off the beach, shells continued to scream overhead, from out at sea but also from German positions inland. The 18th were now ordered to capture the tiny town of Colleville-sur-Mer, half a mile inland, an objective originally given to the now decimated 16th Infantry, but although their part of the beach was now clear, there was no let-up in the fighting. Both Dee and Tom were now busy laying telephone lines and were doing so under constant fire. No sooner would a line be laid than shellfire would rip it apart again. Off Dee and Tom would go, with their buddies, feeling along the wire until they found the break in the line. Every time they heard a shell scream over, they would fling themselves flat on the ground and hope for the best, then get up again, dust themselves down and get on with the repair work. After one particularly close explosion, Tom realized he'd lost his helmet. He looked around everywhere, but couldn't find it. Soon after, he found another and so put it on and continued repairing the lines. 'Where the hell d'you get that helmet?' asked his wiring buddy, John Lamm.

'I just found it lying about,' Tom told him. He took it off and looked at it, and saw the eagle painted onto it, and the name 'Taylor' on the back. It was Colonel Taylor's, of the 16th Infantry. Tom shrugged, picked up some mud and covered up the eagle and the name. 'I wasn't going to give it up,' says Tom.

For his work that afternoon, Tom was awarded the Bronze Star. 'Private Bowles, despite heavy enemy fire, proceeded across vulnerable terrain and repaired the wire. His heroic action contributed materially to the success of the invasion,' noted his citation.

By the end of D-Day, the Americans had gained a tenuous foothold. Tom and Dee were with the rest of the battalion just outside Colleville-sur-Mer; they had almost achieved the day's objective. But while the battle for the beaches was over, the battle for the hedgerows was now to begin, as Dee was about to discover to his cost.

The following morning, on 7 June, Dee and his buddy Private Kirkman had been laying some wires and were heading back down a track towards one of the battalion's companies, when a hidden German machinegunner opened fire from twenty yards. Kirkman was shot through the wrist, while Dee was hit twice in the arm, the back and his side. The force knocked them both backwards, off the road and into a ditch that ran alongside. Incredibly, both were still fully conscious; lying there, Dee felt numb and was unsure where he'd been hit or how badly. Together they managed to crawl about fifty yards until they reached some shrubs out of sight of the enemy gunner. They then both got to their feet and walked back up the road and managed to get some help.

Tom had been lying in a ditch trying to get some sleep when he was told the news. Hurrying up to the aid post, he found Dee still conscious but lying down on the ground.

'Are you going to be all right?' he asked.

'Well, I think so,' Dee told him. Medics were giving him morphine and checking his condition.

'Can you lift yourself onto the stretcher?' one of the medics asked Dee.

'Yeah, sure,' he told them, but when he tried to lift himself up, found he couldn't really move at all. Having been placed onto the stretcher, Dee turned to Tom and asked him to take off his belt and canteens. 'I won't need that Scotch after all,' Dee told him. Tom was relieved that his brother could still joke. Perhaps Dee wasn't too badly hit. Perhaps he'd be OK soon enough. Even so, both realized Dee would be heading straight back to England.

'Well, so long,' said Tom. Then Dee was put onto a jeep and taken away.

For all his cheeriness in front of his brother, however, Dee had been seriously wounded. Soon after, he passed out and when he woke up again, he was already on a ship heading back across the Channel. There were stretchers of wounded men all around him and he was struggling with a desperate thirst. 'But they wouldn't give me no water,' he says. 'They didn't know how badly shot I was.' Eventually, after much pleading, they gave him a wet rag to put in his mouth. 'The next thing I know, I'm in the naval hospital in Southampton.'

In England, Dee underwent a number of operations. 'Only one of those bullets was real,' he says. 'And that went clean through my arm. The rest were all wooden. It's probably what saved me.' Even so, for some time he remained in a critical condition. There were complications; more operations followed, then infection set in. He managed to come through that, but his arm was still not working properly, so he had yet another operation and they found a further wooden bullet still stuck there. Dee began to realize just how narrowly he had cheated death.

Back in France, Tom was worrying about him. 'Of course, I thought about him all the time,' he says. 'If I'd have ever met a German at that time, I would have shot him – I wouldn't have taken no prisoners.'

Not until Dee had been gone a month did he hear any word, and then it was from his sister, back in the States. Both brothers had been writing to each other, but the transatlantic mail service proved quicker and more reliable than that across the English Channel. At least the news seemed to be good: his brother was alive, he was doing well – mending slowly but surely.

There was little let-up for Tom and the rest of the 2nd Battalion, however. Over the weeks that followed D-Day, the Allies pushed forward but only slowly; German resistance, despite Allied air superiority, was fierce. By 12 June, the 18th Infantry were just over twenty miles inland, holding a salient around the town of Caumont. 'It was mainly little skirmishes,' remembers Tom. 'The Germans would try and push us back and we would fight them off.' Two, three, or more times a day, he would be sent up to the front to repair lines. It was around this time that his great friend Giacomo Patti was killed. 'An artillery shell hit him,' says Tom. Not too many of those who had landed in North Africa were still around. There were more and more new faces in the 2nd Battalion – more men, and more equipment too, as the Allied war machine gradually built up strength for the next push.

They were in this holding position at Caumont for the best part of a month, but by the middle of July, the Cherbourg peninsula had been captured by Patton's First Army, and the Americans were finally ready to launch their breakout from the Normandy bridgehead. The 18th Infantry were in reserve, ready to go through the 9th Division once the initial breakthrough had been made. On the morning of 25 July, Tom watched open-mouthed as wave after wave of Allied bombers carpet-bombed the German positions around the town of St Lo. He'd never seen so many aircraft in all his life. Red flares had been set off by the troops on the ground as markers for the bombers, but soon these were clouded by the dust and smoke caused by thousands of exploding bombs. 'You never saw so much dust,' says Tom. 'It was so bad you couldn't see nothing.' The bombers couldn't see much either, and didn't realize that a breeze was blowing the dust back over their own lines. Each new wave of bombers released their bombs over the drifting cloud of dust until, tragically, they began bombing their own troops. They killed over 150 American soldiers, and St Lo lay in ruins. 'That town was nothing but rubble,' recalls Tom. 'Even our tanks couldn't get through, it was so messed up.'

By the third week of August, the battle for Normandy was over, however. On 25 August, Paris was liberated, but the men of the 18th Infantry were not there to witness it. Instead, after a few days' rest, they began an epic journey across northern France, covering three hundred miles in just over a week. They ran into the Germans again around the Belgian crossroads town of Mons, but after a series of small battles, the enemy retreated. In early September, the battalion moved forward again, this time east towards Germany itself.

For the first time, Tom was able to fully experience the joy of the liberator. They drove through Charleroi past streets lined with cheering crowds. 'Those people just about pulled us off the Jeeps,' says Tom. 'They'd get in with us, and the girls were handing us flowers, grabbing us and kissing us. It was really something.' These were moments to savour. Tom could not know it then, but ahead lay the toughest, most brutal fighting he would take part in during the entire war.

Tom reckons that that battle for Aachen, King Charlemagne's capital in the Middle Ages and the first major city inside Germany, was the worst he ever fought. 'That topped D-Day for me,' he says. By the beginning of October, the Big Red One had moved into Germany and was holding a line roughly south and east of the city; the attack was to be launched on 2 October, with the 2nd Battalion of the 18th Infantry given the job of capturing the town of Verlautenheide to the east of the city. Having done this, they were then to prepare defensive positions against possible counter-attacks from the German garrison in Aachen itself.

Tom was given a glimpse of what was to come when he first approached the edge of the town on an eerily misty October morning. A knocked-out car lay to the side of the road and sitting on the roof was a body – with no legs, no arms, and no head. 'The torso was all that was left,' says Tom. 'I thought: this is going to be rough . . . ' The town was taken later that day, but Verlautenheide stood perched on the eastern end of a long ridge, and the fight for this ridge and the neighbouring Crucifix Hill was bitter and hard-fought with the Germans repeatedly counter-attacking. Headquarters Company was based in a three-storey building in the town, and Tom says that for four days and four nights he barely slept as they came under almost continual bombardment and had to repair damaged wires throughout the fighting. One night, Tom and his buddy had to mend a line down to H Company. Slowly, they inched forward, feeling their way through the darkness, the line as their guide. They stopped by a large tree that had been felled by the bombing near a building where H Company had set up their machineguns. They traced the wire, made the repair, and then called back to Company HQ to test it. But the line was still dead. So they crawled forward again. By now, they were doing everything they could to avoid being out in the open – at night, they were all too aware that one of the H Company machinegunners might mistake them for Germans and open fire. They mended another break, but again, the line was still dead. Eventually, they crawled all the way to the wall of the building and, sitting crouched under a window, could see that the wire led right inside. They called up Company HQ again. 'The wire's good,' Tom told them, 'so we'll go inside and try and find out what's going on.' Suddenly, machinegun fire opened up from the windows above them.

'Get yourselves back!' Company HQ told them as Tom and his buddy frantically pressed themselves against the wall. 'H Company's not in that building anymore – the Germans are!' As stealthily and quietly as they could, they crawled back to the comparative safety of the tree, then feeling their way along the wire, scampered back to safety.

Another time, Tom was crossing the cemetery next to the building where Company HQ was based, when two shells screamed over, one exploding only fifteen feet from where he was. The blast knocked his helmet forward and cut his nose. Otherwise he was fine, but as he got up again he heard someone shouting. 'They'd just been bringing up some replacements,' says Tom, 'and one of them was hit.' Tom hurried over and helped the man to the aid station. 'I had his blood all over me as well as my own blood from my nose, so as I laid him down, these medics rushed over and asked me how badly I was hurt,' says Tom. 'It's not me,' he told them, 'it's this guy here.' He has no idea whether the man he helped survived. Replacements were now coming in all the time, and, as he points out, 'you were half-gone by loss of sleep'; there was little or no energy left to worry too much about others. It was whilst still at Verlautenheide that he helped another wounded GI. The man had been hit in his half-track and Tom was asked to help get him out. The man was heavy and it was not easy lifting him up, but Tom did his best and managed to get him to the cover of a building and lay him down. No sooner had he done so than the man gasped one last time and died. Tom looked down at him and saw he was wearing a crucifix round his neck. 'I looked up,' recalls Tom, 'and said, "Well, he's yours," like I was talking to the Lord.'

By the time Company HQ moved again, only the basement of the building they'd been in remained. The storeys above them had vanished into a pile of rubble. Tom received a second Bronze Star – an oak leaf cluster – for his bravery under fire at Verlautenheide.

The fighting around Aachen lasted for the best part of a month, but later, after it had finally fallen, Tom and a friend took a jeep into the city where they came across a former German barracks and stopped to have a look around. The place was a mess – papers, clothing and furniture strewn everywhere. But Tom noticed a box on the top of a locker and reaching up, took it down. Inside was a very large Nazi swastika flag. He has it still to this day.

After Aachen, the First Division were sent south into the Hürtgen Forest, and there, with winter closing in, they suffered a brutal month. The forest was dense, full of mountains and hidden ravines, ideal country to defend, but nightmarish terrain through which to try and attack. During November, eight US divisions had tried to break through the Hürtgen Forest. 'All,' noted the First Division history, 'had emerged mauled, reduced, and in low spirits.' Casualties amongst the 18th had been as high as at any time during the war – a thousand dead and wounded. But what Tom particularly remembers is the near constant rain and the terrible, ghostly darkness. 'I never saw such a dark place,' he says. 'If you went twenty yards from your foxhole, you'd get lost.' The forest, he noticed, played tricks. One night, he was on guard duty and it was raining heavily. Near a road, he thought he could hear troops marching past. But he couldn't see a thing, so he stepped towards the road and held out his arm to see if it would touch somebody's raincoat as they marched past. He felt nothing. 'It sounded as real as could be – tramp, tramp, tramp.' But it was just the sound of the rain on the pine trees.

At the end of November, the depleted 18th were pulled out of the line and sent to a town in Belgium for a week's R&R. It was their first proper rest since D-Day. They'd only been there a few days when someone came up to Tom and said, 'Guess who I've just seen back at the depot?' Tom didn't have to guess – he knew who it was already.

After nearly six months in England, Dee was back. He could have been given a posting back home, but he was not having any of that. He wanted to be with his brother; and in any case, the 18th *was* home. Tom had mixed feelings about seeing Dee, however. On the one hand, he was thrilled to see him again – and looking so well – but on the other, he worried about him being back at the front. The experience of Aachen and the Hürtgen Forest had shown that there would be no easy victory. At least, though, they had this period of rest ahead of them, and with the shortening days and weather becoming even colder, it looked as though the front might stabilize for the winter.

And then a strange thing happened. They were talking in Tom's room in the house where he was billeted and Dee had just handed over a bottle of Scotch that he'd brought back from England for his brother, when someone shouted, 'Fire!'

'And the building was on fire,' says Dee – just an accident, it later turned out. 'So we grabbed our rifles and every doggone thing else and got out of there.' From the road outside, they watched the fire spread, then suddenly the window in Tom's room blew out. 'There goes that Scotch,' Dee told Tom ruefully.

It was on 16 December that the Germans launched their last big offensive of the war, and it took the Western Allies by complete surprise. Under the cover of low cloud and misty, overcast conditions – the 'season of night, fog and snow' – the Germans had managed to gather, undetected, thirty-six divisions for a massed drive through Belgium to Antwerp, a thrust designed to split the Allied forces in two and sever their supply lines.

The 18th Infantry were still on R&R when, the following day, the news of the German attack reached them. Their leave was over: by three that afternoon, they were packed into trucks and were beginning to hurry to the front. The 2nd Battalion found itself holding a position south of the town of Bütgenbach, on what was soon to become the northernmost limit of the Ardennes salient – or 'bulge'. By Christmas Eve, the German attack had run out of steam, crippled by lack of fuel, but what followed was two months of appalling attritional warfare. In the Ardennes, the war soon began to resemble the worst horrors of the Western Front over twenty years before.

On Christmas Day, the big freeze started, and then came the snow, covering everything in a deep white shroud. The temperatures dropped below freezing and stayed there, and the Americans, with too much cotton clothing and not enough wool, began to suffer badly as they crouched in their foxholes and listened to the shells screaming overhead.

There's another photograph of Tom and Dee, taken around this time. There's still an air of swagger about them, but they look more serious, older even, although this may have something to do with the Errol Flynn moustaches they're both sporting. Standing ankle-deep in snow, they're wearing thick scarves around their necks and white camouflage covers over their tin hats. 'The worst part of the Bulge was the snow and my clothes being froze,' says Dee. 'Course, we had thick pants over our other clothes, but we didn't have snowshoes or anything. We just had our regular boots and a field jacket and anything else we could find.' Their clothes became so frozen they would grate together like paper. They also suffered from German V1 rockets, or 'buzz-bombs'. They could hear them coming, like a persistent drone, then all of a sudden the engine would cut and they would hurtle into the dense fir forest where the battalion was crouching. 'You didn't know where they was going to land,' says Tom, 'so you'd lie there waiting for the bang.' Huge craters would be formed, obliterating everything in their wake, and propelling shards of stone and lethal tree splinters in a wide arc.

But the guardian angel that had been watching over the twins since the day they joined the US Army continued her good work, although Tom and Dee both had their close shaves. Dee was even wounded again on their way back to the front. Having just passed through Bütgenbach, their column was attacked by Allied aircraft. One bomb landed no more than twenty feet from Dee, blowing him up into the air and onto the bank of the road and showering him in mud.

Tom found him a short while later, standing in the doorway of a building in Bütgenbach, covered in mud and blood. 'But just by the way he was standing, I could tell it was Dee,' says Tom, who then took him down to the aid station. After being cleaned up and bandaged, Dee rejoined Company Headquarters. 'I didn't go to hospital or anything,' he says. 'I'd already been separated from my brother once, so I just stayed with the outfit. I was fine soon enough.'

Tom had another eerie experience during the Bulge. He was with a new wire-man buddy, a replacement named Private William White, and they were laying wires when shells started whistling overhead and exploding nearby. Taking cover by a fence, they waited for the barrage to lift, then heard voices up ahead.

'I'm going to take a look at what's going on,' Tom told White. 'You wait here and I'll holler for you.' Moving cautiously forward, he soon found a couple of badly wounded Germans. One had already passed out but on seeing Tom, the other asked him to shoot him to put him out of his misery.

'No,' Tom told him, 'I'm not going to shoot you.' He then called back to White, but there was no answer, and so he shouted again. But White still did not appear. So Tom went back to the fence where he had left White, but he was gone. 'That son of a gun,' thought Tom, 'he's deserted on me.' He felt like shooting his buddy when he next caught up with him. Heading back to the command post, Tom reported that White had gone missing.

That night, it snowed again, and the following morning they moved positions, passing within a few yards of where Tom had been the previous day. He saw two mounds where the Germans had been – evidently they had both died and been buried under the snow. 'I just looked at them and didn't say nothing,' admits Tom. Soon after, White was found, dead. 'When I left him there,' says Tom, 'there must have been some Germans still in the area and they grabbed him after I'd gone forward.' Later, as White had tried to escape, he had been shot. 'It could easily have been me,' says Tom.

The Bulge was the last major action the twins fought, although there was still much fighting right to the very end. Tom remembers seeing a twelve-year-old German soldier during the last weeks of the war. He's got a photo of him. 'Most of the time you never knew who you was fighting against,' he says, but claims he never felt any great animosity towards the Germans. Nor did Dee. 'At the end, they just wanted to get away from the Russians,' he says. 'We wasn't their enemy. The Russians was their enemy.'

When VE Day finally arrived, the twins were in Czechoslovakia. The Americans told everyone in the town to turn their lights on so that the German troops still up in the hills would know that the fighting was over. 'I guess they got that signal,' says Tom, 'because the next day they were coming home in droves.'

They got to celebrate the war's end a short while later. Earlier, they'd passed through Bonn and had found a cellar full of wine and even whisky. Backing up an army lorry, they had helped load the drink onto the back. 'Boys,' the officer in charge had told them, 'when the war's over, you'll get all this.' Neither Dee nor Tom believed a word of it. But once the fighting was over, they pulled back to a bivouac area and lo and behold, there was the lorry still full of the drink. 'So they was good as their word,' says Dee. They all had a skinful that day. 'We was glad it was over,' says Tom. 'Of course we were.'

A month later, they were heading home. The war in the Pacific might not have quite been over, but after three invasions and fighting through Africa, Sicily, France, Belgium, Germany and Czechoslovakia, the Bowles twins had more than done their bit. The Army was happy to let them go and get on with the rest of their lives.

In May 2005, Tom and Dee came back to Europe for the first time since the war. I'd first met them eighteen months before, at Dee's place in northwest Alabama, and even then I was struck by their laid-back, easy-going approach to life. They seemed pleased that someone was interested in their wartime experiences, but when I asked them whether they had ever been back to Normandy they said no, they'd not thought about it too much. And do you think you might some time? I asked. They looked at each other and shrugged. 'I don't know about that,' said Dee. 'Tom's son Tim has been talking about it for a while, but I'm not so sure . . . '

Tom lives in Lake Charles, Louisiana, but since his wife passed away he's been spending more time with his brother and sister-in-law. They're as close as they ever were and it's still almost impossible to tell them apart, even now that they're both in their eighties. When they came back, I wondered, after the war, did they ever talk about their experiences as soldiers? No, came the answer, hardly ever. 'We just forgot about it,' said Dee. 'We talked more about before the war, growing up and stuff.' Instead, like millions of others, they simply came back and got on with their lives. They learnt a trade and became electricians. Dee married and had two daughters, Tom married and had five boys. Most of the boys became electricians too, all except Tim, the youngest. He works in IT.

Then in 1994, there was a notice in the local newspaper in Lake Charles. The fiftieth anniversary of D-Day was approaching and veterans were being asked for their memories. Tom called them and a reporter came out to talk to him, wanting to know about his war record and how he came to get two bronze stars. It was the first time Tom had thought about it in years; he hadn't even got his medals. He'd never bothered; nor had Dee.

They began to realize there weren't so very many of them left and started thinking it might be a good idea to get some of their memories down for their children and grandchildren. They ordered their medals, joined the Big Red One Association and got in touch with a few of their former comrades-in-arms. In 2000, the D-Day Museum in New Orleans opened, and the twins went down there with their families and joined a parade with other veterans.

Some time after I'd visited them, Tim finally persuaded them to make the pilgrimage, and so in May 2004, a couple of weeks before the sixtieth anniversary celebrations began in France, the men of the family – Tom and Dee, and Tom's five sons – flew over to England. It was the first time the twins had ever been in an aeroplane and their first time out of the United States since returning after the end of the war.

Since I live not so very far from their old camp near Broadmayne, I had been to the New Inn in West Knighton and had sent Tom and Dee a photograph of the pub, and so now, on this visit, they naturally wanted to see the place again for themselves. They called in at my house, then together we all drove down towards Dorchester. It was a warm and sunny May day, just as it had been when the twins had taken their picture at the pub, a couple of weeks before D-Day. The roads narrowed as we drew closer, the hedgerows rising and bursting with green. Then there we were, pulling into the courtyard, opposite the front of the pub. It's remarkably unchanged on the outside, still instantly recognizable from the black and white picture taken all those years before. The twins got themselves a beer then posed outside for a new set of photographs. Watching it was a profoundly moving experience. It seemed incredible to me that sixty years before, two young men had stood there – unknowing – on the eve of one of the most significant moments in world history and yet now, with the world such a different place, here they were again. It was very humbling.

VILLAGE PEOPLE

Dr Chris Brown

Growing up in the 1970s and 1980s, I was certainly very conscious of 'The War', and like many boys at that time, I made model Spitfires and Tiger tanks and read *Commando* comics. Grown-ups rarely talked about it, but they did often *refer* to it, although usually as a means of implying that we younger generation did not know how lucky we were – which I suppose was true. My mother, for example, would mention the war in the context of food. If I ever took too much butter for my bread, she would say, 'That's enough to have lasted a week in the war!'

What I never bothered to consider, however, was that most men I knew who were then in their fifties and sixties had probably served during the war, and that everyone I knew of that age had lived through it. The only person I knew who was happy to talk about it at length was the Classics master at school, who used to regale us with tales of the war in Burma. 'Did you kill any Japs, sir?' we would repeatedly ask him, then rush off to re-enact our own version of jungle warfare in the trees and bushes at the bottom of the playing fields.

One person who certainly kept his war record pretty quiet was the village GP, Dr Brown. Like most young children, I was forever coming down with stomach bugs, chest infections or needing stitches, so I knew him better than most other adults in the village, and was as familiar with the inside of his surgery, with its green waiting-room chairs and smell of antiseptic, as any place outside my own home.

Dr Brown was truly a pillar of the community. Kind, with a gentle, soothing voice and a warm smile, he did so much more for the village than tend the sick, whether it be helping with the various village sports clubs, writing a musical (revived every ten years), or allowing the villagers to use his swimming pool. Just a short walk down the road from my childhood home, his pool was where I learnt to swim.

But I never thought of Dr Brown in any other light. I liked him enormously, but to me he was simply the village GP and that was that. Only many years later, however, did I discover that he had served with the Chindits in Burma. His wife lent me his wartime diary, and for a moment I was quite taken aback as she handed me the thick exercise book, with its homemade brown wrapping paper dust jacket. Within its pages, neatly written up in blue ink, were his remarkably detailed – and human – wartime jottings, as well as a number of newspaper cuttings and photographs. The Chindits were the stuff of wartime legend; it seemed strange that the man I remembered had been part of that special force of jungle warriors.

Many myths have grown about the Chindits. The romance and derring-do of these soldiers are often all most people know about the war in Burma, and to many they are still seen as the SAS of the jungle war, the 'green ghosts that haunted the Jap'. Like the SAS, they operated deep behind enemy lines, but there the similarity ends. The SAS were a small band of men, but the Chindits, although also special forces, were made up from ordinary infantry brigades; nearly 10,000 troops took part in the Second Chindit Expedition in 1944.

They were the brainchild of Major-General Orde Wingate, a charismatic and unorthodox soldier who had been brought to the Far East in 1942 by General (and soon to be Field Marshal) Wavell, then Commander-in-Chief of India. The war against Japan was not going well: Singapore and Malaya had been lost and so had much of Burma. With the Japanese knocking on the door of India itself,

Wavell decided he needed someone with fresh ideas, unconstrained by notions of military orthodoxy, to help plan the reconquest of Burma and at the very least inflict serious damage on the Japanese lines of communication. He had first met Wingate in 1938, during his time as C-in-C Middle East, and found him to be a mercurial officer with plenty of energy and determination. Wavell's early impressions were not misconceived. In 1941, and with only a few hundred men, Wingate famously bluffed 12,000 Italians into surrender during the Abyssinian campaign.

Wingate arrived in India having recovered from a recent suicide attempt. A manic depressive, he nonetheless found himself re-energized by the task Wavell had given him, and after reconnoitring northern Burma, began developing his ideas for 'Long-Range Penetration' (LRP). Mistrustful of paratroopers, he nonetheless believed that with the help of supply drops from the air directed by radio on the ground, it should be possible to maintain a force that could operate within the 'heart of the enemy's military machine'. His theory was that by keeping constantly mobile, his forces could avoid facing any concentration of enemy forces.

Wavell gave the go-ahead for an expedition using the 77th Indian Infantry Brigade. Split into seven different columns, they set off in February 1943, managing to penetrate 150 miles behind enemy lines. They blew up sections of railway, gathered some helpful intelligence and to a certain degree distracted the Japanese, but as one battalion history put it, 'Never have so many marched for so little.'[1] Strategically, the expedition was certainly of small value, while the many who became sick or were wounded along the way had to be left where they were – a horrible fate considering the brutality with which the Japanese treated such men.

The First Chindit Expedition was, however, a propaganda dream, and Wingate and 'The British Ghost Army' were fêted around the world in the Allied press. Crucially, Wingate had also come to the attention of

---

[1]   Cited in *Burma: The Forgotten War* by Jon Latimer, p.167.

the prime minister, Winston Churchill – so much so that he was called to Canada to outline his ideas on Long-Range Penetration at the Quebec Conference in August 1943, a gathering that was attended by Churchill, President Roosevelt and the British and American Chiefs of Staff. An impressive orator, Wingate persuaded the Combined Chiefs of the value of launching another expedition. Even the Americans agreed to it, for although they had no interest in Britain's colonial empire, they were keen to help the Chinese, who they believed could make a difference in the war against Japan. They had already sent troops under General Joe Stilwell to lead the Chinese Nationalists operating on the border of northern Burma. With this in mind, Wingate was given the task of cutting the lines of communication to those Japanese forces opposing Stilwell's men. Wingate agreed, although privately he also hoped to reconquer the whole of the north of Burma.

Wingate also achieved another coup when the American Chief of the Air Staff, General 'Hap' Arnold, offered to lend him an air force of transport planes, gliders, fighters and bombers, to support the expedition. This was to be called No 1 Air Commando, or 'Cochran's Flying Circus' after its commander, Colonel Phil Cochran. This generosity from Arnold enabled Wingate to think on an even bigger scale. With comprehensive air support, his men would not be left to fend for themselves; furthermore, they could be flown deep behind enemy lines to start with rather than tramping hundreds of miles through thick jungle. With air support, it would be possible to maintain many more men, and with many more men, the effectiveness of the Chindits would be even greater. That was the theory, at any rate.

Like many others, Captain Dr Chris Brown had been impressed by the accounts and coverage of the Chindits' exploits, so when he saw a request for volunteers for a further expedition, he decided to put his name forward. 'I could never face my conscience again,' he wrote in a letter to his parents, 'if I didn't do something about it.' A young doctor in the Royal Army Medical Corps (RAMC), he spent a fortnight assigned to the 4/9 Gurkhas, before joining the 2nd Battalion, the King's Own Royal Rifles, at Dukwan Dam, near Jhansi in India, on 1 December 1943.

Part of the 111th Indian Infantry Brigade, the battalion left Dukwan by special train on 15 January 1944, crossing into Assam six days later. From the railhead at Silchar, they had to march across country to Imphal on the India–Burma border where they were to begin training. A taste of things to come, it was tough going, but Chris was fit and young, and as a boy growing up in Scotland, had always loved mountains and the outdoor life. On a morning of rain and mist – 'Scottish weather' – his first view of Imphal Plain reminded him of Rannoch Moor. Imphal itself, he noted, was 'no more than a glorified village, tho' at present it is the main military base, and there is a constant and staggering flow of trucks'.

Amidst this hive of activity, they began their preparations. As with the first expedition, the main fighting unit was to be the 'column', which was formed by splitting a battalion of roughly 800 men, such as the 2nd King's Own Royal Regiment, into two, and then adding a number of mules, ponies and bullocks. Each column had its share of rifle platoons, mortars, engineers, reconnaissance, and, of course, medical staff, albeit just one doctor and four medical orderlies. The 2nd King's Own was divided into 41 and 46 Columns; Chris was assigned to the latter.

Training principally involved getting fit and practising marching through thick and often precipitous jungle, and crossing rivers. Getting men across water was not usually too much of a problem – it was persuading the mules that was tricky, and ensuring that none of the equipment became wet and damaged in the process.

General Wingate himself visited the brigade and inspected their progress in February, just a few weeks before the expedition was due to be launched. 'We watched his arrival in a light plane with some awe,' noted Chris. '[He was] a small figure in a pale khaki suit and an enormous old-fashioned topee.' That evening, Wingate held a conference for all the brigade officers – Chris included – in which he outlined his plans. Nearly 9,000 men would be used for the Second

Chindit Expedition, he explained, initially made up from five infantry brigades of which 111th Brigade was one. As a deception, they were to be called the fictitious '3rd Indian Division'. Formally, they were 'Special Force'; informally, they were simply Chindits, a name derived from *Chinthé*, the name of the mythical griffins that were supposed to guard Burmese temples.

'His main principle was age-old,' noted Chris, 'to outflank the enemy.' This Wingate was going to do by inserting these brigades by glider or plane far behind the enemy lines. Once there, each brigade would make a base – a 'stronghold' – that would be inaccessible to wheeled vehicles but which would include a hastily constructed airstrip and drop-zone (DZ) for resupplying the brigade and for evacuating the wounded. The enemy was to be encouraged to attack the stronghold while 'floater columns', operating like guerrillas in the jungle, would assault the Japanese in turn.

Wingate's abilities and character have been the subject of fevered discussion ever since the war – some claim he was a genius, others that he was militarily myopic and too eccentric for his own good. This is not the place to join the debate, but Chris Brown, for one, was deeply impressed by him. 'His speech was magnificent and enthralling . . . He made everything appear so straightforward and easy,' wrote Chris, who was won over despite Wingate's 'very anti-doctor' comments. 'The presence of doctors, he thought, made the men soft, illness-conscious and apt to "give up the ghost",' recorded Chris. After briefing the officers, Wingate talked to all the men as well, and, noted Chris, 'took them from suspicion to quite enthusiastic support'.

As February drew to a close, Chris began to sense there were 'big things in the air'. He knew their 'show' was about to start, but there were also rumours that the Japanese were about to launch an attack on Imphal and Kohima, the gateways to India. 'We used to look eastward over the hills and wonder what the Japs were up to,' he noted, 'and if they really were coming.' Then on 5 March, as they sat over their evening fires, they heard planes going east and looked up to see shadowy gliders following behind. Operation Thursday, as the launch of the expedition was called, was on.

Wingate had originally planned for there to be four landing-zones (LZs) established on areas of clear ground, to be called Piccadilly, Chowringhee, Templecombe and Broadway. Using gliders, men and even small bulldozers were to be dropped into these four places and an airstrip hastily constructed at each so that the rest of the troops, mules and equipment could be landed in the heart of the jungle. The 111th Brigade was due to be dropped at Piccadilly, but at the last minute, aerial reconnaissance showed it had been blocked by newly felled trees. Instead, 41 Column was sent to Chowringhee, and 46 to Broadway.

Chris watched 41 Column loading and taking off on the evening of 8 March, 'with that deep roar of the twin engines and the head-lights sweeping past us down the runway'. And then the following evening it was their turn. Chris was in charge of four plane-loads, each consisting of three animals, thirteen men and packs of equipment and supplies. At midnight, four Dakotas came back from Broadway and Chris and his party hurriedly began loading them up again for their second trip that night. The mules were naturally reluctant to get aboard, but 'with a little coaxing and much pulling of ropes and pushing of hindquarters', they clambered in.

With the animals and supplies securely tied and after a roll-call, the doors were shut, the engines opened, and Chris felt himself bumping along the runway, with a dryness in his throat and nerves mounting. 'Really off now,' he noted, 'no turning back, fingers crossed, please God we all come out of this all right, Mum and Dad!'

They landed safely in the early morning of 10 March. 'Burma!' wrote Chris. 'Was it really possible this was it and we were now miles behind the Japs?' The landing-zone was dry and dusty, filled with men, supplies, animals, planes and even field guns. But already the mission had changed somewhat. The brigade had been due to head to an operational area near Indaw, picked out by Wingate as an important railway junction. Nor was there much talk of establishing 'strongholds' – which were to be inaccessible to wheeled vehicles. Rather, they were to establish 'blocks' instead, defensive positions along key lines of communication, such as roads and railways, from where they would carry out demolitions and ambushes. 111th Brigade's task had been to operate south of Indaw in support of 16th Brigade, who were the only columns travelling entirely by foot and who were to secure the two Japanese airfields at Indaw. But by landing at Broadway and Chowringhee, rather than Piccadilly, 111th Brigade now had much further to travel to the Indaw area and were already behind schedule to link up with 16th Brigade. Broadway, where Chris and 46 Column had landed, was more than fifty miles from Indaw as the crow flies – and much further than that when marching through the jungle.

Despite this, after a day resting and gathering themselves together, they set off, crossing the west end of the airstrip just as the first Spitfires came in to land. This, Chris noted, was 'thrilling to watch', although when he saw the large number of wrecked gliders he was glad they had landed by Dakota.

After marching just two hours, he began to feel thirsty and a slight sinking feeling came over him. 'What on earth will I do with the seriously ill and wounded?' he wondered. Even in 1944, he felt they lived in such a protected society that 'it is hard to grasp the fact that from now on there's no hospital around the corner, no ambulance to give a ring for, no surgeon to ask for an opinion, or policeman round the corner if the Japs start getting tough'. He felt a very long way from home and as a doctor, completely on his own. Whatever the problem – illness or wound – he would have to deal with it himself.

At the end of their first day's march, having travelled a little over five miles, they bedded down where they were, and got stuck into their American K-rations, universally despised by GI and Tommy alike. Short of calories, K-rations did not give the men the nutrition and energy they needed when undertaking punishing jungle marches. They were boring too, but they had one overriding virtue: they were light and easy to carry.

Chris woke the following morning feeling terrible, with both vomiting and diarrhoea. But he had to soldier on and after heading through tall teak trees and along a beautiful grassy path, he began to feel better. At lunch they looked back and saw Japanese planes bombing Broadway and the Spitfires climbing to meet them. It reminded Chris of watching the Battle of Britain in Kent during the summer of 1940. A Japanese Zero roared low over them as they pushed on. The going improved in the afternoon, so that by the time they stopped for the night, Chris reckoned they had travelled '11–12 miles for the day'. There was, however, still a very long way to go.

They continued their march through the jungle for the next fort-night. Progress was often slow. All ranks carried heavy loads, even doctors. In addition to rifles and other weapons, they had a 40lb pack each, using pre-war designed webbing that had no padding, frame or waist-belt, or any of the comforts that modern-day hikers would take for granted. On only their second day of marching, Chris noted, 'So stinking hot, and the big pack feels like lead by the end of an hour's march.' The mules were also slow, weighed down by huge packs. Each radio – the one link the column had to the outside world – was so big and cumbersome it took a staggering three mules to carry.

The lack of water and food was a constant problem. 'One bottle of water per day is not sufficient in this heat,' he noted. 'Should have 7–8 pints.' Most water came from streams that they passed, but if they could not find one with clear water they were in trouble. 'No water anywhere,' noted Chris on 19 March, 'so spent a beastly thirsty night.' Food, on the other hand, was dropped by air. Their first was on the evening of 13 March. Chris had been lying under a tree dreaming of cool beers when a plane came over. 'Another seven K-rations to carry,' he noted in his diary, but often they had to wait several days for supply drops. Sitting exhausted at the end of the

day, they would watch planes tantalizingly come over and fly away
again. When a drop was finally made on 17 March, the packages
landed far and wide and were difficult to gather; then they had to
wait a further week for their next drop and had even resorted to
sending an SOS. Four light aircraft then found them and delivered
a case of emergency rations.

Inevitably, more and more men became sick. Jaundice was a particular problem. Those afflicted by it were left sapped of energy, but
there was little Chris could do for them except arrange for them to
be relieved of their packs. 'Poor lads can't eat a thing,' he wrote, 'and
how they manage to keep up in this march is a miracle.' Another man
was kicked by a mule and had broken his elbow, which Chris splinted
as best he could. The following day another man fractured his ankle;
he had to be carried by mule, but it was clear both men were now
useless as fighting soldiers and Chris hoped to have them flown out
as soon as possible.

Although during their training they had been repeatedly told that
complete silence was to be maintained at all times, this soon proved
impossible. Chris was initially alarmed by the loud crunching noise
they made as they marched through the jungle. But despite this,
during the first part of their journey they encountered no Japanese
at all. Two men disappeared when looking for supply boxes and were
never seen again, while a few days later four further men vanished.
'Hard though it is to believe,' noted Chris, 'they must have deserted
and returned to the last village.' Later, he added, 'They were never
heard of again.'

Finally, 46 Column reached their rendezvous, some twenty miles
southwest of Indaw, on 27 March, having slogged well over a
hundred and twenty miles and having safely crossed a main road and
railway line without incident. When they got there, however, they
discovered no sign of Brigade Headquarters, whom they were supposed to meet, but did hear the news that General Wingate had been
killed in a plane crash. 'We all felt pretty upset,' wrote Chris, 'as tho'

the life had gone out of the campaign before it had properly started.' And there was further bad news: the Japanese had finally invaded India and were assaulting both Kohima and Imphal. With this change in the situation came new orders: the brigade was no longer to concentrate on the railway south of Indaw, but to move further west; north of Indaw, the 16th Brigade were to establish a block with an airstrip to be known as 'Aberdeen'.

By 2 April, when they finally linked up with Brigade HQ, 46 Column had reached their area of operations. The following afternoon they set off to prepare a roadblock. The going was hard and it was dark before they reached their destination. Chris had to walk through a hornets' nest in order not to lose touch with the people ahead and was badly stung. When they eventually reached their forming-up point for the block, the column was split into two: a fighting and tail group. Normally Chris was at the tail of the column but in the anticipation of battle casualties was sent up front to join the fighting group.

It was just as well. Later in the night they heard the 'most foul and nerve-shattering screaming' coming from the tail. For a moment Chris stood petrified, then dived for cover as shots and explosions rang out. After the initial confusion, a platoon was sent to the rear to help the tail group who, it seemed, had been attacked. 'It was an eerie night,' wrote Chris. 'We lay for hours listening to spasmodic firing and staring out into the moonlit trees, imagining one heard Japs' footsteps coming over the crunchy leaves.'

Morning brought news of the previous night's events. A platoon of men at the tail had become slightly separated from the main column and had inadvertently walked straight into a party of Japanese. Chris's great friend Captain John Busby had been cut down by a sword and killed along with several others. 'I put up a thankful prayer that I was not marching in my normal place behind John,' wrote Chris. 'How I pray he didn't suffer too much. Felt hellish that I hadn't been there to look after him when he most needed me.'

The next day they had their revenge of sorts. Having established their block, they waited for any enemy traffic to come their way.

Sure enough, late in the afternoon a number of trucks rumbled towards them, the first blowing up as it struck a booby trap and in turn detonating explosives that had been laid under a bridge across the river. 'What a gorgeous sound,' noted Chris. 'I felt like yelling in excitement, and kept thinking, "That's one for John Busby, you bastards."'

After holding the block for forty-eight hours, they were on the move again. Chris had had a busy time tending to wounded from their first encounter, treating ongoing sicknesses, and also one casualty who had been badly concussed when an air drop – a box of hob-nailed boots – landed on his head. As they headed west they crossed another road and accidentally walked into the middle of a stationary column of Japanese vehicles. 'I was never so surprised in my life,' wrote Chris, 'when I found we were walking past a camouflaged truck.' Fortunately, the Japanese seemed to be more alarmed than they were and fled into the jungle, the men of 46 Column firing after them. Later that day they had another run-in with a Japanese patrol – and again came out on top. 'Very close fighting this is,' noted Chris.

The next day they captured a Japanese-held village, but their promised air support arrived too late and opened fire on them instead. Two men were shot. One was not too badly hurt, but the other had been hit in the liver, a wound Chris knew would prove fatal. In the night, the man died.

The next few days they were constantly on the move, but Chris was discovering that marching was now much more of a burden. 'Not only are we all tired,' wrote Chris, 'but I have to stop so often to pick up sick men who've fallen out.' He would then have to get them onto a pack mule or pony and then catch up the rest of the column. By 16 April, he had two men desperately ill with cerebral malaria. Chris called for a light plane to evacuate them, but it didn't arrive until the following day, by which time their condition had worsened. Both men died as they were being carried towards the nearest airstrip. And as if disease and exhaustion weren't enough, they had the added strain of almost daily run-ins with Japanese patrols.

New orders arrived. The role of the Chindits had changed yet again and they were now under overall control of the American General Stilwell, who was planning an attack from the north to take two important Japanese railheads at Myitkyina and Mogaung. Indaw, for which the 16th Brigade had sacrificed so much, was now to be abandoned. So too was Broadway and the blocks at Aberdeen and White City. The latter had also been fiercely fought over, but now the main effort was to be further north: the Chindits, while continuing to make life as difficult for the Japanese as possible, were to try and link up with Stilwell's US–Chinese forces. In the meantime, 111th Brigade were to set up a further block on the road and railway south of Mogaung at a clearing to be known as 'Blackpool'.

But 46 Column faced a long, circuitous and arduous march to reach Blackpool, made worse by several torrential downpours, the first sign that the monsoon was on its way. Sore feet were now getting damp too. 'I am giving poor comfort to a line of sick men,' wrote Chris on 27 April. 'They seem to be sitting everywhere with their big raw feet held ready for inspection. Flavine, elastoplast, more elastoplast, iodine, and they put their boots back on and hobble off.' A man with a temperature of 104 degrees was given decent treatment; a man with a temperature of only 101 was given a dose of sympathy and told to get back in line.

On they went, one day catching some fish by lobbing hand grenades into a pool, another day getting completely lost. After rendezvousing with several other columns, the officers were called to Brigade HQ and given a briefing on the situation. Afterwards Chris noted, 'It looks as if we will have some fighting now.' How right he was. First, though, they still had to reach Blackpool. The closer they got, the harder the march. Climbing a particularly steep hill, one of Chris's medical mules slipped and somersaulted twenty feet back down into a thicket of bamboo. It took two hours to free it and get it back on its feet again. 'Yes, very bad country,' noted Chris. '*Very* slow progress.'

They finally reached Blackpool on the evening of 7 May and Chris was given a patch of ground just below the crest of a ridge facing north for his regimental aid post (RAP). He and his orderlies immediately started digging in. The following morning, Chris clambered to the top of the ridge behind him and got a better picture of their situation. 'Looking west there is a steep wooded slope down to the paddy fields where our airstrip is to be,' he wrote. 'The ground is already littered with white chutes of the supply drop last night. Beyond this, and about a mile away, is the road and railway . . . Our positions are all among fairly thick bamboo and when I sit at my RAP, it is impossible to see any of the defence positions right below me.'

During the day, everyone was busy, preparing perimeter defence positions, digging weapons pits and slit trenches. A railway bridge was blown up, and machinegun and mortar positions set up covering the road. The following day, after a small probing attack by the Japanese in the night, the airstrip was built. Gliders arrived, crashing into the clearing, but brought with them more equipment – even bulldozers.

The preparations of the Blackpool Block continued. The perimeter was lined with wire and booby-trapped. There was continual digging. Some days they were left alone by the Japanese, while on others, light attacks were made and the position would resound with rifle and machinegun fire. Japanese raiding parties attacked on five nights in a row and although they were always cut down, it meant a severe lack of sleep for many of the troops. But fighting was not Chris's job, and he was able to spend the time establishing his RAP and rebuilding his strength. 'The weather was good,' he wrote, 'plenty of food, morale very high and personally I am enjoying the bustle and interest of all that is happening.'

He found the nights difficult, however, and would often lie awake listening to the sounds of the jungle and particularly a small insect that tapped the bamboo down below him. 'As is well known,' he wrote, 'tapping on the bamboo is the method by which Japs keep in touch at night, and it didn't take long before one began to hear foot-steps crashing through the dead bamboo.' One night he watched in 'breathless excitement' as the first planes landed on the new airstrip, bringing with them 25-pounder field guns, ammunition and later evacuating the sick.

Then finally, a week after they had arrived at the block, Chris heard his first shell. He was sitting at his RAP when there was a dull 'crump' and a few seconds later a 'horrid whine' as the shell whistled over them. Unbeknown to Chris, the reason the brigade had largely been left alone was because the Japanese 53rd Division was heading north to meet them, and once there they began digging in their guns in positions that would dominate the newly built airstrip and much of the Blackpool defences.

To begin with the Japanese shelling was inaccurate but they soon found their range, and pounded the main positions. Two officers from 46 Column were killed almost immediately, as were many more men. Even more were wounded. Chris hurried to the brigade dressing station, a couple of miles behind the block in the jungle, and where the brigade's Senior Medical Officer, Doc Whyte, was in charge. 'The scene was certainly gruesome,' jotted Chris. 'Stretchers wherever a flat bit of ground allowed, with dead and others dying. Dressings and blood everywhere.' Chris did what he could, dividing his time between there and his regimental aid post treating a number of men who had been wounded during a counter-attack. 'Pt Wall had his chest opened wide and there was little I could do,' wrote Chris. 'He died that night. Sgt Young had a six-inch gaping wound from behind his ear to his Adam's apple. At the bottom of the wound I could see the Carotid artery beating, quite intact, but I wasn't half scared. He was staggeringly plucky and I was fortunately able to fly him out the same night.'

It was just about the last plane to fly out from Blackpool. During the next day, the perimeter was breached and the airstrip captured. The brigade was now being bombarded almost constantly. Chris was dashing repeatedly between his RAP and attending severely wounded where they lay. He was, however, quickly learning to distinguish the different sounds of shellfire:

> Bang – all right, our own mortar. Bang – hello, grenades down in Dickie Jones's area – what's brewing? Faint crump – Jap 105 which gives me about 10 seconds. If I'm at the RAP, I can afford to sit on the edge of my slit trench for a few seconds trying to gauge where it will drop. If I'm further off, run like hell and undignified leap into the trench, landing any old how with my heart beating like mad. Just in time! Crash! And little splinters go whirring and crackling through the bamboo overhead. Crump – here's another coming. Oh, God – is this the one for me this time? Listen – no. No, it's going to the right. Thank God. And crash, whoomp, it lands somewhere near Joe Green. And so on and so on. Horrible and degrading to find oneself so frightened that even tho' a long term agnostic, I offer up a little prayer to God – just in case he is there.

In fact, Dickie Jones, another of the platoon commanders in the column, was also killed during another pointless counter-attack. Then, as the rains finally began to fall, the King's Own were pulled out of the front line and replaced by the Cameronians. The battle of Blackpool was already all but over, however. It had never been more than a block, but while the 111th Brigade were being blown to bits, news arrived from the north that Stilwell had not yet reached Mogaung. 'Stilwell's name was mud,' noted Chris. On 25 May, they were given the order to evacuate Blackpool entirely. It was a hair-raising process, with the whole brigade leaving by a single narrow path. While mortars and shells fell around them, they slowly inched their way out – but many of those wounded had to be left where they were. The brigade commander even issued an order that those unlikely to survive should be shot rather than leaving them to be tortured and bayoneted by the Japanese.[2]

---

[2] The commander of 111th Brigade was Major John Masters, later famous for his adventure books and for his own memoir, *The Road Past Mandalay*.

At midday, news arrived that the block had fallen. It was, felt Chris, an unbelievable moment, 'like "Tobruk has fallen", and with our rations finished, the near-future looked rather gloomy'. Chris and another of the doctors made their way forward to help Doc Whyte at the brigade dressing station. 'I think it was the most miserable sight I ever wish to see,' wrote Chris. 'Poor lads – roughly bandaged and huddled under the trees, with no blankets and some with no shirts or trousers or boots, and the rain pelting down as if the heavens had burst.' There was, of course, little they could do. Chris went round giving morphine and applying dressings. He found his friend Les Milne, another platoon commander from the column, who was suffering from a bad wound to the wrist. As Chris undid his friend's filthy bandage, the radial artery began spraying blood. 'It was a tricky job searching for it in the mass of shattered tissue but between all of us we managed to get a pair of forceps on the bleeding vessel and tied it off successfully, much to everyone's intense relief. Not a murmur from Les. What a hero he was.'

The following morning, they packed up at first light, getting the walking wounded moving and the rest onto stretchers and what mules remained. They moved painfully slowly up a series of steep climbs and through thick mud, but the Japanese never attempted to follow them and by the middle of the day, the going had substantially improved. Four light planes arrived with emergency rations, much to everyone's relief. 'How the planes found us was a mystery,' noted Chris. 'A marvellous feat which gave us all a meal and one we're not likely to forget.'

A day later they were on the downhill trail and the rain had stopped. By two o'clock, the column had reached Makso where there was an airstrip and a rearguard party waiting with hot cups of tea. Fortunately, the weather remained good and over the next few days, the sick and wounded and most of the remainder of the brigade were flown out.

But not so Doc Brown and the rest of the medical staff. They were to be sent north to help 77th Brigade. With Stilwell's forces still battling around Myitkyina, the remaining Chindit units –

especially 77th Brigade – were given the job of capturing Mogaung. As Chris prepared to move off once more, news arrived that D-Day had been launched in Normandy.

His diary ends at this point, but he did not finally make it out until July, by which time he had been in the jungle for four and a half months. When the end eventually came, he was put onto a Dakota and was soon flying out over the hills and trees and paddy fields; just two hours later he touched down back in India. 'The change was so rapid,' he wrote, 'it was hard to grasp . . . How we looked forward to this day. Everything has been laid on splendidly for our reception: baths, clean clothes, food, a bottle of beer, and a huge pile of mail awaiting us. It is almost too good to be true.'

Physically, he was remarkably fit and well – and one of only four officers in the battalion to have come out with no record of sickness or having never been on a mule or pony. He was, he confessed, glad to have had the experience, but vowed he would never volunteer for anything like it again.

The Second Chindit Expedition achieved much more than the first, especially helping Stilwell in his advance from the north; 111th Brigade managed to destroy 'nearly 200 tons of stores and 20 vehicles, and inflicted 430 casualties', during the weeks before Blackpool.[3] The casualty rate throughout the force was terrible, however, and the expenditure in manpower and aircraft was enormous. Despite this, no one can doubt the incredible courage and tenacity of the 'Ghost Army', and by the time Chris was back in India, with Imphal and Kohima saved, the tide in the Far East had definitely turned. It would be another year of bloody and bitter fighting, but Japan would be defeated – and the Chindits had more than played their part.

Doctor Brown died, too young, in 1985, and his passing was deeply mourned in the village. His diaries are, of course, fascinating on

---

[3]   Cited in *War in Burma* by Julian Thompson, p.268.

many levels, but reading them, I was interested to discover that the humanity and kindness of the man I knew shone through so clearly. 'He never talked about it,' his widow, Bobby, told me. 'Never. No one did.' He was rightly proud of what he'd done, however, and in a book about the Chindits that Bobby lent me, first published in 1981, I found the correspondence between Doctor Brown and the author. 'I wish I'd had the opportunity to talk to you during the research stage of my book,' the author had written. Me too, I thought, although I'm glad I have had the chance to know the man a little bit better through words written down more than sixty years ago.

Bill Laity

Bill passed me a cutting from a wartime magazine, *The Sphere*, dated 30 May 1942. It was an artist's reconstruction of two Royal Navy destroyers, *Jervis* and Bill's ship, *Jackal*, at sea off the coast of Libya. The picture was certainly dramatic: *Jackal*, listing and low in the water, was ablaze with fire and smoke billowing into the night sky, while *Jervis*, rescue nets already slung over her side, had come alongside to help rescue crew off the stricken vessel.

'Yes, it was like that,' Bill told me. 'We were all on the upper deck, and they came alongside and took us off. The decks were that hot, you couldn't bear to stand. I went down into the engine room and got Harry Hayes out. I got badly burnt getting him back up and he died in agony on the upper deck. He was just like a bit of bacon.' Bill looked away a moment, then said, 'That poor bloke, he did suffer, I'll tell you that. I have bloody nightmares about it every May.'

Bill and his wife Linda now live in a bungalow across the road from the pub, The Queen's Head, in the heart of the village, but when I first met them I was just three years old and back then they lived in a thatched cottage in the hamlet of Stoke Farthing, just a mile or so away. They were the grandparents of my best friend at nursery school, Greg, and we had gone there to have tea with them. I can't say I remember much about the occasion, except that both Bill and Linda were there, even though Bill was still working hard back in

1973 – as foreman and dairyman for Joe Waters, the farmer at Stoke Farthing. I was surprised then, to learn many years later from a friend in the village that Bill had been at sea during the war. 'He went right the way through,' the friend told me, 'and survived at least one ship going down. Bill had a hell of a war.' As I was to discover, this was something of an understatement.

Bill was born on a farm in Cornwall, not far from Penzance. The oldest of four children, three boys and a girl, he began helping his father at an early age, looking after the horses. He liked horses, and was a natural and gifted rider, and as a teenager used to compete in local point-to-points. Once he even took part in two different point-to-points in one day – one for his uncle and one for his father. 'My old man was a brilliant horseman,' said Bill. 'He was very kind to a horse, but if I had a bad one, I'd give him hell.' One day, his father caught Bill giving a difficult horse 'hell' and so promptly gave his son 'a bloody good hiding'. Bill was so angry and upset he ran away and joined the 15th/19th Hussars. For six months his family had no idea where he'd got to until he was quizzed one day by the battalion adjutant. 'What is your name, Trooper?' the adjutant asked him.

'Laity, sir,' Bill told him.

'That's a Cornish name,' the adjutant said. 'Do you know a William Laity?'

'Yes,' said Bill, 'that's my father.'

'What's his address? He was my major in the Great War when I was a lieutenant.'

Bill told him and a week later the adjutant called for him again. He'd written to Bill's father and had had a reply. 'How old are you?' the adjutant asked Bill.

'Eighteen, sir,' Bill replied.

'No you're not,' the adjutant told him. 'You're sixteen and your father wants to claim you out. So with respect to your father, go and pack your bags and go home.'

LEFT Bill Byers with his navigator, Bill Morison. Together with the rest of the crew, they flew thirty-four bombing missions. The two Bills remain close friends to this day.

ABOVE A Halifax Mk II, like the one flown by Bill Byers, is loaded with bombs ready for another mission over Europe.

RIGHT Bill Byers and his crew on the port-side wing of their Halifax, 'Z' for Zebra. Dick Meredith, without the cap, is on the left, Bill is next to him, with Bill Morison to his right.

ABOVE Tom and Dee Bowles at Fort Benning, Georgia, shortly after they joined the US Army in 1940. Identical twins from Alabama, they joined the Army after struggling to find work in their depression-hit hometown.

ABOVE Having fought through the campaigns in North Africa and Sicily, Tom and Dee, along with the rest of the US 1st Division, were posted back to England to train for the invasion of France. Just a week before D-Day, this picture was taken at the New Inn at West Knighton in Dorset, close to where the Big Red One were based. There would be few opportunities for beer drinking in the long months to come.

ABOVE Tom and Dee during the bitter Battle of the Bulge in the winter of 1944–5. Dee had only just rejoined his brother after being seriously wounded a day after the Normandy invasion.

ABOVE Tom Bowles, third from the left, in Germany. He reckoned the battle for the German town of Aachen was the worst fighting he witnessed throughout the entire war.

RIGHT Almost sixty years to the day, Tom and Dee return to the New Inn. It was the first time they had left the US since going home to America after the war.

ABOVE Attending the wounded on the Second Chindit Expedition. The few doctors on the expedition were kept busy, treating numerous diseases, broken limbs and other ailments brought on by harsh jungle trekking, as well as a multitude of battle wounds. They often had to make do with insufficient equipment and limited amounts of medical supplies.

ABOVE Doctor Chris Brown. This picture was taken after his safe return from the Second Chindit Expedition.

ABOVE The drop zone and landing ground at Broadway, deep behind enemy lines. Incredibly, bulldozers and other equipment were landed by glider in jungle clearings such as these, enabling troop-carrying aircraft to land just a couple of days later.

ABOVE How to keep a force on its feet many miles behind enemy lines. The efforts of 'Cochran's Flying Circus' ensured the Chindits were not only regularly re-supplied, but also meant the wounded could, for the most part, be safely evacuated.

LEFT Bill Laity as a Petty Officer soon after the end of the war.

ABOVE HMS *Kashmir*, Bill's first ship. He spent over a year on *Kashmir* as a stoker in the boiler room and sailing on Home Waters as well as on the Arctic and Mediterranean convoys.

LEFT *Kashmir's* sister-ship, HMS *Kelly*, under attack off the coast of Crete, May 1941. The following day, the *Kashmir* was sunk and Bill found himself being machine-gunned in the water by German fighter planes. After swimming for more than four hours, he was finally picked up by HMS *Kipling*, another destroyer from the same flotilla.

RIGHT Royal Navy K-class destroyers at war. The ship alongside is Bill's second ship, HMS *Jackal*.

RIGHT HMS *Jackal* aflame, as depicted by *The Sphere* in May 1942. Bill rescued his badly wounded friend, Harry Hayes, from the inferno, but to no avail; Harry died in agony soon after. After these heroics, Bill remained on the ship, one of a few left trying to save her, until the upper deck became so hot it started to melt.

ABOVE The telegram John's parents received when he was made a POW. 'Imagine receiving that,' John said. 'It was so cold and formal and told them almost nothing.'

LEFT The commandant of Mukaishima Camp hands over his sword after the Japanese surrender. It would, however, be a few weeks more before the prisoners were rescued from the island.

ABOVE John Leaver. This mug-shot was taken by the Japanese and was part of his POW identity card. He and his friend Fred Walsh fared better than some Allied Japanese POWs, but even so, one in four at Mukaishima camp died – most because of their nightmare journey to the island on the hellship, the *Dai Nichi Maru*.

ABOVE Fred and John at a beach whilst convalescing in Australia after their ordeal. Both men later agreed that their deep friendship and the support they were able to give each other had saved their lives.

ABOVE Bing Evans and Frances Wheeler become engaged. They are smiling here, but both faced a long journey before they were finally able to marry four years later.

ABOVE Bing Evans in Scotland in the summer of 1942, when he was singled out as the 'typical Ranger'. In the years that followed, Bing took part in four major invasions, made five seaborne landings and fought in seven campaigns. He was shot in the head, wounded by a grenade, taken prisoner, escaped three times and had been due to be executed as a spy before the war finally came to an end.

LEFT Cisterna, where, on a suicide mission, two US Army Ranger battalions were almost completely wiped out.

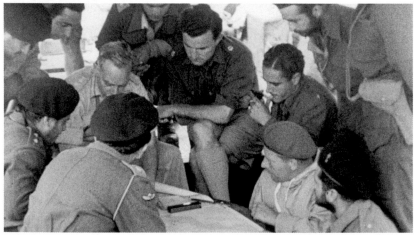

ABOVE George Jellicoe, centre, briefs his men before an attack on one of the Dodecanese Islands. An inspirational commander and fearless soldier, Jellicoe had an extraordinary wartime career, culminating with him capturing Athens on a bicycle.

ABOVE 87 Squadron pilots at Lille in France in 1939. Although the RAF squadrons were unable to prevent the fall of France, Bee Beamont, third from the right, learnt invaluable lessons in the art of air combat during the fierce fighting of May 1940, experience that would help him become an outstanding fighter pilot and commander by the war's end.

ABOVE Bee cutting a dash as he stands by his Typhoon. Playing a key part in the Typhoon's development, he pioneered its role as a powerful air-ground attack aircraft.

ABOVE The Hawker Typhoon. Big and ungainly, it was nonetheless a very fast and powerfully armed single-engine fighter aircraft.

RIGHT Klaus Adam by his Typhoon. One of the few Germans to fly for the RAF, his Jewish family had fled Germany for Britain in 1934. Flying with 609 Squadron throughout 1944 and right up until the end of the war, Klaus was known as 'Heinie the Tank-Buster.'

ABOVE Klaus by his captured German staff car. It was in this car that he toured the Falaise Gap and saw the devastation wreaked by the Typhoon squadrons.

ABOVE 609 Squadron pilots at B.7 airfield in Normandy. Like many RAF squadrons at that time, 609 was a polyglot collection of pilots that included Australians, Belgians, New Zealanders, Canadians, and an Argentinian, as well as a number of British and one German. Klaus is seated second from the right.

ABOVE A rocket leaves the wing of a Typhoon as 609 Squadron pilots make an attack on German vehicles on the road below.

LEFT German dead and destroyed vehicles along a road in the Falaise Gap. This signalled the end of German resistance in Normandy.

'So that was that,' Bill told me, 'but when I was eighteen I went and joined the Navy.' Why the Navy? I asked. Bill shrugged. 'I don't know. I couldn't bloody well swim either and when I was doing my training I wondered why I'd ever joined.' But, I pointed out, as a farmer, he was in a reserved occupation; he needn't have joined up at all. 'Yes, but I was never a coward,' he replied. Nor was he going to join a ship without being able to swim, so every night, after his day's training was over, he took himself off to the nearby public baths and learnt how to – a decision he was to be eternally thankful for.

Training was only eight weeks long and pretty basic, although it was during this time, in the first months of 1940, that Bill discovered he was pretty handy with his fists. Boxing was a routine part of physical training – recruits took it in turns to go a few rounds with the physical training instructor – or PTI, as he was known. 'Right, you long-armed bugger,' the PTI said as Bill put on his gloves, and punched him hard. Considerably riled by this, Bill belted him back. 'I got stuck in,' said Bill. 'I hammered him all round the gym. I knocked him down the first time and he got up like an India-rubber ball – but he didn't get up the second time.'

After he'd finished his basic training in the spring of 1940, Bill was sent to Portsmouth to join the destroyer HMS *Kashmir*. 'She was a lovely little ship,' said Bill. 'One of the K-class destroyers built in 1939 – and she was quick, too. Could do thirty-six knots, comfortable.' Destroyers had been developed at the end of the nineteenth century as a counter-measure against small, fast, motor torpedo boats. Later they became the principal anti-submarine vessel. Comparatively heavily armed with both anti-aircraft guns and depth charges, they were fast, highly manoeuvrable and extremely versatile, with crews of under two hundred men. During the war, destroyers were the mainstay of the Royal Navy – there were more destroyers than any other type of ship by some margin.

Bill was sent below decks, becoming a Stoker 2nd Class in the boiler room. They were a four-man team down there: a petty officer, a leading stoker and two further stokers. Fortunately for Bill, he thought the world of his new boss, Petty Officer Joe Coney. 'He was brilliant,' Bill told me. 'He would tell you something – explain it to you. And he wouldn't ask you again for about a week or so, and then he'd say, "Tell me how that works." And you'd have forgotten.' As punishment, he would be given some onerous task, like repainting part of the boiler room. 'I'll tell you, after that, you never damn forgot again, and when I became a petty officer later on, that's the way I trained my men.'

For much of 1940, *Kashmir* was patrolling home waters. They missed the Dunkirk evacuation, however, because shortly before, another ship had collided with them in thick fog and so at the end of May and beginning of June they were in dock in Hull, undergoing repairs. Soon after, Bill heard about the fate of his old regiment, the 15th/19th Hussars. 'They became mechanized and went to France eight hundred strong, but only thirty-nine came back, so I'm bloody glad I never rejoined them.'

Although Bill suffered terribly from seasickness to begin with, he liked the majority of his fellows, found the work interesting and soon began to enjoy life at sea. In the boiler room there was a strict daily routine: the morning watch was from 4 a.m. until 8 a.m.; the next was from 8 a.m. until noon, then noon until 4 p.m. Four o'clock to six o'clock and six until eight were two-hour watches, then it went back to four-hourly. All the stokers would work one watch on and then two off. Essentially, their job in the boiler room was to make sure engine pressure remained constant. In between, Bill would try and get some sleep – he had a locker for his belongings and a hammock which he would string up. Then, when he'd finished sleeping, he would wrap it up again and hang it back in the hammock racks. There was a mess deck, where all the sailors ate. 'The food wasn't bad at all,' said Bill. In between sleeping and eating, he'd play cards, write letters, or wander up onto the upper deck for some fresh air, although not during the Russian convoys. Bill went on his first trip up through the Arctic towards the end of 1940. 'It was that rough, you couldn't get on the upper deck,' he remembered. 'It was ice-cold. Bloody terrible.'

In April, as part of Captain Lord Louis Mountbatten's 5th Destroyer Flotilla, *Kashmir* was sent to join the Mediterranean Fleet. On the 28th, the flotilla had reached Malta from where they were to operate as a fast anti-shipping force, part of the so-called 'Malta Strike Force'. Unfortunately, tragedy soon struck. Just five days after their arrival at Malta, the flotilla was returning from a night sortie in search of enemy convoys when the destroyer HMS *Jersey* hit a mine at the entrance to Grand Harbour and blew up, blocking the harbour entrance. Mountbatten, in his ship HMS *Kelly*, was stuck inside the harbour along with two others, while *Kipling*, *Kashmir* and the cruiser HMS *Gloucester* were left outside. 'We picked up some of the survivors of *Jersey*,' said Bill. 'She went down right in front of us.' The flotilla was now split up, but because it was too dangerous to stay where they were, the ships stranded outside the harbour – *Kashmir* included – hurried back to Gibraltar.

Although this meant a premature end to the Malta Strike Force, the 5th Flotilla was back together by 10 May, when they took part in the bombardment of Benghazi in Libya and followed it up with another sweep along the Axis convoy routes. They soon came under attack from German dive-bombers, but although some bombs fell uncomfortably close, none of the flotilla was hit. This attack, however, was nothing more than a taster of what was to come.

On 20 May 1941, German paratroopers invaded Crete, and while it was the general opinion amongst the British commanders that it might be possible to defend the island against an airborne assault, it was feared the Axis might also try a seaborne invasion as well. The task of seeing off that threat was given to the Royal Navy, the 5th Flotilla included. This was always going to be a perilous operation because the Mediterranean Fleet had almost no air cover – there was very little available on Crete itself and the Fleet's aircraft carrier could not reach the area until 25 May at the earliest. In contrast, the Axis forces could call on large numbers of bombers, dive-bombers and fighters to support their invasion.

The 5th Flotilla left Malta late on 21 May, rendezvousing with
the battleship HMS *Warspite* southwest of Crete the following
afternoon. 'We knew we were heading for bloody trouble,' said Bill,
'but that's all. We didn't know much about what was going on.' In
any case, he was busy below decks in the boiler room. During battle
stations, the normal daily watch routine went out the window, and
so for most of the time Bill was working hard to keep *Kashmir*
running to her full potential. They found themselves in the thick of
the action straightaway – a ferocious battle was developing, every
bit as vicious as the fighting on the island itself, and already naval
losses were mounting. Within the first few hours of their arrival off
Crete, *Kashmir* helped search for survivors of the sunken cruiser
Fiji, patrolled off the island's coast, bombarded Maleme airfield,
(by that time mostly in German hands), and, along with *Kelly*, fired
at and destroyed two German caiques, small vessels full of enemy
troops.

At first light on 23 May, the flotilla was ordered back to Alexandria.
Having finally come off watch, Bill was up on the upper deck just
before eight o'clock when a swarm of twenty-four Stuka dive-
bombers hove into view. In moments the Stukas had split into two
groups and were screaming over both the *Kelly* and *Kashmir*, bombs
whistling and exploding all around them. The Stukas were attacking
them in waves of three, one from directly ahead, the other two diving
down from each side of the ship. Bill was at his action station at the
stern of the ship when a bomb hit the upper deck, just in front of the
funnel. The bomb then exploded deep inside the ship, breaking
Kashmir's back almost immediately.

The ship split in half. In less than two minutes, *Kashmir* had
almost completely sunk. Those who could jumped into the sea. Bill
dived overboard, only for another bomb to land in the sea just a few
yards away from him. The explosion flung him high into the air
again and severely damaged his eardrums, but otherwise he seemed
to be all right. He resurfaced just in time to see the stern and the bow
of the *Kashmir* upended and almost touching. 'The propellers were

still going round as she slid under the water,' said Bill. Eighty-two men were lost – nearly half the crew – including Joe Coney and Bill's colleagues from the boiler room.

The *Kelly* had also been hit, and survivors from both ships were now struggling in the water. 'The Germans were out to sink us, and we were out to shoot them down,' Bill told me, 'but when we were in the water and had nothing to hit back with, they machinegunned the hell out of us.' He could scarcely believe his eyes as the first Messerschmitts swept overhead, guns roaring. Bill quickly discarded his lifebelt, overalls and shoes so that he could dive more easily when they were being shot at. The ploy worked for him, but nearby, a young seaman had been hit in the shoulder, so Bill swam over to help, clutching the wounded man and making sure they kept both of their heads clear above the water, even when the 109s came back for another attack.

Despite now having no lifejacket, Bill managed to keep himself and the young sailor from drowning for over an hour. 'You could trace the blood,' said Bill. 'And then eventually he died and I just had to let him go. Now you don't forget things like that. Those Nazi bastards went back and re-armed and had another go and that's why I bloody hated them and I still bloody hate them today.' At this point, he stopped talking for a moment. The image of that young boy bleeding to death in his arms, haunts him to this day. As far as Bill is concerned, the lad's death was nothing less than murder. Slightly changing the subject, he told me he was very glad he'd learnt to swim, and by then he'd become a very good swimmer. 'But when I was in the water with that lad and he died,' he added, 'that really took the will to live out of me.'

Nearby, however, was another destroyer from their flotilla, the *Kipling*, which had spent several hours dodging bombs and picking up survivors. 'If I hadn't been near the *Kipling* then,' Bill confessed, 'I would never, ever have made it.' In fact, he was the last person the *Kipling* picked up. Having been in the water for more than four and a half hours, he was exhausted, but managed to heave himself up the nets that were slung down the side of the ship. He was wearing nothing but his underwear and one sock.

There were still plenty more bombs to dodge as they set full steam for Alexandria, but luck was now with them, and they made it safely to port. As they inched into harbour, those ships already there sounded their horns and klaxons in salute, while the crews cheered. 'They gave us a real heroes' welcome,' said Bill.

We were sitting at the back of the bungalow, in a conservatory that Bill's son David built for them. His wife, Linda, had joined us too, and I was glad she was there because some of Bill's memories were so obviously painful for him; somehow, her presence made it easier to talk more freely. Bill's hearing was not particularly good – something he blamed on the bomb that exploded near him as the *Kashmir* was going down – but in all other respects, however, he seemed extremely fit and well. Sunlight poured through the window, highlighting the swirling smoke from his pipe. 'Of course, I never smoked at all during the war. I used to hate smoking. Didn't drink either. Never have done.' He always used to draw his daily rum ration, however, but would give both that and his ration of cigarettes away. Why didn't you ever drink, I asked? He shrugged again, although earlier had admitted his father had been a drinker. 'My father was all right when he was sober,' he'd said, 'but when he was drunk, he'd leather us kids and beat my mother.'

But back to 1941. On his first night in Alexandria they were kept aboard the *Kipling*. Playing cards, Bill won a fair amount of money and used some of his winnings to buy a camera from a fellow sailor. The next day they were all given new kit and taken ashore to a rest camp at Dekheila, just outside Alexandria – 'bloody tents in the desert' – and there Bill promptly lost the rest of his money; his luck with the cards had temporarily deserted him. With no money left he decided to try and pawn his new camera, but having looked around the centre of Alexandria he realized there were no pawnshops anywhere. He found himself ambling into a gunsmith and admiring a

Purdey that was on display – he'd been a keen shot as a boy – and soon got talking to the shop's owner, a French–Italian called Louis Bonnet. Eventually Bill asked him whether he'd consider giving him 300 piastres – one pound – for the camera. Bonnet readily gave him the money, but not only did he refuse to accept the camera, he also invited Bill to come duck shooting. 'I'd love nothing more,' Bill told him, 'but my ship's just been sunk and I've not got much money.'

'Oh, it won't cost you anything,' Bonnet told him. 'We'd have been invaded by the Germans by now if it wasn't for the likes of you. You will be my guest.'

Bill was thrilled and having been given permission duly went out on the shoot. He was lent an old gun, and put in a punt with an Arab to glide him through the rushes and marshes of the Nile Delta. 'I went back with a load of ducks,' grinned Bill. His skipper from the *Kashmir* then approached him. 'I've got an estate in Scotland,' he told Bill. 'Is there any chance you could get me a day's shooting? I'd pay whatever it cost.'

'So I went to Louis Bonnet,' said Bill, 'and I said, "I've been put in a funny position. The skipper's got an estate in Scotland so I imagine he's a fair shot and he's wondering if there's any chance of having a day's shooting. I hate to ask, but . . . "'Bonnet cut him short. 'By all means,' he told Bill, 'but there's one condition. If you don't come then nor does he. Tell him that.' Bill smiled again. 'He treated me like a son, he did.'

In due course, Bill was sent to another ship, a destroyer called HMS *Jackal*, and which he already knew and on which he had several friends. On his first day back at sea, Bill was between watches and was playing cards on the mess deck when the warning bell was sounded. They all flung down their cards and ran to their action stations, which in Bill's case was right next to the tiller flat – in the stern – from where the ship would be steered if the bridge was damaged in action. But he suddenly realized he didn't have his lifebelt on and so raced back to the mess deck, grabbed it, and was just heading to the back of the ship when a torpedo hit, blowing off the stern. Another half-minute, and Bill would have been a dead man.

On this occasion, the *Jackal* survived to sail another day. Having limped back to Alexandria, she was given a new stern, and then just a few weeks later they were sent back out to sea, operating very successfully in the Mediterranean as part of the 14th Destroyer Flotilla for the best part of a year.

On 10 May 1942, however, the 14th Flotilla had been sent out from Alexandria to intercept an Axis convoy that was heading towards Benghazi in Libya. The destroyer force had been told to turn back if it was spotted by enemy aircraft. This they did when two enemy aircraft flew over on the afternoon of 11 May. By then, however, it was too late. A couple of hours after, at around four-thirty in the afternoon, six German Junkers 88 bombers, crewed by men especially trained for anti-shipping duties, flew over and struck HMS *Lively*, which sank in minutes. While *Jervis* and *Kipling* picked up survivors, *Jackal* carried out an anti-submarine patrol. Just before six, the remaining three destroyers set off again at full speed, with German bombers dogging them repeatedly.

The sun had almost set when at just after eight o'clock, a further ten Junkers 88s came to attack the destroyers again. The fading sky was peppered with the black smudges of anti-aircraft fire, and huge fountains of water leapt into the sky as bombs exploded. Bill was with the Engineer Officer by the after boiler room when a stick of bombs hit the ship. One went through one of *Jackal*'s motor boats, on into the upper deck, the No 2 Boiler and out through the bottom before finally exploding directly under the centre of the ship. 'It lifted and bounced the ship like a toy,' Bill recalled. 'The Engineer Officer and myself were stood three feet from the motor boat, so had it been an ordinary bomb and not armour-piercing, we would have been blown to bits.' He sighed and muttered, 'Bad days,' then added, 'I was lucky.' And he was also extremely fortunate not to be badly injured when he went to rescue Harry Hayes from the engine room. 'You don't think about it when you're doing it. If your mate's injured, you try and help him. It's only after that you think, "What a bloody idiot I was." When I went to get Harry, someone said to me, "Don't go down there mate – you'll never get back up." I said, "He's my friend and I'm bloody going down there."' Bill also volunteered to stay on board after *Jervis* had first come alongside at around half-past-ten that night. Initially, it was hoped that *Jervis* would be able to tow the burning vessel back to port. Those who remained tried to man the ship and fight the fires, but it was to no avail. 'Flames were leaping from the funnel up to forty feet high,' said Bill. By four in the morning, *Jackal* was very low in the water, and with the fires spreading, she was a lost cause. The decision was made to cut the tow, and *Jervis* came alongside again to take off the remainder of the crew, Bill included. They then moved away from the burning wreck and fired a torpedo into her so that she finally sank.

Bill could have been forgiven for suffering a severe dose of *déjà vu* as he returned to Alexandria once more, short of clothes and without a ship. For the second time, he was rekitted and sent to a rest camp in the desert. He also renewed his acquaintance with Louis Bonnet. On one occasion Bill and two of his friends were invited to the Bonnets' house for a meal. They had an Italian maid who, Mrs Bonnet told them, could tell people's fortune. At first the maid was reluctant to do so. 'Is she going to tell me I'm going to get blown up?' Bill said, then asked her again. 'It's all right, you can tell me,' he told her. 'I can take it.'

'All right,' she said. 'You will go on a long and dangerous journey, but you will make it home.' She was reluctant, however, to say anything about the other two.

'You're going to tell me I'm not coming back home, aren't you?' said one of Bill's friends.

'Yes,' said the maid.

'And he bloody didn't,' Bill told me. 'I'd never have believed it – but it did happen just as she said.'

Rather than being drafted onto another ship, Bill was in fact sent home on leave, and it was there that he met his future wife. He explained to me that at the time, he'd already become engaged to a girl called Iris. She lived in Salisbury, so once back in England – after a long journey round the Cape – he went to see her. One night, they went to a dance at the Cadena Café in Salisbury, and that's where he saw Linda, who was working there at the time. 'I fell in love with her the moment I saw her,' Bill told me. 'She was the prettiest little thing I ever saw. The girl with the laughing eyes, I called her. Iris was a very nice girl and I loved her very much at the time, but when I met Linda I loved her more. I changed ship, look.'

'I was being bothered by that American,' said Linda, joining the conversation once more.

'Yes, he was drunk, and he kept saying, "What's your name?" and then he turned to me and said, "Hey, Jack, do you know her name?" So I said, "Look here, she's my sister, and if you know what's good for you, you'll bugger off."'

Linda thanked him and later they had a dance. 'It was the Lambeth Walk of all things,' said Linda. 'And he said he'd like to see me the next day, and we did. We went for a walk round Victoria Park.'

'But that wasn't the end of it with that American,' Bill added. Before they'd left the Cadena, he'd gone into the gents and the American had been there. 'You had a lot of mouth in there,' the GI told him. 'Let's see if you can back it up.' 'So I said, "No problem!" Bang, bang and that was it. I laid him out.'

As the American had discovered, it was not a good idea to try and take Bill on; those who did invariably ended up unconscious on their backs. Mediterranean Fleet boxing champion in 1941 and 1942, Bill would never go looking for a fight, but if he felt someone had done him an injustice he was quite happy to make the offender think twice about crossing him again. 'When I was on *Jackal*,' he said, 'if we ever went anywhere – in port or whatever – they'd always put me in charge of the patrol.' If any of the sailors got into trouble, they'd have Bill to answer to. He also told me of an occasion in Algiers, at the time of the Allied invasion of Northwest Africa in November 1942. Bill had been drafted into a naval brigade and on landing they had found themselves separated from their officer. As leading hand, Bill suddenly found himself in charge, although his authority soon came under question when a large Welshman wanted to head off into the town to look for food. 'You're not going,' Bill told him. 'Who's going to stop me?' asked the Welshman. 'I'll bloody stop you,' said Bill, who then knocked him to the ground. He had no more trouble after that.

Another time, towards the end of the war, Bill had a run-in with some Germans. By this time, it was 1944 and he was serving on the American-built destroyer, HMS *Inglis*. They had been escorting an aircraft carrier and one of the planes from the carrier had shot down a German bomber. *Inglis* paused to pick up five German survivors. As the men heaved themselves up the netting, a midshipman who had only just joined the ship called out to one of the cadet officers to help the Germans clamber aboard. Seeing this, Bill grabbed hold of the first German and said to the cadet, 'Catch hold of his legs, and one, two, three, sling him into the middle of the deck.' Watching this was the new midshipman. 'What do you think you're doing?' he asked Bill angrily.

Bill turned to him and said, 'Are we fighting this war or nursing these Nazi sons-of-bitches?' Reported to the captain, Bill was let off with a warning to abide by the rules, but a few days later, to his disgust, he saw the German pilot line up his four men and give them the Nazi salute. 'Don't you heil Hitler on one of His Majesty's ships!' Bill told him. 'Do that again and I'll put you over the bloody side!' Two days later the German pilot deliberately brushed into Bill with his shoulder. 'I bloody belted him,' Bill told me, 'and he went flat on his back. He could speak better English than me, and he said, "Never do that again." But after that, if he ever saw me coming, he got out of my way.'

By the time he joined HMS *Inglis*, Bill was a petty officer. He'd spent six months in Algiers, then returned home in the summer of 1943 to take his petty officer's course and to do some further electrical training. It meant he could see Linda again and soon after his return, they became engaged. They'd written regularly to each other while he'd been in North Africa. 'We had a code,' Linda told me, 'because when he went back overseas just after we'd met, he didn't know where he was headed. So he said to me, "When I write, take the first letter of each paragraph and that will tell you where I've been posted." And when I got his first letter, it spelt out the word "Algiers" so that's how I knew where he'd gone.'

They were married on 14 June 1943. 'I didn't really know him very well,' admitted Linda. 'But I knew all right,' said Bill. 'As soon as I saw her, I said to myself, that's the girl I want to spend the rest of my life with. We've been married sixty-three years and it don't seem a day too long. You couldn't wish for a better wife if you searched the world over.'

Bill stayed with the *Inglis* until the German defeat, then was transferred to an LCT (Landing Craft, Tanks) and sent to the Far East for the invasion of Japan. 'We were steaming through the Red Sea when they dropped the atomic bombs,' said Bill, 'and I admit I was quite pleased about it. I didn't want to invade Japan.' They continued their journey, however, ending up in Singapore. With the war now finally over, Bill was faced with several possible careers. The first was to become a professional boxer. In Singapore he went three rounds with the Australian middleweight champion, but didn't win outright. 'There's no draw in amateur boxing,' said Bill, 'and I always said that when I got beat, I'd never put a pair of gloves on again.' But the Australian tried to persuade him otherwise. 'He said to me, "I'm used to going ten or fifteen rounds, but that was the hardest three rounds I ever fought." He said I should think about taking it up professionally, but I wasn't going to do that.'

The second opportunity he had was to go on an engineer's course and become a permanent officer in the Navy, which he also turned down. 'The Commodore said to me, "The day will come when you'll regret this – you're an idiot. You're throwing your chance away."' Bill sighed, remembering. 'I wish I had my time over again – he was right. But you come to a crossroads in life and you make a decision. How often do you go the wrong way? Quite often, and that was one of those times.'

Instead, he bought himself out of the Navy, intending to go back to farming. It took some wrangling, but his father was keen for him to take over his farm. 'My parents had got divorced and I felt a bit sorry for the old man,' Bill explained. 'But by the time I finally got home, he'd bloody given it up – he'd sold the farm and bought a smallholding. I was that bloody mad, I could have turned round and gone back into the Navy.' But he didn't. He wanted to go back to the land and to be with Linda and so he took a job as a dairyman in Somerset, then later moved to a farm near Salisbury, before ending his working life at Stoke Farthing.

Understandably, Bill looks back on his time with the Navy with pride. A glance at his service record confirms what is obvious from talking to him: that he was a very professional and competent sailor, who worked hard, listened to what he was told, and who always took his own responsibilities very seriously. From the start of his naval career to the end, his character is described as 'VG' – very good, and his efficiency rated as 'superior'; in 1943, he was also mentioned in dispatches. And like many men who lived and died in the Second World War, he had an absolutely unshakeable sense of honour towards his friends and shipmates. 'If I've got a friend,' he told me, 'he's my friend for life and I'd give my life for my friend. But if he's my enemy . . . ' He let the sentence trail. There are ghosts there, and he still can't forgive those German pilots for what they did after the *Kashmir* went down. Linda then turned to me and said, 'You know, he was sitting there the other day and he said, "Please Lord, cleanse my soul of all this hatred."'

Bill nodded. 'It's all right for people to talk,' he said, 'but what happened – it leaves a scar. You can't remove it.'

FRIENDSHIP

John Leaver & Fred Walsh

No matter how grim or brutal the Second World War might have been, most combatants were able to draw a few positives from the experience. Chief amongst these was the sense of camaraderie that developed amongst men thrown together entirely because of the war. When young men were living, sleeping, eating, and fighting for their survival together the intense bonds of friendship that developed were often all that kept them going.

Very many terrible things could befall a young serviceman in the Second World War, but for sustained misery and pain, becoming a prisoner of war of the Japanese was a notably unfortunate fate. Most faced brutal treatment by their guards, extremely harsh conditions, as well as starvation and disease. The death rate of Allied prisoners in German POW camps was around four per cent; in Japanese camps, this figure was between twenty and thirty-seven per cent – at best a one in five chance of survival. A good friend could make the ordeal easier, however; good friends could offer one another solace, humanity, and physical and mental support during the darkest of moments. Sometimes, a pal could make all the difference between living and dying. And this was most certainly the case for John Leaver and Fred Walsh.

John was born and raised in the cathedral city of Salisbury in Wiltshire, the middle son of three. His father had been to sea in the

First World War – a petty officer on minesweepers. He had survived and on reaching home again, had got a job working as a mechanic during the week and as a chauffeur to a farmer at the weekends. 'He was a lovely man, my father,' says John. 'A very charming man, and brilliant with his hands. He could make anything.' It was tough for almost everyone in the 1930s, but although they were poor, they were a close family, and John grew up a happy, stable and contented lad.

At fourteen he left school and began work in an outfitters' shop. He was still there when his call-up papers arrived in May 1941. Two brothers were already in the army, but John was told he would be joining the RAF. After initial training – square-bashing and route marches in Weston-super-Mare – John was due to begin an armourer's course when, in September 1941, he suddenly received orders to report to Liverpool Docks. He, along with a number of other RAF groundcrew, was to be shipped overseas.

As instructed, John reached the quayside and reported to a hut alongside the docks. The only other person there was another man of similar age, who immediately came over, shook John's hand, and introduced himself as Fred Walsh. They got talking and immediately recognizing a kindred spirit in one another, stuck together until they boarded their ship the following day. In fact, they remained pretty inseparable throughout a very long three-and-a-half-month journey.

They had been told they were to become the groundcrew for 84 Squadron, but catching up with the squadron proved to be something of a wild-goose chase that took them round the Cape to Durban – where Fred introduced John to his wealthy uncle – then on to Bombay, back through Iraq, Syria, Palestine and Egypt and eventually, at long last to the Far East, by which time, John and Fred had become extremely good friends.

Fred was from Guernsey in the Channel Islands, the son of a policeman. He'd left the island before the Germans occupied it in June 1940, and although not much older than John, was already married with a young son. The voyage was a very new experience for them, for although Fred had been to sea when crossing the Channel between Guernsey and the south coast of England, neither had ever really spent much time away from home and neither had ever left the United Kingdom before. Nor did they have any idea how long they might be away or when they might next see their families. The knowledge that there was a good friend to share this adventure across oceans and continents made the separation from home much easier.

They never did catch up with the rest of the squadron, however. By mid-February 1942, they were steaming towards Singapore, when news arrived that the British there had surrendered to the Japanese. Their ship was promptly diverted to Sumatra instead, in the Dutch East Indies. 'We couldn't believe Singapore had fallen,' says John. 'We had enough manpower there. If they'd just stood firm . . . It still irks me, because I think they should have fought on, I really do.'

John and Fred arrived in the Far East amidst the panic and mayhem of the biggest military defeat in British history. On Sumatra, the squadron's groundcrew were split up. Half were told they would be sent to Rangoon in Burma, the other half were to stay on Sumatra. John and Fred were amongst those told to stay, although four days later they were on the move again. Against the advice of the ship's captain, who suggested they sail straight on to Australia, the RAF officer in charge decided they should do as they'd been ordered, and fight on in the best way they could. That meant landing at Morak in Java and helping the Dutch pilots at Bandoeng airfield, who were still desperately holding out against the Japanese onslaught. Once again, the squadron was divided: some of the men were ordered to man the guns around the airfield, while the rest worked on the surviving planes. But yet again, John and Fred stayed together, singled out to help keep the aircraft flying.

Theirs was now a lost cause, however. John remembers that one day they were attacked by no less than seventy-two Japanese bombers. 'Lucky for us, they all attacked the far side of the aerodrome from where we were,' he says, 'but you could see hundreds and hundreds of bombs coming out of these planes, then the most terrific explosions and the ground shuddering. The aerodrome was flattened – the hangars were down, the planes there were on fire and there were bits of bodies all over the place.' They held out for a few more days, cannibalizing the wrecked aircraft to keep the remaining two planes airborne, until on 8 March, several British army lorries reached the airfield. 'Don't you know there's bus-loads of Japs coming?' the soldiers yelled at them. On the back of the trucks were several Bofors anti-aircraft guns, but instead of training them on the advancing Japanese, the soldiers were heading for the port. 'They balked,' says John, 'and that really sticks in my throat. They were being bloody yellow.' With nothing left to fight with, the groundcrew grabbed whatever kit they could and clambered aboard the lorries. 'I suppose the idea was to try and get a ship to Australia,' says John. But there was no ship to take them, and they were left with no option but to wait for the Japanese to arrive and then surrender. Both John and Fred could scarcely believe what was happening. 'I felt bloody sick about it,' admits John. Their active contribution to the war effort had lasted less than three weeks.

After they had surrendered, they were ordered back to Bandoeng airfield to fill in the bomb craters. When they got there, they saw that those men from the squadron that had been ordered to man the guns had been killed. 'They were all dead,' says John. 'Every one bayoneted.' But despite such scenes, John says he had little idea then of how they would be treated as prisoners of war. 'Actually to begin with, they weren't too bad,' he says of the guards, although conditions were far from comfortable. He, Fred and the remainder of the squadron's groundcrew were initially put into a holding compound on Java; then in August, they were moved to another POW camp at Batavia, where around two thousand Allied service-men were interned. Fred had kept an occasional diary ever since leaving England, and incredibly he managed to keep it going throughout their incarceration, writing with whatever he could find on scraps of paper. 'Food scarce,' he noted on their arrival at

Batavia on 17 August 1942. 'Bad sanitation and cramped billets . . .
Rumours that we will not be here long.'

The rumours were correct. Towards the end of October they were
herded onto a ship and taken to Singapore. Once there, they were
disembarked, hosed down, then ordered to board another ship, an
old, rusting hulk called the *Dai Nichi Maru*. It was a freighter, built
on the Clyde in Scotland at the end of the previous century and not
designed to take passengers at all. The Japanese, however, were planning to carry more than a thousand prisoners and slightly more
Japanese troops on board. Keeping close to one another, John and
Fred climbed the gangplank up onto the deck then followed the line
of prisoners slowly descending a vertical iron ladder into one of four
holds on the ship. John and Fred were two of nearly three hundred
men crammed into their hold, and it quickly became very apparent
that the Japanese viewed the prisoners as nothing more than cargo,
no different from the damp bed of bauxite (aluminium ore) that lay
at the bottom of the hold and onto which the bewildered men now
stood and squatted.

Conditions had become progressively worse the longer they had
been in captivity, but the *Dai Nichi Maru* was truly appalling, a
degrading, dehumanizing, claustrophobic hulk. There were only a
few toilets and these were wooden structures built on to the outside
of the boat. In order to use them, a prisoner would have to climb up
the iron ladder onto the deck, then clamber over the side to the
latrine. The holds were also dark and dank, with tarpaulins covering
over most of the open roof. Food was given twice a day in large tubs
lowered from the deck and was usually a thin, watery gruel or red
fish. The men ate it with whatever they could – an old mess tin or
enamel mug, for example. There was no way of cleaning them afterwards. The water ration was also severely restricted and the water of
bad quality. 'We got two cups of water a day,' says John. 'One in the
morning and one in the afternoon and that was it. Your mouth was
parched up dry – it was horrendous.' As for the fish – well, he cannot
even look at a fish bone now. 'It's daft, but I still hate red fish,' he says.

'To me they're vile.' To make matters worse, most men, like John and Fred, were still dressed in KD – khaki drill, the RAF's twill cotton tropical kit – with no spare clothes. Facing a journey of uncertain length to an unknown destination, in winter, and in a ship that was so inadequate it would disintegrate the moment it was hit by a torpedo, John and Fred could do little but pray their ordeal would soon be over.

The *Dai Nichi Maru* was one of the notorious 'Hell Ships' that transported Allied prisoners from the Philippines, Dutch East Indies and Singapore to camps elsewhere in the Japanese Empire. Apart from the infamous Burma–Thailand railway, these ships were the greatest cause of death amongst Allied POWs. Japanese reports suggest that more than 10,000 of the 50,000 prisoners transported in this way died *en route*.

John remembers the voyage as one of barely comprehensible horror. Many prisoners had boarded in a weakened physical condition, but soon disease became rife, with dysentery crippling many just a few days into the voyage. The stench – of faeces, sweat, oil and fish – was appalling. 'By God, it was terrible,' says John. 'You've got those with dysentery, being sick all the time, and plenty that were dying. And the moaning – that's all you could hear.' Later, Fred noted in his diary, 'More and more chaps were fainting daily. I shall never forget it. There were no medical supplies on board. Chaps were lying sick and dying all around.'

The first man to die in their hold was an army captain. They couldn't leave him there and so they tied a rope around him and two men clambered up the vertical ladder and hauled up the body. One of the officers then said a few prayers and they tipped his body over the side. 'I still get bloody bad dreams about that,' admits John. 'Towards the end there were three or four deaths every day, regular as clockwork. Sometimes even five or six.' Some prisoners, John says, simply gave up the will to live. 'You saw their spirit drain away.'

After calling into port at Formosa (now Taiwan) they continued northwards and ran into storms, which brought more misery.

Huddling together to keep warm as the ship rolled, the condition of many of the prisoners dramatically worsened. The food – both the quantity and quality – deteriorated further, as did the water available. Although few men had the stomach to eat anything, they were slowly but surely dying of starvation and thirst, as well as dysentery.

They finally docked at Moji in Japan on 24 November, nearly a month after setting out from Singapore. John was in better condition than most, but Fred had started to become ill; a few more days aboard and the death toll would have been far greater. 'We were lucky,' says John. 'Because Fred and I were put in the same hold, we were able to keep each other going.'

At Moji, a hundred names were called out, and once again, good fortune ensured that both John and Fred were among those listed to be taken to a small new POW camp on the tiny island of Mukaishima, some thirty miles east of Hiroshima. The Japanese had built the camp there for two reasons: first, it was almost impossible to escape, and second, the prisoners provided a very useful labour force for the Hitachi Shipyard on the island.

Not that they were in the best physical shape after their ordeal on the *Dai Nichi Maru*. Fred was taken to hospital with serious stomach problems, but most of the seriously ill were, as he noted in his diary, 'too far gone'. Within a few days of their arrival at the end of November, the first man had died. John helped the medical orderly measure up the dead man. Soon after, the Japanese produced a rough coffin. 'We had to carry him out of the camp and up a track,' says John, 'then dig a hole and fill it with wood. Then we put the dead lad on top and set fire to it.' Further deaths swiftly followed. By the end of the year, twelve men had died; by the end of March 1943, that figure had risen to twenty-one.

Life on the island was monotonous in the extreme. The camp itself was small, a compound of about 75 feet wide by 150 feet long, enclosed by an eight-foot-high wooden fence. The prisoners lived in long huts, made of rough wood, unpainted inside and out and without any form of heating. The men slept on a raised wooden deck; the latrines were outside: a wooden box with six holes covering a concrete pit that had to be emptied every week. The urinal was tacked onto the end of the living block, separated only by a partition wall, and particularly unpleasant for the prisoners sleeping at that end.

Every day, they got up at around 6 a.m., then were marched the two miles down to the port. The working day began at seven. They were allowed a ten-minute break in the morning and half an hour for lunch, or 'tiffin' as it was known, and another ten-minute break in the afternoon. They finished work at 4.30 p.m., and then were marched back to the camp. Every four weeks, they were given a day off. Fred worked in the welding shop all day long, but John was part of a work-gang who pushed carts of supplies from the ships around the island. 'There was one guiding the front,' he says, 'two each side on the ropes and two at the back pushing.' As slave labour went, it wasn't too bad. 'At least we were on the move all the time,' he says, although the work was exhausting. 'In the summer we were black as the ace of spades,' says John. 'We'd sweat like hell and we were absolutely knackered all the time. Your legs would go. There'd be blokes screaming at night their legs hurt so bad.'

As John is the first to admit, their camp was not as brutal as some. 'Ours was a doddle compared to what some had to contend with,' he says, but even so, theirs was still a very tough, uncomfortable existence. The summers were hot, but the winters were cold; they only had one set of clothes, which were filthy and worn. The island was fairly bare: grassy with sandy soil, and with few trees. During the monsoon they got absolutely soaked with little opportunity to get their clothes dry, whilst in the summer there was almost no shade at all.

Nor were they ever given enough food. Meals consisted of a tiny bowl of rice each first thing in the morning and some watery soup, the same again at lunch and on their return to the camp in the evening. 'Sometimes they put these tiny minnows – dried fish – in as well,' says John. On a good day they'd eat maybe as much as 700 grams of food, but it could easily be as little as 350 grams. It simply did not provide enough energy for the kind of hard physical work they were doing. John says they spent much of their time dreaming and obsessing about food. 'You would be lying on your bunk at night and you'd say, "I could really do with a nice plate of beef," and someone else would say, "I could murder a treacle pudding," then others would shout, "Shut up!"' Every day on his march down to the port, he would pass a small factory. He had no idea what was made there, but the smell tantalizingly reminded him of his mother's treacle pudding. 'Every day I had to smell that,' he says. Only once the war was over did he discover they had made mustard pickle there.

Any opportunity to supplement their meagre rations was readily taken. One Saturday in winter, they were marching past a field of frozen swedes. There was a guard with them who was kinder than most and he told them to hide behind a wall where no one could see them, then passed them some swedes. 'We struggled to break the bloody things,' says John. 'We smashed them against the wall and trod on them and eventually got some bits, and we sat there chewing them.' Two hours later, however, they all suffered terrible stomach-aches.

On another occasion, John was helping take cartloads of wooden faggots to the kitchens at the dockyard. 'We got there just after a mealtime,' says John, 'and this Jap was scraping the crust of rice off the edge of his wok, and he gave it to us.' They all ate a small bit, then carefully hid the rest in their clothes and took it back to the camp. Once there, John told Fred about his extra rations and together they went to the latrines to eat it. 'We took it in turns to eat it while the other kept watch,' says John. 'Can you imagine? It was horrible in there – it really stank. The things you did for a tiny bit of food.'

The second time he was given some rice scraps, he was caught, however. By this time, John had been in the camp long enough to know what to expect. Sure enough, he was taken out and beaten with a pick-axe handle. 'It was like being hit with a baseball bat,' says John. They hit him on his body and across the back of his head, which knocked him out. 'When I came to,' he says, 'I was in a wheelbarrow being pushed back to our barrack block.' Punishments were frequent and often for the slightest misdemeanour, and although prisoners were not beheaded or used as bayonet practice as in other camps, their guards could still act with ruthless cruelty. 'A favourite punishment was to put people in a box,' says John. This would be just a few feet square and the prisoner would have to sit crouched up. 'The agony would start after half an hour,' says John, 'but you could be in there for days.' On 9 November 1944, Fred noted, two prisoners were put in boxes for ten whole days for breaking into stores near their billets. Another punishment was to make prisoners kneel on strips of bamboo, with further strips placed on the back of their legs with the weight of the body resting on them. 'There was no way you could relieve the pain,' explains John, then adds, 'God, they were sods for what they did.'

And whilst some of the guards were all right, others were most definitely not. Towards the end of 1943, one of John's friends, John Yateman, became ill. One day, John was talking to him in their barrack block when one of the guards came up to them and told Yateman that he'd heard the doctor talking about him. 'You're going to die very soon,' the guard said with relish. 'They can do nothing for you.' 'Yateman was a big lad,' says John, 'about six-foot-four, but when he heard this he just cried and cried. He was a hell of a nice kid, and he didn't want to die. I was so angry I could have grabbed that guard's rifle and stuck his bayonet into him right there. The bastard.' Sure enough, Yateman did die – of tuberculosis – on 7 January 1944. 'I'll never forget it,' says John, 'seeing him crying his heart out.'

Occasionally, Red Cross parcels would reach them, which would be shared out. Typically, these included clothing and tins of meat, cigarettes and chocolate, but it was not until April 1944, a year and a half after they first arrived on Mukaishima, that the first letters from home reached the prisoners. The sense of isolation and of being out of touch with all that was familiar could easily sap morale, but as John points out, the ongoing friendship between Fred and himself helped sustain them. Then in the summer of 1944, Fred became ill again. He had never properly sorted out his chronic stomach problems that had begun during the voyage on the *Dai Nichi Maru*. Incredibly, he had been taken to hospital early in 1943 but the operation had not been a success. In August 1944, he left the island for another operation, and to John's great relief, not only did he return soon after, but his treatment appeared to have been a success.

Although more than a hundred American prisoners joined them in September that year, the British prisoners knew that by then the tide of the war had turned. One of them knew Japanese and he used to read out bits of Japanese newspapers to the others. 'We heard about D-Day and so on,' says John, 'and about the Americans retaking the Mariana Islands. After that we started to see the Superfortresses flying over.' He remembers one time when he was down at the dockyards and suddenly a huge din of aero engines could be heard. 'We looked up and saw 80–100 aircraft coming over. It gave us the most incredible lift.'

But the closer they got to the end of the war, the worse their condition became. By the autumn of 1944, both John and Fred weighed well under nine stone, and rations were getting worse. Red Cross parcels gained ever-greater importance. The prisoners were almost delirious with excitement when 200 parcels reached the island – almost one each! – but having unloaded them and carried them up to the camp, the camp commander told them they could only have a small portion of them every two months. The rest were locked up. John shakes his head at the memory. 'We could have murdered them for that.'

The twenty-third prisoner out of the original one hundred died in February 1945. Mukaishima may have been less severe than other camps, but nearly a quarter of them had died. The victim had contracted pneumonia, as had several others. Most had suffered chest infections and other ailments during what had been a particularly cold winter. But somehow the surviving prisoners had kept going, bolstered by the knowledge that the Allies were slowly but surely winning the war. On 9 May, just a day after VE Day, word reached them that the war against Germany was over. Meanwhile, they were seeing more and more American aircraft flying over. Moreover, there was less and less work to do at the dockyards and, John noticed, nearly all the Japanese workers on the island had gone – presumably called up as replacements for the Imperial Army. 'It suddenly went very quiet,' says John. 'There was hardly any work being done and then one day one of the guards said, "Yesterday one bomb, 120,000 killed." He looked like he could kill us there and then because we were happy. So we shut up quick.' In fact, after the first atomic bomb, the whole island, prisoners included, were told to stand by to evacuate. The order to leave never came, but some of the Japanese guards told the prisoners they would kill them all. 'We were scared,' admits John. 'We really thought they might.' Nor was John in good physical shape. His weight had dropped further and he was suffering the vitamin deficiency disease, beri-beri fever. For ten days they waited with mounting apprehension. Then at one o'clock on 17 August 1945, the camp commander told them the war was over. A minute later, the British officer in charge led the prisoners in a rendition of 'God Save the King'. 'I have never heard it sang so well before as it was today,' noted Fred in his diary. 'A wonderful feeling . . . so came the day we had been waiting for for three and a half years.'

There was a short while to wait until the Americans came to liberate them, but on 12 September, they left the island for good, and were taken to Yokohama Harbour. From there, they boarded an American aircraft carrier that took them to Sydney. 'There were thousands on that ship,' says John, 'but even then Fred and I were called out and put on the same deck and mess table together. It was incredible but that's how it was throughout the whole war.' When they reached Sydney there was no ship to take them back to

England, so the Red Cross billeted the former prisoners with Australian families while they waited for their passage home. Once again, John and Fred remained together. 'They were the nicest people,' says John of the family that took them in. 'And to be honest, staying with them was just what we needed to get back to normal. They took us out – to the opera, to the races. Looked after us like we were their own family.'

After a month of recuperation, they boarded a ship bound for Southampton. The two of them had been together almost every day from the moment they left Liverpool in September 1941, to the moment they arrived home in January 1946. 'Fred was a hell of a nice man,' says John. 'The best friend in the world. In all that time we never once had a cross word. Not once.'

With the war over, however, they finally went their separate ways. Reunited with his wife and son, Fred initially returned to Guernsey. But his father had died and Fred found it hard to settle down. He had been very taken with Australia, however. Furthermore, the family he and John had stayed with in Sydney had told them that if they ever wanted to move to Australia, they would guarantee them both a job and a place to live. 'They were as good as their word,' says John, 'and they sorted Fred out, and he stayed there for good.'

The world is a much smaller place now, but in the decades following the end of the war, it was no easy matter keeping in touch with a friend on the other side of the world. And anyway, John had his own life to sort out. His return was marred by the news that both of his brothers had been killed in France shortly after D-Day. 'That knocked the stuffing out of me,' he admits – for a year and a half, he'd had no idea they had been killed. Unsurprisingly, their loss also left his parents heartbroken. John remembers coming home one night and seeing his mother crying at the kitchen table. 'She could barely hold a cup of tea,' he says. 'I talked to my father about it and he said, "She's like this most days."'

John, on the other hand, initially adjusted well. Soon after the war, he met and married his wife, Jean, and together they had four 'super kids'. He had a good job and was content, living in Salisbury with his parents nearby. But then one day, some years later, he suffered a sudden and catastrophic breakdown. The combination of his wartime experiences and the loss of his brothers had finally got the better of him. He was in hospital for months. 'I'd never talked about the war, and nor had anyone asked me about it,' he says. 'I later discovered that people had been told not to ask former POWs about what they'd been through. I'd always wondered why they hadn't.' Gradually, however, he began to improve, although for years after he was taking Librium, 'like they were Smarties', a drug he fears may have done him more harm than good. 'It affected my memory,' he says. 'There's quite a lot I can't remember from when the kids were younger.'

He was fortunate to have a very close and supportive family, however, and made a full recovery, but as the years passed by he often wondered what had become of his old pal who had helped him through the long years of war. He regularly made enquiries but it took a number of years before he finally tracked Fred down via their respective Rotary Clubs. That was in 1982; they had not heard from each other for thirty-seven years. With the friendship now rekindled, a few years later, in 1989, Fred made a trip over to England and the two were reunited. Fred spent a month in England, 'and we got on as well as we'd ever done,' says John.

But by then Fred's health was in decline; he had recently had yet another stomach operation. 'You see, the war affected my nerves,' says John, 'but it affected Fred too – with his ulcers and ongoing stomach problems.' Fred's visit to England was the last time the two saw each other. In 1998, John received a call from Australia to say that his friend had lost his battle with Motor Neurone Disease and had passed away. 'I've never cried in my whole life,' says John. 'Not when I heard my brothers had died nor when my mother and father passed away. But when I heard that Fred had gone, I sobbed my heart out.'

During Fred's last visit they spent a lot of time reminiscing and talking about the war years. They recognized that they had been lucky to have survived, but they were both in agreement as to why. 'Fred said to me, "Without you, I don't think I would have lived,"' remembers John, 'and I know that but for Fred, I wouldn't have made it either.'

LOVE AND WAR

Warren 'Bing' Evans & Frances Wheeler

Bing Evans and Frances Wheeler were finally married on 5 August 1945, just two weeks after he'd returned from three and a half years away at war. Three and a half years in which Bing had taken part in four major invasions, had made five seaborne landings and been involved in seven campaigns. He'd been shot in the head, wounded by a grenade, taken prisoner, escaped three times and finally been due to be executed as a spy. Somehow, he'd survived, but he was no longer the same man Frances had promised to marry four years before. Physically, he was a shadow of his former self. A tall, athletic, six-foot-three and weighing 225 pounds when he left for war, by the time he was standing at the altar, he had only raised his weight back up to 160 pounds. He was also still struggling with malaria and after they said their vows, Frances could feel the feverish perspiration on his face as they kissed.

'We should not have gotten married so quickly after he came back,' says Frances now. 'It was just too soon, and we had to get acquainted again after we were married.'

'She had waited for me all that time,' says Bing, 'but after what we'd both been through we were complete strangers. Each of us married a dream. But I've never regretted it. She's been my life – the most wonderful being in the world. And all through the war, even during the darkest moments, thoughts of her kept me going.'

Two weeks after their wedding in Frances's home town of Brookings, South Dakota, they were far away in Hot Springs, Arkansas, at an army rehabilitation centre for former prisoners of war. There, Bing had a thorough medical examination, but as Frances points out, they were checking him for any physical effects of his incarceration, not psychological damage. And despite the weight loss, physically, he was more or less all right. Psychologically, he was in trouble. 'I was having nightmares,' admits Bing. Shortly after they were married, he was standing up in bed screaming and Frances leant over and touched him. 'I knocked her clear across the room,' says Bing. 'That's when she learnt never to touch me in the middle of one. From then on she just . . . '

'I learnt to get away and call your name,' Frances cuts in. 'I still do. He still has them – not as often, of course, but when he starts moaning, I just get away.'

These dreams are always the same. 'There's one I hesitate to talk about, because usually if I do, I have a nightmare about it later.' Well, please don't, I say as we sit in the living room of their home in Indiana. Frances then points out that the damage is already done: he's started thinking about them, so he might as well continue.

Bing sighs. 'Probably my most miserable nightmare . . . there are two really miserable ones, actually. The first is from when I'd escaped prison camp the second time.' Bing had been a prisoner at Aflag 64, in northern Poland, some fifty miles south of Gdansk, but in January 1945, with the Russians getting ever-closer, the Germans decided to evacuate the camp and move the prisoners west. With the petrol shortage the Germans were now suffering, the men were to march to their new camp, nearly 350 miles away. It was freezing cold and Bing began getting painful chilblains on his feet – he still has a problem with his feet to this day because of that march. After a few days, he and two others decided to try to escape. This they did as their prisoner column passed through a town – they simply ducked out of the line and hid in a deserted building.

Heading for the Russian lines, they suddenly found themselves caught in the middle of a battle between the German and the Soviet forces. Neither Bing nor his comrades spoke Russian, so they decided to hide until the battle passed. Finding a mound of potatoes in a frozen field, they discovered that next to it was a kind of cellar, where potatoes were stored during the winter. There they hid, eating raw potatoes until they were found by a young teenage boy. On seeing the Americans, the boy ran away but returned later with some hot soup for them. The following day he brought civilian clothes and a few blankets. For a few days, the three Americans continued to shelter in the cellar, the battle raging intermittently above them. But in the fighting above and around them, the Germans briefly managed to push the Russians back. Soon after, Waffen-SS troops found not only the potato cellar but the escaped prisoners and the boy down there too. 'And the next day they lined this young fellow up and they'd gotten his whole family too. There were five of them,' says Bing. 'Two younger kids – one of them couldn't have been more than five or six – and the mother and father. And they made us watch as they shot them, one by one. And that nightmare still haunts me today.'

The three Americans were separated – Bing is unsure what happened to the others – but he was tried for being a spy. 'It was perfunctory,' he says. 'I was in civilian clothes and I didn't have a leg to stand on.' Inevitably, he was found guilty and told he would be shot on 22 April 1945. In the meantime he was kept in solitary confinement in a heat cell. 'They had heaters down one wall, and I was in there, stark naked,' he says. 'The heat was on and you couldn't stand it, you could barely breathe, and of course, there were no ablutions or anything – you had to urinate in the corner.' Eventually, the heat would be turned off and then the interrogations would begin. After enduring this repeated torture several times, his German captors realized Bing had nothing to tell them, and so he was flung into a compound with a number of Russian prisoners until the date of his execution. 'And I'd thought they'd mistreated us Americans!' says Bing about the Russian prisoners. 'They were starving.' His second terrible nightmare derives from this experience. A horse-driven cart comes past, filled with horses' bones. The bones are tossed into the compound, and because Bing is in better shape than most of the Russians, he manages to snatch one of the larger bones, break it open and suck out the marrow. 'I fought those Russians over the bones of an old dead horse,' he says. 'I mean, how low can you get?' He sighs again. 'Those are the two dreams that make me cry.'

Before he met Frances, Bing's early life had hardly been sweet-smelling roses, either. From Aberdeen, South Dakota, he was just four years old when his father had died of cancer, a tragedy that left his mother to raise both him and his younger sister on her own. She did what she could by waiting tables, but they were always broke. Time and again, unable to pay the rent, they would be kicked out of their home. 'I don't ever recall living longer than six months in any one place,' he says. Then his mother became ill. Bing got a job selling newspapers. 'I had the best block in town,' he says, 'but the only way you kept that block was to fight for it.' But he was strong and resourceful and never lost a fight – he couldn't afford to. It did get him in trouble, though. One time, he put an opponent in hospital and found himself before a juvenile court. Fortunately, the judge looked upon him kindly and secured him a job as a salesman on the understanding that he give up fighting. Bing jumped at the chance – the $18 a month was enough to keep him and his sister alive all the time his mother was in hospital.

When his mother's health improved, Bing went back to school and life began to pick up. He excelled at sports, especially American football – six-foot-three was unusually tall back then – and he won a sport scholarship to South Dakota State. He was also a pretty decent baritone – which was why he gained his nickname, after the crooner, Bing Crosby. In fact, so good was his voice he was also offered a scholarship to the New York School of Music, and would have gone there rather than South Dakota State had he not broken his nose playing baseball. This affected his voice, and unable to afford the surgery he needed, he opted to play football instead. This was to prove a fateful decision, because it was at South Dakota State in Brookings that he met Frances Wheeler.

Frances had been raised on a ranch near Brookings, one of five children – four girls and a boy – and although life during the Depression-hit 1930s was hard, they always had enough to eat, slaughtering whatever cattle and sheep they needed for themselves from their own farm. All the children were expected to help out and Frances worked hard, ploughing fields and learning to drive two horses at one time. During harvest time, they would link up with other farming families and help one another to do the threshing, working in crews that would move from farm to farm.

Living out on the ranch, she would take the family's Model A Ford and drive herself into Brookings every day to attend high school, although once she began college at South Dakota State, she and her two sisters moved into a flat in town. And it was during her first year at college that she met Bing: Thanksgiving Weekend, November 1940.

The football scholarship had given Bing a room, two meals a day and tuition, but he still had no money, so he had joined the National Guard. A dollar a week for a bit of drill on Thursday evenings seemed like easy money. But his twin commitments of sport and National Guard meant that Bing did not have time to try and hitch 180 miles back home to Aberdeen for Thanksgiving. Still, he wanted some fun and there was a dance that Saturday night. The problem was, his current girlfriend had gone home and he had no one to go with, so he asked a friend if he knew any local girls who might accompany him. His friend suggested Frances Wheeler.

When Bing called her, Frances agreed. She already knew about him because of his footballing prowess, and her current boyfriend was also out of town for the weekend. 'Sparks flew even that first night,' says Bing, who thought his pretty blonde date was just about the most beautiful girl he'd ever seen. 'It was pretty much love at first sight,' agrees Frances. Afterwards, as they were saying their goodbyes, Bing plucked up courage to ask her to the dance the following week, but she turned him down; she was already due to be going with her boyfriend. He did get to dance with her again, however. 'I was with my date and he was with his,' says Frances, 'but every third dance he danced with me.'

'And then we didn't really see each other too many times after that for a little while,' continues Bing, 'until word came to me that she had broken up with her date and I was in the process of doing the same and so that's when we got together for good.'

Within a very short space of time, he knew he'd found his soul-mate, but his new-found happiness was soon shattered. No sooner had he found her than he was having to let her go, for in February 1941, he was inducted into the Army. His sole motivation for joining the National Guard had been the dollar a week; suddenly, the money no longer seemed worth it. At that time, his obligation was only a year of service, but although it would be a further ten months before the attack on Pearl Harbor, Bing felt sure war was inevitable. In his heart of hearts, he knew they would be kept apart for more than one year.

Frances went to the train station to see him off, promising to wait for him. Bing was to join the 109th Engineers, part of the 34th Infantry Division, and their initial training was at Camp Claiborne in Louisiana. She had no idea when she would see him again, and driving back home, she admits, she cried so hard she could barely see the road.

As it happened, they would see each other again just once in four and a half years. That was at the end of the summer of 1941, when she and Bing had one short, but precious, weekend together. To be with him for those brief couple of days, she had driven all the way to Louisiana from South Dakota – over a thousand miles. Bing took her to the Roosevelt Hotel in New Orleans, and, having saved up his pay for several months, produced a diamond ring and asked her to marry him. She accepted.

They hadn't really talked about a date for getting married, but then shortly after Pearl Harbor, in December 1941, the 34th Division was posted to Fort Dix in New Jersey. This was an embarkation camp. The penny quickly dropped: before long the division would be posted overseas. Bing was distraught. It had been bad enough leaving

Frances in South Dakota. Now he would be heading to an unknown destination for an unknown period of time. Possibly for years. God only knew how long the war would last. Perhaps, Bing suggested, they should get married straightaway. Frances asked her parents. 'If it'll make him a better soldier, then perhaps you should,' they told her, and so she packed up her wedding outfit and prepared to travel to Fort Dix while Bing bought a ring and the wedding licence. It was fifteen hundred miles from South Dakota, but Frances managed to get a ride in a car with two of the officers' wives who were going to visit their husbands before the battalion set sail. But it was winter, and there was snow on the road, and having driven through the night they had only reached Rockford, Illinois, when they were hit head-on by another car. The driver had been drunk and asleep. Frances's travelling companions were badly hurt, but although Frances was flung from the car, she suffered no more than a cut lip, chin and broken arm. Far worse was seeing her wedding clothes strewn across the road and struggling to get them back into the suit-case. All three were taken to hospital. The officers were given leave to visit their wives, but because Bing was, as yet, unmarried, he had to stay behind at camp. There would be no wedding after all, nor a chance for the two of them to see each other and say goodbye.

Three days later, a heartbroken Frances left hospital and began the bus journey back to South Dakota. Bing was already on the ship sailing out into the Atlantic. In the black of night, he went out on deck, tore up his wedding licence and tossed the ring into the ocean. 'I figured it was bad luck,' says Bing. He could only hope that Frances would, as she had promised, wait for him to return.

Despite his reluctance to leave Frances, Bing took to soldiering like a duck to water. Intelligent, physically tough, and a natural leader of men, he had been promoted to staff sergeant by the time he headed overseas, and was one of the very first to volunteer to join a new elite fighting unit, the 1st Ranger Battalion, formed in Britain in June that year, and based on the same principles as the British Commandos.

'I thought it seemed like a challenge,' says Bing, who was interviewed in person by his future commanding officer, Lieutenant-Colonel William Darby. Bing was impressed. 'He had charisma,' he says. 'He led from the front – he was a soldier's leader, and if the going got tough, he was part of it.' Bing also impressed Darby: he was among the first three hundred selected on 11 June.

Bing and the new battalion were soon sent to Scotland, basing themselves at Achnacarry Castle, in the shadow of Ben Nevis near Fort William. A Commando Training Depot had already been established there – 'Castle Commando, we called it' – and although the Americans were trying to distance themselves from the Commandos, they were initially trained much the same way and for similar purposes. They were even instructed by Commandos. It was tough, both physically and mentally. As well as learning hand-to-hand combat, the Rangers were expected to climb mountains, carry out speed marches, river crossings and swim in ice-cold water, in addition to developing scouting and small-unit tactics. Amphibious training was also extensively carried out, usually with live ammunition.

Throughout his training, Bing continued to do well, and by August 1942, had been singled out as the 'archetypal American Ranger'. As First Sergeant of E Company, he was due to take part in the first aborted Dieppe Raid in August. He missed the eventual attack because by then he had been promoted again to Sergeant-Major and Darby refused to risk him on such an obviously fateful mission.

So instead his first combat was during the TORCH landings in Northwest Africa in November 1942, when a joint American and British force carried out the largest seaborne invasion the world had ever seen. The Rangers led the successful assault on the Algerian town of Arzew – and were at the thick of the fighting for much of the campaign in Algeria and Tunisia, operating along the front, and behind enemy lines during large parts of the fighting.

They were also amongst the first troops ashore during the invasion of Sicily in July 1943, and again when the Allies landed in southern Italy in September that same year. Not for nothing had the

Rangers become known as the 'Spearheaders'. 'The first time we landed, I felt a sense of anticipation,' admits Bing. 'The second time, I felt less anticipation but a little apprehension. The third time, a great deal of apprehension.'

By then, Bing had seen more combat than most in the US Army. He'd had his fair share of close calls too. He mentions an occasion in Tunisia, in February 1943, when the Rangers were ordered to infiltrate deep behind enemy lines and make a night attack on an Italian garrison in the mountains at a place called Sened.

The Rangers' attack caught the Italians completely by surprise. One group of Rangers ran straight into the barrack block, where sleepy disorientated Italians were just beginning to wake up. With their Commando knives, the Rangers cut the Italians' throats. Outside, flares were arcing into the sky. Suddenly, the place was lit up and Bing turned and saw an Italian emerge from the shadows and rush towards him. 'He was intent on killing me,' says Bing, 'and I looked into his eyes and saw they were big and frightened and bewildered and I just couldn't pull the trigger on my .45. I froze.' Then a shot was fired and the Italian slumped in front of him. Bing turned and saw his friend Tommy Sullivan. Tommy had saved his life.

There was a lucky escape on Sicily, too. The Rangers had just made their landing there. Having marched three miles inland behind enemy lines, they were attacking the port of Porto Empédocle when they met an enemy outpost. By this time Bing had received a battlefield commission and was now First Lieutenant of F Company in the recently formed 3rd Ranger Battalion. A sniper had obviously spotted he was the senior officer and so singled him out. The shot hit Bing's helmet above his left eye, penetrating the steel, but miraculously the bullet got caught in the lining, so that by the time it hit his skull, the force of it was largely spent. Instead of blowing his brains out, the bullet merely scored the top of his head. His wound looked a lot worse than it was: blood poured down his face and his men thought he was in serious trouble. After applying sulfabromide on the wound, however, and wrapping a bandage round his head, he put his helmet back on and kept going. 'But,' he says, 'I had a hell of a headache later on.'

Others were not so fortunate. Battlefield casualties amongst the Rangers were high, largely because they were always in the thick of the action. Bing lost many good friends. 'For the most part, you just had to put these deaths behind you and go on,' says Bing, 'but there were definitely some you lost that hurt more than others.' Like Tommy Sullivan, who'd saved Bing's life in Tunisia, but who was killed during the fight for the Chiunzi Pass in the Salerno beachhead, when the Rangers fought off twelve major counter-attacks. Or like Ronnie Kunkle, one of Bing's greatest friends in the Rangers. 'He was my First Sergeant,' says Bing, 'and he was an old timer. We had so many green troops by the time we were in Italy, but Ronnie would always look after them. And we'd been together enough so that he read my mind a lot of the time. I'd give an order and he'd be there.' Ronnie was killed on 30 January 1944, at Cisterna. 'I remember a kind of cold, empty feeling when I knew that Ronnie had been killed,' says Bing.

But sometimes it was the death of comparative strangers that got to him. In Sicily, he lost one of his second lieutenants, a Texan named Slim Camel. 'I didn't know Slim that well,' admits Bing. 'He came as a replacement, but he was gung-ho and anxious to prove himself and so I let him do something I shouldn't have and he was killed as a result. I've always felt bad about it, but then on the other hand, if I'd sent one of the more experienced guys and they'd gotten killed, I wonder what I would have felt then.'

He then mentions an episode that took place towards the end of 1943. The Rangers were fighting in the Venafro Valley north of Naples, but their progress was being blocked by enemy forces dug in on the top of a mountain. Every time they tried to advance, the Germans opened fire, stopping the Americans in their tracks. After being held up for several days, Bing was told to take a patrol up the mountain to assess both the enemy strength and what was needed to knock them off. The next night, Bing took a small section of men up the mountain but found the summit all but deserted. Reporting back, he was then ordered to take his company up there and make the mountain secure.

The very next night, Bing went up the mountain again. 'We infiltrated right in amongst them and took the mountain without too much trouble,' he says. 'But when daybreak came, we saw why it had been easy.' Under the cover of darkness, they'd not realized there were two summits, rather than one, divided by a narrow gully fifty–seventy yards wide and a hundred-odd feet deep. As dawn broke, they could see German troops moving about on the other side. Having told his men to take cover, he then sent a small patrol to see if there was any way of reaching the other summit without being detected, but they soon came under fire. 'We'd taken their observation posts,' Bing explains, 'but because of this gully we couldn't get at them and they couldn't get at us.' Radioing down to Colonel Darby, Bing told him the task was not going to be so easy after all. 'Lieutenant,' Darby yelled, 'I don't give a damn what you do, but I want you to take the other side of that mountain, d'you hear?'

'Colonel, it's impossible,' Bing replied. 'It'll take me time to work out how I can get round there but there's no way I can frontal assault that and take it.'

'Lieutenant, those are your orders,' Darby told him then signed off.

Bing thought for a moment, then shouted out across the gully, 'Is there anyone over there who can speak English?'

'Yes,' came the reply.

'Good, well let's call a truce,' Bing suggested. 'You alert your men, and I'll alert mine, then let's talk this situation over.'

The German agreed, but insisted Bing stood up first. Taking a deep breath, Bing did so – and then so did the German. Bing explained he'd been ordered to take the mountain, and suggested the Germans give up now. If they did, he promised, he would introduce them to some sweet Red Cross girls and make sure they all got a steak dinner. The German laughed, but Bing's ploy failed. Over the next few days, however, they began to regularly hold similar truces. Bing found out the German was called Hans, that his parents ran a hotel in Leipzig, and that before the war, they'd sent him over to the USA to the Kellogg Center at Michigan State on a hotel management course. And when Bing asked to speak to the officer in charge, Hans told him there was no officer, but that as the senior NCO, he was in charge. But no matter how much they talked to one another across the gully, Bing could not persuade him to surrender.

Every night, however, Bing's Rangers were carrying out further reconnaissance of the German position, and after a few days had pinpointed all their guns and machinegun positions and were almost ready to make their renewed assault. After four days, some American paratroopers were sent up to join the Rangers. Bing explained the situation to a colonel from the 82nd Airborne, and told him what they'd learnt about enemy dispositions, but the Colonel angrily said, 'Well, I don't see a damn thing!' and told Bing he could not understand why they had not attacked earlier. Suddenly Hans called out from the other side, 'He hasn't been here long, has he, Lieutenant?' The colonel was so startled he tripped backwards and fell over.

After this, the colonel agreed to let Bing's men carry out their own infiltration and assault of the German position before his paratroopers took over. The night attack was entirely successful, but although Bing had given orders that Hans should be taken alive, the following morning he discovered to his dismay that the German was amongst the dead. 'It's kind of difficult when fighting at night to determine who is who,' says Bing, 'but although he was my enemy, I felt really sad about his death.'

Bing made his final seaborne invasion at Anzio in January 1944, the ill-fated Allied attempt to break the deadlock further south at Cassino. By that time, Bing says he just felt numb. He mentions the opening of the film, *Saving Private Ryan*. 'Do you remember when the guy lands he seems to be operating in a vacuum, with no sound? Well, when I landed in Anzio, I was in that vacuum. I did everything I was supposed to do. I didn't experience fear, I didn't experience apprehension, I just operated in a vacuum. My mind just closed everything else up. It's a strange feeling.' Unsurprisingly, Bing is anxious to make it clear that he thinks little of war films. 'But that bit,' he says, 'they got right.'

The landing was initially successful but the Allies missed opportunities to make an immediate thrust for Rome, thirty miles to the north, and the Germans soon counter-attacked in force. A week later, the 1st and 3rd Ranger Battalions were given a mission to infiltrate behind enemy lines and attack and capture the town of Cisterna, a few miles inland. But the enemy strength there had been massively underestimated – Bing knew that because his scouts had reported otherwise. Setting out on the night of 29 January 1944, he knew they were headed on a suicide mission, and so it proved. By noon the next day, both battalions had been largely wiped out. Bing's memory of that last day is hazy, but he remembers ordering his men to open fire on German troops guarding a column of American prisoners. Then there was an explosion and suddenly the ground was rushing up to meet him. What happened over the next few weeks is a complete blank; his next memory is of being a prisoner of war in Germany.

Frances, meanwhile, stayed home in South Dakota. She had wanted to do something active for the war effort and intended to join the WAVES (Women Accepted for Volunteer Emergency Service) or the WACS (Women's Auxiliary Army Corps) but when she suggested this in a letter to Bing, he begged her not to. 'He'd heard too many stories about women in the services getting involved with other men,' she says and so honouring his wishes, became a court reporter instead in Watertown, some sixty miles from Brookings, which, she says, kept her 'very busy'. Living in a house with two girlfriends, they all spent many hours in the evening listening to the radio and trying to follow what was going on in the war, and in Frances's case, especially what was happening in the Mediterranean theatre. 'We also got our news through the movies at that time,' she says. One night she had gone to see a film when a newsreel was shown and she spotted Bing; she could scarcely believe it. 'I went to that movie every night for five nights to see him on the newsreel,' she says.

Then came the news that two Ranger battalions had been destroyed at Cisterna. Frances had been in her room when the news was announced on the radio. Her two girlfriends had been listening, but didn't dare tell her what they had heard. Only when she got to work at the courthouse and the judge came over to console her did she finally learn what had happened. 'I remember going out in the hall in the lobby and walking around,' she says. 'I think I was crying. Nobody came near me. The judge went back into his office. He was so sorry he had said anything, but I had to know.' [4] At that time, she had no way of knowing whether Bing was dead or a POW. An agonizing month passed until a card arrived from Germany stating that he was alive and a prisoner.

Not until September 1944 did she hear anything more. It was another postcard, addressed to 'Mrs Warren Evans'. The card had once again been pre-printed, although Bing had been able to cross out any words that did not apply. It also said, '*I can receive mail from you, my next of kin.*' 'I got it,' says Frances. 'So I started sending my letters to him, always with the return address of Mrs Warren Evans.' Later she was notified that she could mail one package a month out to him, and so she sent him warm clothes, socks, cigarettes and candy and filled any spaces in the box with popcorn and cookies. Only two of these parcels ever reached him.

Wondering where he was, and worrying about when and if he would be home, wore Frances down. She was still very young – a smart, beautiful girl with her life ahead of her. One of the girls she lived with was engaged but broke it off when she began dating a pilot instead; there were many other broken engagements as Bing was well aware. But although she still went dancing, Frances continued to turn down every date she was asked on. She had promised Bing, and she meant to stick by him. 'It was,' she says, 'a long, hard wait for me.'[5]

---

[4]   *Heroes Cry Too* by Marcia Moen and Margo Heinen, p.168.
[5]   Ibid., p.185.

* * *

With his execution date looming, Bing managed to successfully escape – his third bid for freedom during his time as a POW – and by hiding by day and travelling by night, he and another American eventually reached the River Elbe. They swam the first part of the river easily enough, but the final twenty yards were deep, with strong currents. In his present physical state, Bing doubted he would be able to make it but then they spotted an American half-track, and yelled to them to get their attention. 'This guy waded out as far as he could go and handed his rifle out to me,' says Bing, 'and I grabbed the end of it and managed to get the rest of the way across.' His friend then did the same. At long last they were truly free.

After crossing the Elbe, Bing was taken to Leipzig, a German city recently captured by the US First Army, and put in a hotel. He soon got thinking: hotel, Leipzig, and the German called Hans on top of the mountain in Italy. He asked a few questions. The American military police at the hotel told him it had been owned by an old couple, but no one knew where they were now. But Bing persisted and eventually he was given an address and went to see them. They were living in a small apartment but they were happy enough to talk to him. And the more they talked, the more Bing was convinced that, incredibly, they *were* Hans's parents. Their name, he discovered, was Schüller, and one day Frau Schüller said to him, 'You know something about our Hans, don't you?' 'And so I told her the story about the mountain top,' says Bing, 'and it was one of those times I cried. And she put her arms around me and said, "We understand."'

When Bing eventually made it back to the US, it was July 1945. As soon as he could, he called Frances and heard her voice again for the first time in three and a half years. It was as though a miracle had occurred. Not only was he alive, she was still there, waiting for him as she'd promised she'd do. They agreed to meet halfway, at Minneapolis, and when she got off the train, she saw him further along the platform, anxiously checking each carriage. 'I recognized him right away,' says Frances, 'but what a sight! His neck looked so shrunken and his uniform was just hanging off him.' She started running towards him and then he spotted her and began running too until at last they reached one another and fell into each other's arms. The long separation was finally over. 'And we were married two weeks later,' grins Bing.

It's been a long and happy marriage but the war has always haunted Bing, and, in a way, Frances too. On his return home, he made the most of the GI Bill and went back to college and eventually ended up working for an agricultural supply firm, the Ralston Purina Company. It kept him busy and he did well, working all round the United States; in one fifteen-year period they lived in nine different states and eleven different cities. He was on his way to the top of the company, had three great boys, and a beautiful wife, but with every passing year, he found it harder to put those terrible experiences of the war years to one side. He wanted to forget, to move on; but a part of him wasn't going to let that happen.

Around twenty-five years after the end of the war, Bing reached his lowest ebb. 'The company was very good to me,' says Bill, 'because a lot of times I just disappeared. I didn't want to see people, didn't want to be with them. I'd be holed up in some motel and no one knew where I was. It was a terrible time in my life.'

What he didn't realize until later was that he was suffering badly from post-traumatic stress. Eventually, he went to a Veterans of Foreign Wars meeting, and stood up and talked: about the war, about his experiences – a confessional of kinds. 'It was packed, that place,' says Frances. 'And when he talked there wasn't a sound. It was so quiet you could have heard a pin drop.'

That night there was no miracle cure, but it marked a turning point. From then on, life began to improve again. Together, he and Frances worked through it, until in 1993, they both went to Italy with a few other former Rangers and their wives. They visited some of the battle sites and the American cemetery at Nettuno, near Anzio, where

7,861 fallen soldiers lie. Wandering through the rows of white crosses, Bing found the graves of many old friends, men who'd been cut down when he had somehow survived: Tommy Sullivan, Slim Camel, Ronnie Kunkle and others he'd known and fought beside.

'The bus was loaded and waiting,' says Frances, 'but they just quietly waited for him. And I stood off to one side and watched him as he went down those rows and saw the names he was looking for.'

That was a cathartic experience for him and although a dozen years on he still suffers the occasional nightmare, he is now at peace with his past. 'If you'd asked to talk to me about all this stuff twelve years ago,' says Bing, 'I'd have told you to go jump in a lake. But I've been a very fortunate man really, to have gone through what I have and still come out being able to enjoy life like I do.' And as far as he's concerned, there is one person above all, who has made that possible. 'I was so lucky to find her,' he says. 'Frances. She's been my rock, I tell you. She's been my rock.'

DERRING-DO

George Jellicoe

A retired general who commanded a brigade during the Falklands campaign and has since become a distinguished military historian, once told me that there are essentially four categories into which soldiers divide themselves. At the bottom are the 'failures' – a small number who either desert or simply fall to pieces. Next are the 'survivors'. This group makes up the vast majority, who cling on by their fingernails, doing what they are told but nothing more. On the third rung are the 'stickers' – those who are utterly reliable and who do more than is required of them. Typically, they are good, solid officers and NCOs, and without them, any army would fall apart. And at the top are those he termed the 'thrivers' – a very small minority of men who relish the challenges of war and tend to excel, whatever situation they are placed in. It is into this final category that George, 2nd Earl Jellicoe, falls.

For some strange reason, his wartime exploits are less well-known than they might be. At the time I first wrote to him, there was no biography in print, or personal memoir, while other books and documentaries in which he has featured were notable by their lack of any quotation from him. And yet George Jellicoe had been second-in-command of the SAS, first commander of the SBS, had taken part in two of the most famous and outrageous SAS raids of all time, and later in the war had captured Athens by riding into the city on a bicycle.

I met him, at his suggestion, at the House of Lords, one dark winter's afternoon, where, as Father of the House, he has served longer than any other peer. He was even Leader of the House under the Heath Government in the early 1970s and although the right of hereditary peers to sit in the Lords was abolished in 1999, he was immediately created a life peer, as Baron Jellicoe of Southampton, enabling him to continue taking an active part in politics. Indeed, at regular intervals throughout our conversation, he would excuse himself whenever the Division Bell rang, and hurry off to vote, returning a few minutes later. In between, however, he talked freely and quite openly, and with no small amount of humour – he was a man who smiled a lot, both actually and with his eyes – yet his stories were always laced with enormous amounts of self-deprecation. It soon became clear that this modesty about his achievements was the reason why there was so little written about him. 'Shooting a line', to use wartime parlance, was anathema to him; I suspected he would rather die a thousand deaths than for anyone to think he was a glory-seeker of any kind.

In many ways it was surprising that he was ever in the Army at all. His father, Admiral Lord Jellicoe, was First Sea Lord during the First World War and commanded the British Fleet at the Battle of Jutland. As a boy, it was expected that George would follow his father into the Navy. But unlike most boys his age destined for a career at sea, he was not sent to Dartmouth Naval College. 'My father thought Dartmouth was rather restrictive,' Earl Jellicoe told me, 'and thought it would be better for me to go to a normal public school first.' His father was a good friend of Lord Selbourne, a former First Lord of the Admiralty, but who was by then Warden of Winchester College. 'He persuaded my father I should go there,' he said, 'and so I did.'

By the time George had turned sixteen, he had decided that he no longer wanted to join the Navy, however, and so wrote to his father explaining his reasons. 'Because he was a very kind man,' Earl Jellicoe said, 'he didn't raise any immediate objection.' Rather, his father suggested that next time they saw each other, they would have a chat about it. The family home was at St Lawrence on the Isle of Wight, so next time he was back, George was met by his father and taken for a round of golf. They talked about George's decision and by the time they had finished their round and had lunched in the clubhouse, his father had accepted his son's reasons with good grace. 'I can't remember what I said exactly,' said Earl Jellicoe, 'but I didn't tell him the real reason, which was that I was one of those young gentlemen who from time to time peed in their bed. And the idea of peeing in a hammock with somebody underneath me didn't appeal to me at all!'

He had also decided that he would much rather try and pursue a career in the Foreign Office. Although he insisted he was 'not very bright' at school, he still won the Herbert Smith Prize at Winchester and an exhibition to Trinity College, Cambridge. By the time he went up to Cambridge in 1936, he had already become the 2nd Earl Jellicoe; his father had sadly died the previous year. His three years at Trinity College, he told me, were among the happiest of his life. 'I loved it. I think I made three of the closest friends I've ever made,' he said, then added, 'unfortunately all three died in the war.' Peter Pease, whom Richard Hillary wrote about at length in his memoir, *The Last Enemy*, became a Spitfire pilot and was killed in the Battle of Britain; David Jacobson, a top scholar at Eton, was killed in North Africa in 1941; and Mark Howard, who had inherited Castle Howard in Yorkshire, was killed in Normandy in 1944.

By the time George left Cambridge in the spring of 1939, he and his friends were all very conscious that war was looming. His first political stirrings had been prompted by the Munich agreement the previous autumn, to which George had been vehemently opposed. He had also spent time in Germany before going up to Cambridge, touring around and brushing up his German. 'I drove all around Germany with a very nice young chap who was an art student,' he told me. 'I remember him saying that I didn't need to worry too much about the prospect of war. He said, "I'm absolutely certain that if the Führer does decide to do something foolish, the Army chiefs will not allow him to go too far." He was later killed outside Moscow.'

George was staying with his friend Mark Howard at Castle Howard when the news of the German–Russian pact was announced. It was August 1939, and as they realized, the accord meant that war was now inevitable. At Mark's suggestion, George joined the Coldstream Guards, and they were immediately sent to Sandhurst for their officer training. By Christmas, however, George was laid low with pneumonia and by the time he had recovered had heard that the 5th Scots Guards were forming a ski battalion with the aim of going to help the Finns in their war against the Russians. 'I was a keen skier,' said Earl Jellicoe, 'so I didn't bother going back to Sandhurst, but joined the ski battalion instead. We had a marvellous time. On the trip out we left a trail of champagne bottles all along the railway, then had two or three weeks in Chamonix skiing every day.' Most were young well-to-do men like himself, and although there were a number of commissioned officers among them, most, like George, had been more than happy to join the Ski Battalion in the ranks as guardsmen.

'It was a crazy idea,' said Earl Jellicoe, although it was probably fortunate for these eager young men that the Finns, and then the Norwegians, capitulated before the Ski Battalion could be sent into action. Instead, George rejoined the Coldstreams, was posted to a holding battalion and, much to his frustration, spent May and June 1940 stuck at Regent's Park Barracks while the rest of the regiment was fighting in France. To compensate, he began spending more and more time partying in the evening – the Bag o' Nails in Soho was a favourite haunt – and getting back later and later until eventually he was put on a charge and confined to barracks.

His confinement coincided with the formation of the Commandos, they were being set up by Colonel Bob Laycock, already well-known to George as one of the leading huntsmen in the country. George volunteered immediately, as did a number of other friends from the disbanded Ski Battalion. His interview, at White's Club, was straight out of an Evelyn Waugh novel. 'I wasn't used to being interviewed,' Earl Jellicoe admitted, 'and hadn't prepared an answer for the obvious question of why I wanted to join the Commandos. I hesitated, and

Colonel Laycock answered for me: "I suppose you want to have a crack at the Boche?" I said, "Yes, Sir," although really I just wanted to get out of Regent's Park Barracks.'

Training in Scotland was 'good fun – quite a lot of training on ships and rubber boats and that sort of thing', and then in January 1941, they were shipped off to the Middle East as No 8 Commandos, or 'Layforce' as it was known. They were an eclectic bunch that included the Prime Minister's son, Randolph Churchill, Evelyn Waugh himself, and David Stirling, soon to become the founder of the SAS. 'It was the first time I really got to know David Stirling,' Earl Jellicoe told me. 'He slept most of the voyage out, very rarely emerging from his cabin except to play Chemin de Fer in the evening. We called him the Giant Sloth.'

Layforce never achieved its full potential in the Middle East, largely because the Royal Navy, which was to transport them on raiding missions, was particularly occupied at the time with the evacuations from Greece and then Crete. Under-used and losing their sense of purpose, the men became frustrated. The writing was on the wall, but in June, George and Carol Mather, a good friend who had been with him in both the Ski Battalion and Layforce, devised a plan – and were given permission – to make a two-man raid on General Rommel's headquarters at Ain el Gazala, west of Tobruk. Having taken passage to the besieged port, they began making their preparations. Their idea was to sneak out of Tobruk Harbour in a light landing craft known as an 'R-boat', land near Ain el Gazala, carry out their attack, and then make their way back by land, passing through the perimeter of Tobruk held by the 18th Indian Cavalry. 'It was an absurd idea,' Earl Jellicoe admitted, but fortunately, the naval officer charged with landing them at Ain el Gazala was a hopeless navigator, and despite three separate attempts, they were never able to make a landing. Soon after, like the Ski Battalion before it, Layforce was disbanded.

George rejoined his parent unit, still the Coldstream Guards, whose 3rd Battalion was now in North Africa. Despite being involved in the Crusader offensive of November and December

1941, in which the British Eighth Army managed to push the German and Italian forces back several hundred miles across Libya, Earl Jellicoe confessed that he 'very much enjoyed his time with the 3rd Battalion'. He told me about an incident in January 1942. The battalion was on the extreme right wing of Eighth Army, and their role was to carry out night patrols and raids. One day, he was asked to take an early morning patrol across the main coastal road and up into the sand dunes overlooking the coast, and from there establish an observation post. George took a small truck and a handful of men, travelling as far as they could in the truck and then continuing on foot. But no sooner had they set up their observation post than they saw that Rommel's forces were on the march and that the enemy had started their counter-offensive that very same morning.

Hurrying back to the truck, they found it had already been destroyed. They now had no choice but to try and walk back, over-take the advancing Axis forces, and somehow get back to their own lines. They walked for a day and a half, with barely enough water to sustain them, until they eventually spotted a well, but George had got to within fifty yards of it when they were suddenly fired on. Turning back, George was shot through the shoulder. 'It wasn't serious,' he said, 'but knocked me over.' Gathering himself together, he carried on, struggling with a bullet hole through his chest and almost no food or water. 'I'm not entirely sure who it was who fired on us,' he said, 'but in any case we had another day's march before finally meeting some British armoured cars out on a reconnaissance patrol, and they ran us back to Benghazi.'

So how far had he walked, I asked? He shrugged. 'Nothing, really . . . eighty miles, that sort of thing. No, it wasn't epic.'

Having rejoined the battalion, he carried on as normal without any treatment for his wound other than a bit of bandaging. Unfortunately – and unsurprisingly – it did not heal properly and became inflamed, so eventually he had to be sent back along the coast to a hospital in Alexandria. There he was attended by pretty nurses and soon recovered. 'Rather fun, really,' he said.

George was still on sick leave in Cairo when he met up with David Stirling once more. Since the disbandment of Layforce, Stirling, having overcome his bout of sleeping sickness, had been busy forming a new specialist raiding force called L Detachment of the Special Air Service – the SAS. He had realized that the desert was a vast place and that airfields, especially, were difficult places to guard. If they could just get close enough, a handful of men should be able to sneak in at night and, with a few guns and lumps of high explosive, cause serious levels of damage and mayhem. Having managed to win over General Auchinleck, Commander-in-Chief Middle East, Stirling had been promoted and authorized to raise a small force.

Early missions had been disastrous, largely because they had initially depended on parachuting from aeroplanes to reach their targets, and this was too haphazard and lacked the necessary stealth. But Stirling had persevered, and by April 1942, when he met up with George Jellicoe in the bar at Shepheard's Hotel, his achievements had begun to mount. Key to these successes was the help they received from the Long Range Desert Group (LRDG) who had offered them a form of desert taxi-service, guiding them very circuitously to very precise points in the desert from which they could make their lightning raids.

Stirling was now looking to expand his force and so asked George to join him as his second-in-command. 'I told him I'd be delighted and honoured to if my battalion would release me,' Earl Jellicoe recounted. 'And not to my surprise, my battalion had no difficulty about releasing me.' He had 'no idea' why Stirling wanted him as his deputy, but admitted that his ability to speak French might have played a part. 'David was keen for me to take a particular interest in the Free French who had joined him,' he said, 'and I suspect I was very flattered by him asking me to join him.' He was, he admitted, also excited at the prospect of carrying out further raids behind enemy lines, all of which sounded 'rather thrilling'.

George's first raid was not in the Western Desert but on the Axis airfield of Heraklion in Crete, one of four separate attacks planned for the island's air bases. Their aim was to knock out as many aircraft as possible in an effort to reduce Axis air strength prior to a much-needed convoy sailing from Alexandria to relieve the besieged British island of Malta.

Planning of the raid was left entirely to George and the commander of the Free French squad, Georges Bergé. Their attack on Heraklion, the largest of the airfields on Crete, was to be carried out by just five men and a Greek guide: George and Bergé; a French sergeant, Jacques Mouhot; two other Frenchmen, Jack Sibard and a seventeen-year-old, Pierre Leostic; and their Cretan guide, a former Royal Hellenic Army lieutenant called Costas Petrakis. Leaving Alexandria in a Free Greek submarine, the *Triton,* on 5 June, they set sail in great secrecy for Crete, reaching the coast east of Heraklion five days later.

The SAS men clambered into their inflatable dinghies in the early hours of 10 June. They were three miles out, rather than one, as had been planned, and consequently had quite an arduous row, scrambling ashore later than intended. They also then had a tough climb through mountains, and realizing they were overloaded, discarded some of their kit. They were now, however, well behind schedule: the raid was supposed to have taken place on the night of 12/13 June, but although they reached the edge of the airfield by the evening of the twelfth, they had not had time to survey it properly; and in any case, they nearly ran into a German patrol. Deciding caution was the better part of valour, they withdrew to where they could safely lie up throughout the thirteenth and keep a good watch over the airfield.

They soon realized there were more than fifty Junkers 88 bombers at Heraklion, and so once darkness had fallen, set off to carry out the raid. They were nearly caught out again as they were going through the barbed wire that lined the perimeter. George was lying behind Mouhot, and the SAS men thought the Germans had passed, but the last man in the patrol spotted them. Instantly, Mouhot turned on his back and began to snore. Thinking they must be drunken Cretans, the patrol moved on. The raiders had just got through the wire when they heard the patrol return once more, but again, luck was with them. At that precise moment, two RAF Beaufighters attacked the airfield, distracting the German patrol and providing the SAS men with the ideal diversion.

While Bergé and the Frenchmen busily began fixing fused Lewes bombs to a cluster of aircraft, George went off on his own and planted explosives on a fuel dump and a number of vehicles. As the bombs began exploding, the airfield became a sea of flames. Escaping was no easy matter, but in the confusion, they were able to fall in behind a column of German troops and at the perimeter deftly peel off into the shadows. They had not put the airfield completely out of action, but as Earl Jellicoe concedes, 'We had a vast bag – twenty-plus aircraft.'

Despite the success of the attack, they were faced with a difficult journey to their rendezvous, which was off the south coast with a small Royal Navy-manned fishing trawler. They were only three or so miles from the airfield when dawn broke, and in any case, Bergé had been leading them in the wrong direction until George realized the position of the Pole Star meant they had been heading north. As they lay up by day, their Greek guide went off to find some food and returned with news that the Germans had shot fifty Cretans as a reprisal for the raid.

By night they continued their journey across the mountains. By day they lay low, although their hiding places were invariably discovered by inquisitive local Cretans. Eventually they reached the coast, hiding in a sheltered valley near the home village of their Cretan guide. They were again discovered, this time by a local man who offered to fetch them food and drink. Bergé was immediately suspicious, but their guide, Costas Petrakis, assured them he knew the man's family. 'He's perfectly OK,' Petrakis told them.

Later that day, Bergé sent George and Petrakis to go and make contact with the people who were going to take them off the island and row them to the trawler. This they did successfully, but Petrakis could no longer walk – his feet were in a terrible way from the arduous journey across the island – so George made his way back to

the others on his own. It was by now night-time, and in the dark, he
struggled to find the place where they had been lying up. Eventually,
however, as dawn was about to break, he discovered their small
encampment, with their kit looking suspiciously tidy and with no
sign of the Frenchmen. 'I knew immediately that something was
wrong,' Earl Jellicoe told me. Soon after, some Cretan boys ran up to
him, and although he did not speak Greek, he quickly realized they
were telling him to clear out right away – which he promptly did. A
few days later, he and Petrakis were successfully picked up and taken
back to Alexandria.

'The Cretan that Bergé had been so suspicious about had betrayed
us,' the Earl explained. 'He was one of those very rare things: a Greek
quisling.' As Earl Jellicoe discovered, the Frenchmen had been surrounded by Germans, but they had tried to fight their way out until
they ran out of ammunition and were forced to surrender. Tragically,
the seventeen-year-old, Leostic, was killed, and the others taken prisoner. Bergé was eventually sent to Colditz.

By the time George rejoined the rest of the SAS at their camp at
Kabrit in Egypt, David Stirling had begun planning his biggest raids
yet. Armed with new specially adapted American jeeps, they set off en
masse, nearly a hundred men and thirty-five vehicles. To avoid detection, they drove down into the vast chasm of the Qattara Depression,
until emerging again some 150 miles behind enemy lines and some 60
miles south of the coast. Hiding in a series of ridges, Stirling planned
for them to operate in the area for the best part of a month.

Largely because of faulty intelligence from GHQ in Cairo, the first
set of small raids on 7/8 July achieved little. George was leading
another raid on 12 July, however. Heading over open desert in late
afternoon towards enemy airfields at Fuka, their detachment of three
jeeps was spotted and attacked by German aircraft. In moments, two
of the vehicles were burning fiercely, but George had managed to
hide his in a small crevice. It was still badly damaged, however, with
several bullet holes in the radiator. Only by filling the holes with

plastic explosives and by taking it in turns to urinate into the radiator, were they able to stagger back to their makeshift desert camp.

Leaving a small core of men behind to guard their camp, George and David Stirling returned to Kabrit to stock up with more supplies. Eight days later, they were back, with food, cigars, drink, twenty brand-new jeeps, and vital intelligence that one of the Fuka airfields, Sidi Haneish, was in constant use and full to bursting with enemy aircraft. Stirling now planned a massed jeep attack in full moonlight. 'This last attack was very exciting,' Earl Jellicoe told me. 'Instead of carrying out the attack in the normal stealthy way, with just a handful of chaps creeping onto the airfield, we decided to take eighteen jeeps in formation – two columns of seven with four in the middle navigating the way.' It was certainly audacious. The night before, they practised driving in formation, then after spending the following day preparing, they were ready.

They set off at sundown, hoping they would not be spotted by enemy aircraft. The journey was only forty miles or so, but it was more than four hours before they were nearing the airfield – numerous punctures and halts to get bearings ensured their progress was slow. They stopped again just south of the airfield, unsure precisely where they were. By a stroke of good fortune, an enemy aircraft then came in to land. Briefly, the runway navigation lights were turned on and the raiders saw they were only about a mile away.

George was leading the right-hand column of jeeps. Quickening their speed as they approached, they burst onto the airfield and opened fire. 'And then,' Earl Jellicoe told me, 'we just cruised around, shooting up their planes.' It was an extraordinarily successful enterprise. They lost just one man and two jeeps, and as they roared off back into the night, left thirty-seven aircraft burning, most of which were transport planes, of vital importance to Rommel in bringing up supplies along his increasingly lengthy lines of communication. Furthermore, at a time when British successes in the war were few and far between, the men of the SAS had given the Allies something to cheer about.

This was the Earl's last raid with the SAS. He had developed knee trouble and after being operated on in Cairo, was sent home to the UK for two months. There he saw Mountbatten, and gave some lectures at Combined Operations Headquarters, which was responsible for the revitalized Commando units. He was also invited to dinner at Number Ten and asked to recount his exploits at Heraklion. 'And as I was telling Churchill about it,' Earl Jellicoe grinned, 'I could see I'd lost his attention entirely.' Even so, he was soon after asked to spend the weekend with the Prime Minister at Chequers. 'All in all,' he said, 'it was rather a jolly time.'

He had returned to the Middle East in January 1943, and had immediately been given command of the Third Greek Sacred Regiment, which was to be absorbed into the SAS. 'They had been founded in classical times,' he explained, 'but had been reformed from Greeks who had escaped from the German occupation of Greece. And they were a very fine lot, too.' The arrival of the Greeks was just one of many changes since he had been away. David Stirling had been captured and with the North African campaign drawing to a close there was less need for clandestine raids behind the lines. Even so, the SAS had expanded and had been given regimental status. There were now four squadrons, of which the SBS was one.

By April, however, another reorganization was needed, and George, promoted to major, was given command of the newly independent SBS Regiment as well as the Greek Sacred Regiment and moved to Palestine. To his intense frustration, he was no longer allowed to go on raids himself. Since he was privy to the plans for the invasion of Sicily due to take place in July that year, it was considered too great a risk were he to be captured. Instead, he oversaw training and planned raids on airfields in Sardinia.

In September, after the Allies' successful campaign in Sicily, the Italians surrendered, and George, having already made a name for himself not just as a soldier but as someone with considerable diplomatic skills, was sent to Rhodes to try to persuade the Italian garrison there to come over to the Allies. The Germans, however, held the air-fields, and their troops were more concentrated and better armed than the Italians, and so the Italian commander refused George's offer. He did, however, 'behave quite honourably', allowing George safe passage off the island.

George had better success on Leros, persuading the Italian commander to come over to the Allied side, but a fierce battle quickly ensued with a number of his SBS men and troops from the Long Range Desert Group fighting alongside the Italians against a reinforced German garrison. George was captured by some German paratroopers, but managed to give them the slip, and along with forty of his men, took a boat and escaped to Turkey. He eventually made it back to Cairo, where Churchill was visiting, and was ordered to brief the Prime Minister on the situation in the Aegean.

For the next six months, George's SBS and Greek Sacred Regiment carried out more than three hundred raids throughout the Aegean, operating from Palestine and then Bari in southern Italy. He was, he told me, pretty sure that his forces were largely responsible for tying up so many German troops on the Dodecanese islands and on Crete – troops and materiel that could have been used against the Allies elsewhere. 'They were mostly small raids,' he said, 'but they were effective.' They also demonstrated his ability to plan, choose good men to work with and under him, and his flare for taking well-judged risks.

By the late summer of 1944, the Germans began withdrawing from southern Greece. The concern amongst the Allies in the Mediterranean was that if the Germans withdrew too quickly, the Greek Communist partisans, ELAS, would try to take power, over-throw the King of Greece, and cause a civil war. It was thus decided that a neutral British force should harass the German withdrawal and try and prevent a Greek bloodbath in the aftermath. 'I was given command of this force,' said Earl Jellicoe. 'It was a complete mixture: a squadron of SBS, part of a RAF Armoured Regiment, a troop of the LRDG and a number of engineers and various others.' George was now an acting brigadier, despite still being only twenty-six.

Their first task was to secure Patras. 'It was tricky,' said the Earl, 'because there were many more Germans there than us and there were also a number of anti-Communist Greek security battalions, who weren't really pro-German but were definitely anti-ELAS.' Not only did George's force hasten the departure of the German garrison there, they managed to persuade the Greek battalions to withdraw one night and surrender themselves to George's men – and as a result, they were not massacred by the Communists.

With all ELAS groups in the northern Peloponnese now under his command, George's next task was to make sure his troops quickly reached Athens. The Germans carried out quite a strong rearguard action, and George then had to make a difficult decision: whether to drop in the British 4th Parachute Battalion, quite a responsibility since there were strong winds that would make the manoeuvre hazardous in the extreme. He gave the go-ahead. Two were killed and a number of others seriously hurt, but it could have been worse. 'I think it was the correct decision,' he said, 'because it was so urgent to get the troops into Athens.'

The Germans had by now begun withdrawing from the city. The Greek Communist troops had agreed to remain outside the city until a legitimate government was established, but George doubted their word and so with his second-in-command, Major Ian Patterson, took a small boat and landed on the far side of Athens, so bypassing the German rearguard. After watching the last of the German troops leave the city, they found two bicycles on the side of the road, and cycled the twelve miles to the centre of Athens, arriving in the early hours of 12 October 1944. He immediately took control, mediating between the Communists and Royalists and ensuring civil war did not break out in the capital city. When crowds gathered in the morning of 12 October, George appeared on the balcony of the Hotel Grande Bretagne and was cheered rapturously.

With the retreating Germans harried all the way to the border by George's men, and with Athens secure, his time with the SBS came to an end. Warned that he was due to be posted to the Far East as a staff officer in charge of a number of Special Service units, he was sent to Staff College in Haifa in Palestine and was still there when the war finally came to an end. He looked up and smiled. 'All rather boring, I'm afraid.'

He then returned to the subject of David Stirling once more. 'In a fairly long life,' he said, 'I don't think I've ever known anybody with his power of leadership. He really was a very remarkable person. One couldn't help but admire the astonishing way by which more often than not he got what he wanted.' But Earl Jellicoe clearly had exceptional leadership skills himself. Few men his age were given such huge amounts of responsibility, and yet he had excelled in almost every situation in which he found himself.

He admitted that he had rather a good time during the war. Blind fear was not something he ever really experienced. 'I think one is anxious beforehand,' he said about going into action, 'but once one gets involved, one forgets the anxiety.' Raids on airfields, being dropped onto enemy-held islands, or liberating cities on bicycles, was, he admitted, 'rather exciting'. And there was the camaraderie. 'One enjoyed, above all, the fellowships one had,' he told me.

It was by now getting late, but although he had a dinner engagement to go to, he suggested there was time for a drink in the bar. 'Well, I fear this hasn't been of great use to you,' he apologized as we got up to leave. 'I've gone on, rather.'

Naturally, I demurred; but nor did I want to gush, so I kept to myself what I was really thinking: that George Jellicoe was one of the most extraordinary people I had ever met.

FIGHTER BOYS

Roland 'Bee' Beamont

'Oh, it's the way things happen in wartime,' Bee Beamont told me, his eyes twinkling. 'Nobody took life too seriously.' We were in the sitting room of his new house just outside Salisbury, one sunny summer's afternoon, some sixty years after the events he was describing. He looked a lot older than a comparatively recent photograph I had seen of him, and smaller too, but the smile and resolute chin were still recognizable from the picture of the devil-may-care young pilot taken during the height of the Battle of Britain. He wasn't talking about the Battle of Britain, though, but about a funny incident in September 1941, when he was a flight commander of 79 Squadron, stationed at Fairwood Common, near Swansea.

Bee had only been with the squadron a couple of months, when one morning the telephone had rung at the dispersal hut and he had answered. It was not news of flying orders but rather Shirley Adams, a WAAF cipher officer on the station, whom Bee had taken quite a shine to.

'How are we going to Pembrey tonight?' she asked. For a moment Bee couldn't think what she was talking about. 'You haven't forgotten have you?' she asked.

'No, of course not,' he lied, and then suddenly remembered. There was a party on at Pembrey that night – Shirley's old station and although he wasn't invited himself, he'd promised to take her there.

But the problem was that his car was not very serviceable at that point in time; it had only three wheels. There was silence on the end of the phone. *Think quickly, Beamont,* he told himself, then said, 'Look, I know, you come over here with your night kit in a small bag at four o'clock. I'll tell you how we're going when we get there.'

Having rung off, Bee wandered over to his flight sergeant. A month or so before, he'd flown the station catering officer to another base in his Hurricane and it had worked out fine. 'And I'd done that,' Bee told me, 'because I'd learnt through the bush telegraph that this had been done in North Africa when a chap had been shot down in a Hurricane and one of his mates landed on the flat desert alongside him, picked him up, threw the parachute out and then flew back to base.' It was perhaps not the most comfortable way to fly a Hurricane but, it seemed, was perfectly possible over small distances.

'I'll need my Hurricane about four this afternoon,' Bee told his crewman. 'Just need to nip over to Pembrey and back.' The flight sergeant nodded, and at four, when Shirley came over, everything was ready.

'Well, what are we going in?' she asked.

'That,' said Bee, pointing to his Hurricane.

'Good God!' said Shirley. The other pilots could barely contain themselves as they watched Shirley clamber onto the wing and gingerly hoist herself into the seat.

'Where are you going to sit?' she asked.

'On your knees,' Bee told her. Normally, the pilot sat on his parachute and was strapped in tightly; both these measures had to be discarded, but by flying steadily and carefully and without any aerobatics, the flight was a success. Shirley had a great thrill and they landed safely at Pembrey some twenty minutes later. Taxiing off the runway, Bee brought the Hurricane to a halt and with the engine still ticking over, jumped onto the wing and helped Shirley out, then clambered back into the cockpit and set off again. Without either Shirley or a parachute to sit on, he was now lower in his seat than he would have liked, and he had to crane his neck to see properly. Nonetheless, as he took off he spotted her still walking across the airfield and so pulled his Hurricane into a tight turn and flew a diving pass across the air traffic building in order to wave goodbye.

Unfortunately for Bee, Pembrey was a Training Command station and its administration officer had been in the air traffic building, and had watched his stunt. The next morning, back at Fairwood, Bee was summoned to the Station Commander's office. Rather apologetically, the CO told him he was now under open arrest for unlawfully carrying a passenger in a Hurricane. When Bee pointed out that in that case he couldn't command his flight, he was released. 'It must have been one of the shortest arrests ever,' Bee laughed. But that was not the end of the matter, and the following February, Bee found himself being brought before a court-martial. By this time he was attached to the special duties list for test flying at Hawker Aircraft Limited, so he had to ask the chief test pilot for a couple of days off and a Hurricane with which to fly himself back to Fairwood. 'Sure,' the chief told him, then added that he'd been talking about the incident a few days before over lunch with Air Marshal Sholto Douglas, the Commander-in-Chief of Fighter Command. Douglas had made the point that had Bee had the sense to land at a Fighter rather than a Training station, nothing more would have been heard about it.

It didn't make much difference. Bee's court-martial consisted of a long conversation with Group Captain Atcherly, the Station Commander at Fairwood Common, who asked him in great detail about the Hawker Typhoon that Bee had recently been testing. Eventually Atcherly told him he was being severely reprimanded, then sent him on his way. Shortly after, Bee was promoted to Flight Lieutenant. 'In those days,' Bee told me, 'it was an incredibly casual life. This business of flying a girl in a Hurricane was one of the biggest laughs of the century.'

Wing Commander Roland Prosper Beamont, DSO and Bar, DFC and Bar, began his flying career on biplanes capable of little more than a hundred miles an hour and ended it on supersonic jets. His

first flight, however, came at the age of six as a result of a stunt by his
father that backfired. When a rickety old Avro 540 landed in a field
near their home in Chichester offering to take passengers up for five
shillings a ride, Major Beamont thought that offering young Rolo a
flight in this terrifying machine would put his son off for life. How
wrong he was: Bee's obsession only grew. Model aeroplanes were
built and aviation books bought with hoarded pocket money. When
his parents gave him a bicycle for his birthday, he used it to pedal
over to Tangmere, the nearest RAF airfield, where he would spend all
day watching the aeroplanes come and go. His parents, realizing
there was no point in trying to deter him further, then made every
effort to encourage the lad to achieve his dream. At Bee's interview
for Eastbourne College, Major Beamont told the headmaster that it
would be the school's mission to ensure his son secured a place at the
RAF College at Cranwell upon leaving school.

Class work was not Bee's strong point. He failed his first attempt
at the School Certificate and only passed after his father sent him to
a crammer. By then he had missed his chance of going to Cranwell,
but in 1939 was accepted for a short-service commission. Nine
months later he had his wings and was a fully qualified fighter pilot.
Two months after that, in November 1940, Bee was on his way to
Lille in France to join 87 Squadron.

What were the living conditions like in France? I asked. 'Appalling,'
Bee replied. 'Absolutely appalling. We were one of only four
Hurricane squadrons sent out to France and the French off-loaded
us in accommodation that they wouldn't live in.' These were First
World War-era wooden huts, extremely damp and with holes in the
roof. 'We were never warm,' he continued, 'and you couldn't get dry
when you got wet.' The aerodrome was also basic, to say the least:
a grass field, which, by the time Bee arrived, had turned to mud.
Eventually they had to take off down the only road that led into the
airfield and fly to Le Touquet where there was a dry runway. Most of
the pilots became ill, Bee included, who ended up in hospital in
Dieppe with pleurisy.

Life improved once they were transferred to Le Touquet permanently. Digs were now in a hotel by the sea and the novelist P.G. Wodehouse, who lived in a chateau nearby, took them under his wing, entertaining them regularly. There wasn't too much flying, but their main task was to try to intercept the occasional German reconnaissance planes that flew over. It was during one such sortie that Bee had his first combat.

It was another wet morning and Bee's flight flew straight into cloud. Although Fighter Command back in Britain could call on radar, there was no such thing in France. Vectoring the pilots into position was done very basically by two-way radio from ground control; this was pretty haphazard at the best of times, but especially so with thick cloud cover hindering them. Even so, on this particular morning, Bee happened to catch sight of a wisp of vapour trail against the blue of a gap in the cloud, and then he saw the wing of a German Heinkel bomber. They got into firing range at about 18,000 feet, by which time the rear-gunner from the Heinkel was firing at them, with lines of feathery smoke curling past the Hurricane. Bee was fascinated rather than frightened. His section leader then opened fire in turn and the Heinkel immediately dropped its nose and dived, trailing black smoke. Disappearing into cloud, that was the last they saw of it. 'So that was an exciting morning,' Bee smiled, 'and a good reason for starting the evening's party at about noon.'

At around 5 a.m. on 10 May 1940, Bee was sitting in the tent at dispersal, struggling with a virulent stomach upset, when he suddenly heard several enormous explosions and saw enemy bombers roaring overhead. The German Blitzkrieg had begun. But while the other pilots rushed to their planes, Bee was simply too ill to fly. 'All I could think of was the awful frustration and even shame of being stuck on the ground with sickness when what we had all been waiting for – the opening of the fighting battle – had started,' he told me. 'There was a war going on, and my friends and colleagues were flying every day, some not coming back from fierce combat, and I was stuck on the couch with sickness and expressly forbidden to fly.'

It wasn't until three days later that he flew again. Even then he was hardly recovered, but defying instructions from the Medical Officer, hitched a ride from the mess to the airfield. Dispersal was now in a ditch alongside the grass airfield, their only means of communication an out-moded field telephone which was wound up with a handle. Staggering over, Bee found most of the pilots sitting in the ditch waiting for something to happen.

'I thought you were sick,' muttered his Flight Commander.

'Oh, I'm better now,' Bee lied.

'Well, you can fly that one,' he said pointing to Hurricane LK-L.

Just after two in the afternoon, the telephone rang and Blue and Green sections with a further section of the newly arrived 504 Squadron were ordered to patrol the line Louvain–Brussels at 10,000 feet. As Bee grappled with his parachute, oxygen and R/T (radio-telegraphy) gear, he was conscious that it hadn't been a very good idea to come down to the airfield. He still felt distinctly unwell and as he took to the skies he was aware that his vision wasn't quite as good as normal. 'When you're flying in close Vic formation, at several hundred miles an hour, and with your wingtips only three or four feet apart from the next chap,' he admitted, 'poor vision doesn't help.'

As they climbed into the sky, a thought struck him. If they actually got into action, how on earth was he going to be able to cope, feeling as he did? Suddenly a string of aircraft appeared right across in front of them. They were a different colour from their own planes – mainly grey and white. And they had twin fins. He recognized them from his identification charts: they were German Dorniers.

The Flight Commander led them into attack, saying over the R/T, 'Come on, let's get them.' ('There were no tactics at all,' said Bee.) Remembering to turn his gun button on to 'fire', Bee found himself quite automatically concentrating on manoeuvring his Hurricane into a line that would enable him to open fire without hitting his section leader, who was still in front of him. Bee reckoned there were at least twenty Dorniers, so there was no difficulty finding a target. He ruddered his Hurricane until a Dornier three from the end of the formation on the rear quarter filled his gunsight – and then he opened fire. It was the first time he'd seen tracers pumping from his own guns and it was exciting. Wavy lines of smoke began converging on the enemy machine, but then he realized that if he didn't take immediate avoiding action he was going to crash right into it. Selecting the only space between the Dornier and the next in the formation, he dived through then pulled up and looked back to see what was going on. 'This was all over in seconds,' explained Bee. 'But I realized it was my duty to get back into the combat.'

Another Dornier suddenly slanted across his front, only about two hundred yards away. 'He looked very big,' admitted Bee, who immediately rolled back after it and began firing directly into its rear. Suddenly more streaks of grey began darting past him between his cockpit and the roundel on his starboard wing. He wondered where on earth it could be coming from, and swivelling his neck, saw a twin-engine Messerschmitt 110 fighter right behind him busily pumping out all he had – but fortunately missing. 'His guns were actually flashing,' said Bee. 'I was a complete novice. I'd never thought of looking behind me – although we'd been repeatedly told to be aware of what was going on all around, in the excitement of what was happening in front of me, I forgot.' Being attacked put him off his stroke with the Dornier, so he rolled away from the Me 110 and dived for about a thousand feet. Pulling back again, he saw he'd successfully lost the German fighter, but quite a long way off spotted another twin-fin aircraft streaming smoke. 'It might have been the Dornier I'd been firing at – I've no real idea – but he was diving away to the northeast and looked to be heading home in a hurry.'

Bee decided to chase it. He was soon catching up, too, because one of the Dornier's engines was hit and it was steadily slowing. Filled with excitement and with his adrenalin pumping, Bee opened fire at over four hundred yards – 'too far really' – and continued firing until he ran out of ammunition. Even so, the Dornier began diving steeply, disappearing into a layer of cloud. Still swirling around in a very hostile sky, but with no more ammunition, he realized his best option was to dive 'to the deck', and at just a few hundred feet off the ground, hedge-hop his way back to base.

He had begun to work himself on a course that would lead back in the direction of Lille when once again feathery lines of smoke began flitting past his cockpit. Sliding his canopy back in order to get a better look, Bee saw a Dornier on his tail. 'One of these cheeky bastards had decided he was going to chase a Hurricane with his Dornier!' exclaims Bee. 'A bomber after a fighter!' This was, he pointed out, an indication of the very high morale of the Luftwaffe at that time, many of whom were experienced in warfare after Spain and then Poland, 'while we, of course, weren't at all.'

For a moment he couldn't think of what he should do, then remembered that a Hurricane was supposed to be able to out-turn a Dornier. He immediately yanked his plane into a very tight turn, as tight as he could fly it without blacking out and pulled the 'tit', which increased boost for a short period of time. The Hurricane lurched forward and after only half a turn he began to see the rear quarter of the Dornier. 'So there were the two of us,' he explained, 'a bloody great Dornier in a vertical bank, and me in my Hurricane also in a vertical bank on his tail but with no ammunition.' Meanwhile the Dornier's rear-gunner had begun firing at him.

This, Bee knew, was not a healthy position to be in, but at least the enemy now knew the Hurricane had a superior turning circle. If he reversed the turn, he realized, the Dornier would never come after him. And nor did it. As Bee looked back, the Dornier was banking away from his own circle and beginning to level out in the direction of the German lines. 'And as he did so,' Bee told me, 'he waggled his wings. He was saluting. Absolutely fantastic!' He paused a moment, then looked up again, smiling. 'And that was my first proper combat.'

*   *   *

When, in September 1939, the British Expeditionary Force sailed for France, they were joined by four fighter squadrons, part of the Air Component of the BEF along with a number of bomber squadrons. Like the BEF, the RAF's contribution in France was little more than a token gesture. All four squadrons were made up of Hurricanes, easier to repair and more numerous than Spitfires, and although by May 1940 they had been joined by two more fighter squadrons, these were still in the process of replacing their Gloster Gladiator biplanes with Hurricanes. Meanwhile the German Air Force, the Luftwaffe, had several thousand aircraft at their disposal, of which none were biplanes, and amongst their squadrons were men who had gained crucial experience in the Condor Legion during the Spanish Civil War.

Just nineteen at the time, Bee readily admitted he was naïve as well as inexperienced during those intense days of the Battle for France, but he was nonetheless an accomplished pilot by that time. In fact, there were a number of highly skilled pilots amongst the RAF squadrons in France. Bee told me about Dicky Lee, a pilot from 85 Squadron with whom they had shared an airfield. Before the Blitzkrieg they had practised their gunnery skills on old cans of petrol piled high at one end of the airfield. 'They were piled up in a pyramid, and you'd fly round and attack them,' Bee explained. 'If you caught them on fire there would be a huge cheer, but you had to keep going round until you hit them. Dicky was the guy who used to be able to knock these petrol tins off with his first burst of about one or two seconds of fire. He was absolutely amazing and brilliant at aerobatics.' Bee was also quick to point out that they were lucky to have some very good leaders too, such as the CO of 87 Squadron, Johnny Dewar. 'He was a fantastic pilot and a wonderful commanding officer,' Bee told me. 'We'd have done anything for him.'

The problem was that they were hugely outnumbered and tactically some way behind the Luftwaffe. During their time in Spain, the German pilots had worked out a highly efficient flying formation that was based around either two or four aircraft, spaced well apart, with the back of the lead plane being guarded by the second. In contrast, the RAF operated in 'Vics' – formations of three aircraft, which flew very closely together, wingtip tucked behind wingtip. A flight was generally made up of two sections of three, a squadron four. The problem was twofold: first, by being bunched together, they provided an easier target, while second, pilots were concentrating so hard on not collid- ing with one another, there was less opportunity to watch the skies for danger. Bee mentioned an occasion when they flew alongside another squadron that had joined them for the day from England. There were eighteen Hurricanes patrolling the sky over Valenciennes in a tight box of six Vics. Suddenly Bee spotted four Messerschmitt 109s emerge from cloud above and to their left. No one reacted, so he told the CO over his R/T. While he was reporting this, the 109s rolled over vertically and came in behind the formation. 'Two Hurricanes at the back broke away streaming smoke and another rolled on its back and went straight down,' he told me. 'We didn't do a thing. Johnny Dewar couldn't move two squadrons around in time. It was a perfect example of the inflexibility of Vic formations.'

Despite this, the squadron did well, shooting down many more aircraft than they lost. Bee likened the squadron to a rugby club – they'd been out in France for six months, all knew each other well and since most were aged between nineteen and twenty-one, they never lacked energy or enthusiasm. After the first few days of the Blitzkrieg that enthusiasm began to be tempered – 'but not lowered' – by the fact that some of their friends were not appearing at the end of the day. 'The atmosphere was one of confident aggression laced with an enormous amount of humour.' Johnny Dewar was also 'completely unflappable', which gave everyone else confidence. 'It was,' Bee admitted, 'as if we were engaged in a magnificent cause and we were doing better than anybody else.' He smiled, then added, 'Which we weren't doing. We were doing rather badly actually. But that didn't get across.'

Within a week, however, it was plain to all that they were losing the battle. The squadron had lost nine pilots – figures that were being repeated by the other fighter squadrons in France. The British bomber squadrons were suffering even worse. 'We were making big claims,' said Bee – over fifty enemy aircraft destroyed in that first week – 'but the balance was all the other way.' Around the airfield, the roads were becoming clogged with refugees. On 19 May, Bee was at dispersal when at about noon a despatch rider arrived from headquarters. He told Bee he was the fourth sent that day. The CO was at the mess, so Bee sat on the rear mudguard of the motorbike and led the despatch rider to Dewar. When the CO read the message he exclaimed, 'My God, this was timed at 0600 this morning!' It was a movement order – they had been told to move back to Merville immediately. There were now more pilots than Hurricanes, so Bee, along with several others, had to travel to the new airfield by truck with the ground forces. It took them seven hours to travel just twenty miles, and along the way they found themselves the objects of abuse from French refugees who were not at all pleased to see men in uniform heading backwards. 'It was an atmosphere that as a nineteen-year-old I found extraordinary,' Bee admitted.

By the following morning, the Panzers were just a few miles away. Despite this, Bee was stunned when the CO told him he and three others would be flying back to England that day. 'We haven't enough Hurricanes for all of us,' Dewar told him. 'There's a transport heading back at noon.' It was a Dutch DC-2, and the pilot, despite the danger in the skies, insisted on flying straight and level at 2,000 feet. 'I thought we'd absolutely had it, but amazingly we made it, crossing the Channel and into the serenity of Dorset.' It was a Sunday, and everywhere Bee looked, from Dorchester all the way to London, he could see games of cricket being played. 'That was the spirit then. Fighting for one's life a hundred miles away in France, but back home everything was carrying on as normal.'

I was conscious I'd spent a lot of time talking to him about the Battle for France, but Bee was one of only a very few from those times still alive to tell the tale, and his story of chaos, youthful ingenuousness, and the morale amongst this tiny band of brothers fighting in part of such an overwhelming defeat explained much about what was to follow. About a third of the pilots never left France and by the end of the Battle of Britain even more were gone: Dicky Lee, for example, last seen chasing three 109s out to sea on 18 August; or even Johnny Dewar, who was killed over Southampton on 12 September. Most of those originals who survived, however, went on to achieve much in the remainder of their flying careers.

Bee, for example, remains a well-known figure in the aviation world, where he is regarded as something of a pioneer. During the war years he was instrumental in helping develop both the Typhoon and Tempest fighters, and he continued his work as a test pilot after the war, flying the first flights of no less than five major prototypes and sixteen type variants, including the ill-fated TSR2 supersonic jet in the 1960s. This model is widely regarded as the best jet aircraft the British never had: the Wilson government controversially scrapped the project as it neared completion. Most experts agree this was an error, not least Bee, who is not alone in thinking it would still be in use today had it ever entered service.

He also flew all twenty-two different Marks of Spitfire, although it was the Hurricane that he stuck with throughout the Battle of Britain. Most of those who flew in Hurricane squadrons back then are quick to defend it, believing it has had a bad press when compared to the more glamorous and beautiful Spitfire, and Bee was no exception. 'The Spitfire was about thirty miles an hour faster, that was all,' he told me. 'The diving capability was about the same. They both became difficult to control laterally in a roll at about 400 mph. And from deck-level to 20,000 feet, the Hurricane could out-turn a Spitfire with ease. It had superior combat manoeuvrability and was a far better gun platform. Only at heights of over 20,000 was the Spitfire its superior, so really, there was little to choose between them, and if you selected the right area of combat for each of them you got the best out of them.' Broadly speaking, this is what happened: the more numerous Hurricanes were given the job of intercepting the enemy bombers that tended to operate below 20,000, while the Spitfires took on the fighters, usually flying at higher altitudes. However, he was quick to point out that he was talking about 1940. 'By 1941, the Hurricane had become outclassed,' Bee admitted. 'In 1940, the Hurricane had reached the end of its development, while the Spitfire had only just begun.'

The Battle of Britain occurred in several phases. Throughout July and the first part of August 1940, the Germans concentrated on attacking Channel shipping and ports. The all-out attempt to annihilate the RAF began on 'Eagle Day', 13 August, lasting for nearly four weeks, until Göring, the Commander-in-Chief of the Luftwaffe, turned his attention away from Fighter Command's airfields and began concentrating on London and other British cities instead.

Bee's 87 Squadron were not in 11 Group, in the southeast of England and the front line against the onslaught. Instead, they were based at Exeter in the southwest, part of 10 Group. They were still kept very busy, however, and found themselves in the thick of the fighting from the very beginning.

Although they were still operating in Vics, the squadron had learnt much in France. They now rarely flew in larger formations than six aircraft, working on the principle that the fewer they were the more manoeuvrable they would be and the less of a target they offered. The old RAF attack procedures that had been a part of their training had also been shown the door. They also learnt that whenever the enemy was sighted, they would turn towards them. 'Always close the enemy,' Bee explained. 'It's a rule that never changed. And get as close as possible before firing, because you can't afford to waste bullets when you've only got fifteen seconds' worth of ammunition.'

Throughout the summer he maintained that morale remained sky-high. The numbers of enemy aircraft were fantastical, but they knew that so long as they broke up bombing formations and kept knocking enemy aircraft out of the sky, they were doing their job. He told me about flying into what they called a 'beehive'. The sky would be completely clear while through his headphones he could hear the ground controller warning them of the approach of 'a hundred-plus bandits'. Suddenly, he would see glinting lights ahead as the sun flashed over hundreds of aircraft canopies. Soon after, the sky would fill with what looked like an enormous swarm of bees – tier upon tier of Stukas, twin-engine Messerschmitt 110s, and on top, the single-engine fighters, the Me 109s. 'Masses and masses of aeroplanes in your way,' he said. Inevitably, collision became a thought, especially as the closing speed might be well over 500 mph. 'Then the CO would come on the R/T and in a very calm voice say, "Target ahead chaps. Let's surround them."' Bee laughed. 'Six Hurricanes against 120 plus! It sounds like Hollywood, I know, but it actually happened.'

Just after four o'clock on 15 August, two days after Eagle Day, 'B' Flight was scrambled to intercept a large formation heading towards Portland and Weymouth. There were only five serviceable aircraft, but Bee and four others in the flight hurriedly took off and climbed to 12,000 feet. They were over Lyme Regis when they spotted out to sea a huge swarm of well over a hundred enemy aircraft in a spiral between 8,000 and 14,000 feet. Undaunted, the new CO, Squadron Leader Lovell-Greig, led them straight into the lead formation, a mass of over sixty Stukas, Me 110s and 109s. Bee rolled into a section of Stukas as tracers whizzed past his cockpit. A moment later, a Me 110 appeared directly under his nose. Bee was diving vertically as the Me 110 was climbing towards him. Just then the enemy pilot stalled and Bee pressed down on the gun button and felt his Hurricane shudder as bullets tore into the underside of the Messerschmitt at almost point-blank range. There was a flash of flame and Bee thrust his control column forward just in time to avoid hurtling into the wreckage.

A second later he was under attack by a second Me 110 closing dead ahead. A line of his tracer curled past between Bee's cockpit and the roundel on his port (left) wing. Bee opened fire again and as the two aircraft flashed past one another, he saw smoke burst from the enemy aircraft and turning back, glimpsed the pilot baling out. He'd scored two victories in a matter of seconds. It might have nearly been three. Plunging through the mêlée, he saw a lone Stuka and hauling his Hurricane into a tight turn fired his remaining ammunition before nearly blacking out. Levelling out, he could see trails of smoke streaking across the sky; a further Me 110, missing its tail, plunged past him. With 109s dropping down to join the fight, Bee dived beneath the cloud-base and headed back to home.

Emerging through the cloud at around 4,000 feet, he saw he was directly over Weymouth. With the sudden release of tension, he suddenly felt very hot and realized his jacket was dark with sweat. Pulling back the canopy, he allowed himself to be buffeted and cooled by fresh air as he headed back to Exeter, landing a mere three-quarters of an hour after he had taken off. Two others in the flight landed back soon after, also making several claims. A further pilot had been hit, but soon rang up from Weymouth having safely baled out. There was bad news about the CO, however, who had crash-landed at Warmwell and been killed. Despite the loss of Lovell-Greig, Bee and the rest of the squadron returned to the mess, a run-down hotel in Exeter called the Rougemont, and celebrated their successes late into the night.

Letting off steam, either in the hotel bar, or at a nearby pub, was a regular feature of squadron life. Flying in combat was not only exhausting physically but mentally too, while sitting around dispersal, waiting for the telephone to ring, was, as Bee put it, 'very tense-making'. When it did ring, it was more often than not just some minor request for information, but it didn't stop the pilots nearly jumping out of their skins. 'The pressure never stopped,' Bee admitted, 'and the fatigue became accumulative.'

Ten days after the big battle over Portland, the whole squadron, led once more by Johnny Dewar, found themselves caught up in another fierce engagement over the south coast. Bee shot down a Dornier 17 bomber then became caught up in a dog-fight with a Me 109. Out-turning the German, Bee hit his fuselage, so that the pilot half-rolled and dived on his back. Following him, Bee hit him again as the German curled out of his dive, fatally crippling the enemy aircraft. About to fire his *coup de grâce,* Bee could not help feeling impressed when the German pilot out-manoeuvred him with a roll and stall-turn. With smoke trailing behind him, the German pilot belly-landed in a field near Abbotsbury. Diving down towards the Messerschmitt, Bee saw the pilot was already standing on the wing about to set fire to his aircraft. As Bee swooped over, the German raised his hand in salute. Waving back, Bee sped back to Exeter.

By October, the Battle of Britain had begun to peter out. As the days shortened, so the amount of combat flying lessened. Both flights in the squadron took it in turns to carry out duties as night-fighters, Bee adding to his mounting personal score. He finally left the squadron in May 1941, a year after the Blitzkrieg in the west. By that time, it had changed greatly since the days of the Phoney War in France. In those twenty months, Bee had served under five commanding officers and seven flight commanders, and he was one of the last pilots to have been with the squadron since the beginning of the war. Some had moved on, others had been wounded, but a large number had been killed. Bee told me that the first good friend he lost was a terrible blow; the second was felt a little less. By the time half a dozen of his friends had been killed, he'd learnt to put it out of mind and get on with the job in hand. 'I think we gradually developed a protective shell,' he confessed. Despite the intensity of the Battle for France and the Battle of Britain, Bee was to witness greater losses later in the war, by which time he was commanding firstly a squadron of Typhoons and later a wing of Tempests. Principally used for ground attack, these aircraft were consequently flown at much lower altitudes where the chances of safely baling out were much less.

It was Bee who was instrumental in establishing these aircraft for use in ground attack and other low-level operations. He had little to say to me about his time with 79 and 54 Squadrons, or about his first stint as test pilot at Hawker, although he did admit that his intimate knowledge of the Typhoon acquired during his time with Hawker was 'very useful' when he joined 609 Squadron in the summer of 1942. The squadron had only just been equipped with Typhoons. As Bee was well aware, this new fighter was not really ready for operational use at this time. There were teething problems not only with the engine, but also when the plane was put into a power dive; entire tail structures were disintegrating. In its first couple of months with the Typhoon, 609 lost four pilots purely due to engine failure. Bee, however, continued to argue for its retention, twice putting his case forward at Fighter Command HQ. Believing in the Typhoon as an aircraft that could out-manoeuvre, out-gun, and fly quicker than anything the Luftwaffe possessed, he hated the idea of it being permanently grounded. What about the loss of life it was causing, I wondered? Yes, he accepted, that was a tragedy, but he knew that the pressure of operational failures would hasten the speed with which these problems were straightened. Winning the war was the goal – and the Typhoon and later the Tempest, which evolved from the same design – had important parts to play in that victory. More lives were saved, he argued, by sticking with the Typhoon.

He talked about the nature of command. In October 1942, he was made a squadron leader – still only just twenty-two – and took over as CO of 609 Squadron. Morale in the squadron was not high. It was a pre-war auxiliary squadron – the 'gentlemen fliers' – and had achieved a great record in the Battle of Britain, but by the autumn of 1942, with accidents mounting and with little to do other than tedious patrol work, the atmosphere amongst the pilots was at an all-time low.

Bee knew he had a tough job on his hands. For all his experience, he was still very young, but recognized that the potential successes of both the squadron and the Typhoon were inextricably linked to his abilities as a commander. Morale began to improve once they moved to Manston in Kent, however. The Luftwaffe were daily sending over their latest fighter, the Focke-Wulf 190, with bombs strapped beneath it and with its guns full, on low-level tip-and-run raids, targeting coastal towns and airfields. Bee devised a system of standing patrols so that at least two Typhoons were patrolling the coast for intruders at all times. On the very first morning this system was begun, the squadron shot down two FW 190s. This had been doubled by the end of the first week. As if any further proof were needed to confirm the Typhoon's speed, Bee challenged the CO of neighbouring 91 Squadron – equipped with the latest Spitfire Mk XIIs – to a race. Bee beat him by a mile.

Despite these successes against the Focke-Wulf raiders, there were still serious question marks against the future of the Typhoon, and Bee felt very strongly that it was up to him and the rest of the squadron to prove its worth beyond any further doubt. Making the most of the November full moon, he flew a lone night-time mission to Nazi-occupied France, found a military train and shot it up, stopping it in its tracks. Spitfires were being used to attack ground targets by day, so most German war material was now travelling by night. If Bee's Typhoons could make a serious impact, the three successes he craved – his own, the squadron's and the Typhoons' – would be assured. 'I knew that once we'd proved ourselves as night intruders,' he told me, 'Fighter Command would have to admit that ground-strafing was not the work for Spitfires alone.'

In a nutshell, that was exactly what happened. Bee insisted his pilots properly trained for night intrusions before sending them over to the Continent, but they were, 'almost to a man', keen to carry out such operations, even though both the training and the intrusions themselves had to be performed in addition to their daytime tasks.

They could also only be carried out during periods of full moon when there was little cloud cover or else visibility would have been too poor. Despite these limitations, their scores soon mounted. In January and February of 1943, 609 Squadron shot down or badly damaged twenty-three enemy aircraft (mostly FW 190s), forty-five trains, as well as a few vehicles and barges. Bee had personally accounted for fourteen trains. Early in the month, Lord Balfour, the Secretary of State for War, visited Manston. Afterwards, he sent Bee

a letter. He still has it and showed it to me. 'I must send you this line to tell you with what wonder and admiration all of us watched your take-off and flying of the Typhoon yesterday,' Balfour had written. 'Not only did it impress those like myself, who have not got the knowledge of others, but I wish you could have heard the comments of the Spitfire experts. They said they did not realize the Typhoon could be handled like that.' Any questions as to the future of the aircraft had now vanished.

Even so, in early March, Bee suffered engine failure himself, and although he just made it back to land, he badly cut his head as he crash-landed, was hospitalized and off flying for several weeks. On his return, however, he proved the squadron's and the Typhoons' worth again by leading them on an anti-shipping strike, sinking two minesweepers, crippling a third and damaging a motor anti-aircraft ship in the process. By now the fame of the 'train-busters' was spreading. 'Tip-and-run raiders hate the Typhoon', ran a headline in the *Evening News* in early March 1943. A few weeks later the *Daily Sketch* announced, 'Typhoons win 5–0 victory. Better armoured and with a longer range than either the Hurricane or Spitfire, the Typhoon is a single-seater, single-engined plane with a speed of over 400 mph,' a seemingly fantastical pace at the time.

Bee finished his time with 609 in May, and was sent straight back to Hawker as a test pilot. By that time his personal tally of destroyed trains was twenty-five and he was an ace – five kills – nearly three times over. When he was awarded a Distinguished Service Order to go with his Distinguished Flying Cross, congratulations arrived from far and wide, including from Air Marshal Sir Trafford Leigh-Mallory, the Commander-in-Chief of Fighter Command.

By this time, most of the mechanical problems with the Typhoon had been ironed out, but not the structural ones. Bee was put to work helping investigate the tail breakages which continued to plague development. 'It was pretty hairy at times,' he told me, 'and at one point I honestly thought it was safer fighting the Germans than being a test pilot at Hawker.' Fortunately, his role soon changed

and he became the project pilot for the new Hawker Tempest, a faster, improved version of the Typhoon. Final tests on the Tempest were completed by January 1944, by which time Bee had repeatedly flown faster than the world speed record of 464 mph, set by a German in a Messerschmitt in 1939. As Bee had proved during his time with 609 Squadron, the Typhoon was ideal for low-level ground attacks and was now being equipped with rockets as well as bombs; the Tempest, on the other hand, could, with its even greater speeds, fulfil the role of being both an air-to-air and ground-attack fighter.

Job done, Bee was promoted again and was asked to form the first Tempest wing of three squadrons. Air Vice-Marshal 'Dingbat' Saunders, commander of 11 Group, Fighter Command, told Bee it was imperative his wing was fully operational by the end of April. 'He told me, "I don't have to tell you why." Everyone knew the invasion was coming soon,' Bee explained. 'Dingbat was hinting that it would be in either May or June.' He also told Bee to choose one of three air-fields in Kent in which to base his new wing. 'He said, "Think of it as three sides of a triangle. You need to be near the Pas de Calais, near the Normandy coast, and also well-placed between Eastbourne and North Foreland for the V1s."' Bee had read something about these new weapons in intelligence reports, but Dingbat Saunders explained further. They were rockets – 'flying bombs' – and the Germans had been building up launch sites between the Cherbourg peninsula and Antwerp. It was to be the job of the Tempests to try and shoot these new pilotless missiles down.

Bee led the wing over Normandy on 6 June 1944, just over four years after the squadron had left France. 'It was a great feeling,' Bee admitted, and told me how as they left England for France, he looked behind him and saw with a sense of pride and excitement, twenty-four Tempests drawing into formation. 'When I'd left in May 1940 I remember having a very strong belief that although we'd been kicked out of France, one day we'd be back. I know it probably sounds ridiculous, but it was there. And, of course, I was right – although I couldn't possibly have known it back then.'

acting with this sort of panache and unconcern. The nonchalance with which those men could do those things, as though they appeared to be enjoying it. And the calm, quiet way with which they would slap anyone down who started to be negative. I think that played a great part, you know. A great part, particularly during those early years when our backs were against the wall.' He smiled. 'But I'm sure it's still there. If our country was ever in danger again, we'd see that reaction. I'm absolutely certain.'

When I got up to leave, he followed me out and shook my hand, and ever the gentleman, waited as I clambered into my car, closing my door for me. He smiled and waved as I pulled away, lingering in his driveway until I turned the corner. What he had never said was that he was already terminally ill with cancer; just a month after my visit, I was reading his obituaries. Another of our most celebrated wartime pilots was no more.

Ken Adam

Normandy, August 1944. In the six weeks since the pilots of 609 Squadron had moved to France, they had become used to the very different surroundings and living conditions in which they now found themselves. Gone were the days of large, purpose-built air-fields, complete with hangars, repair-workshops, living quarters and, most importantly, a comfortable and well-stocked mess. Instead, theirs was a tented existence of notable impermanence and unset-tlingly close to the front line. They were now at their third airfield since crossing the Channel for good – known simply as 'B.7', a wood-shielded field just outside Bayeux, from where the sounds of battle never seemed to be far away.

The rattle of small-arms had sounded fainter, however, over the past few days, and the thud of shellfire duller. The pilots of 609 had never been busier – sometimes as many as five missions a day, a heavy workload. But all the men sensed the battle for Normandy was now reaching a close. Montgomery's forces had finally taken Caen and were pushing south towards Falaise, while the Americans and Free French, having pushed south away from the main fighting, had turned east and were now driving northwards. The entire German 7th Army and half the 5th Army were trapped in a deadly encirclement between Falaise and Argentan, with only a steadily narrowing corri-dor through which they could escape.

Flight-Sergeant Klaus 'Heinie' Adam[6] had not been too concerned about giving up the comfortable existence they had enjoyed
back in England. After all, it was exciting to be part of this great
invasion force and to feel that they finally had the enemy on the
run. And his tent was comfortable enough: he and his good friend
Norman Merrett had a camp-bed and sleeping bag each and a
canvas washstand to share. They felt a bit more vulnerable at night
– the Allies might have had complete air superiority, but that
hadn't stopped a couple of German fighters sneaking over and
spraying the airfield with machinegun and cannon fire – although
Klaus had slept easier again since going to bed with his tin helmet
covering his most vital parts.

9 August dawned with mist hanging over the airfield, but it promised to be a warm, clear day, and even before the liaison officers
stepped into the large dark-green intelligence tent for the morning
briefing, it was obvious to the assembled pilots that there would be
plenty of flying that day once the early morning mist had been burnt
off by the sun.

At least none of the pilots could ever complain about being kept
in the dark. Daily briefings were held in the 'inter ops' tent for the
two squadrons that shared the airfield and made up 123 Wing – 609
and 198 – providing each and every pilot with impressive amounts
of information about the progress of the Allies. In attendance were
liaison officers from the Army and Royal Navy as well as their own
intelligence officers and the Met Officer. Such detail was essential: the
fighting across the dense *bocage* of Normandy was often close and
intense. Often very little ground separated their own side from the
enemy; the role of the 2nd Tactical Air Force was to help the ground
forces, not hit them by mistake. Klaus listened carefully to the briefing by the army liaison officer, then the Met Officer, until finally it
was the Wing Commander's turn. Around ten o'clock, once the mist
had gone, 609 would send up a flight on an armed reconnaissance

---

[6]   He became known as 'Ken' after the war.

mission over the Falaise area. If they saw any clear targets they were to hit the enemy hard.

Klaus's friend Norman Merrett took part in that first flight of the day. They spotted enemy tanks moving northwest six miles southeast of Falaise, and attacked, knocking out two of them. Another armed recce took off at 1.45 p.m. and once again they found targets, opening fire on an enemy column on the Falaise–Argentan road, and leaving a truck and a further tank in flames.

Klaus was one of eight men in 'A' Flight chosen to fly a third armed recce later that afternoon. Shortly after half-past-four, he was walking briskly towards the large and imposing bulk of his Hawker Typhoon, standing motionless alongside a number of others under the cover of some trees around the airfield perimeter. His ground-crew were already there. Ammunition boxes were stacked nearby, as were piles of rockets. Klaus took the parachute off his dew-sodden wing, and put each fur-booted leg in turn through two of the straps, then brought the other two over his shoulders and clipped them all together into the buckle. A quick glance at the four rockets loaded under each wing, and then he put his boot into the retracting footrest and heaved himself up onto the scuffed, paint-chipped wing-root and clambered into the cockpit.

At seven tons, the Typhoon was the largest fighter in the RAF by some distance. With its thick wings, and huge protruding radiator jutting from underneath the nose, it had none of the finesse and elegance of the Spitfire, or even the Hurricane, but what it lacked in looks it gained in speed. Quite simply, it could out-fly the latest Spitfire or anything the Americans had, and although it had been found wanting at high altitudes and against the best of the Luftwaffe, as a ground-attack machine it had no rival. Its bulk also meant it was an extremely effective gun-platform. In its brief service career, machineguns had soon made way for four high-velocity 20mm cannons. Bombs were then added: it could carry as much as 1,000lb, more than any other single-engine plane. Then in February, 609 Squadron had been transferred to Fairwood Common in Wales, and a new type of armament had been given to the Typhoons: rockets. Eight could be slung to the underside of the wings. Klaus had been impressed by this new addition to their fire-power. Now he was not only flying the fastest aircraft in the RAF but one armed to the teeth with cannon and rockets. And he was good at it too. During training he'd regularly fired his rockets with an average error of between fifty and sixty yards; with eight 60lb warheads exploding, that still created an enormous amount of damage.

In the cockpit, Klaus immediately put on his helmet and, as he always did before a mission, turned the ring on his finger three times. Having given the signal to his groundcrew, he strapped the oxygen mask to his face and fired the starter cartridge. The Typhoon could be a temperamental starter, but this time the huge 24-cylinder Sabre-Napier engine immediately burst into life amidst clouds of thick, acrid smoke. The noise was enormous – far louder than the Hurricane. The airframe shook violently and immediately Klaus switched on the oxygen to avoid breathing in lethal carbon monoxide fumes that swept into the cockpit the moment the engine began to run. Closing the bubble-Perspex canopy, he watched his groundcrew, their faces covered with scarves, take away the chocks and wave him round towards the wire-mesh – PSP – runway amidst clouds of dust whipped up by the propeller.

The Typhoons took off in pairs, his friend Norman leading them on what was his third sortie of the day. By the time it was Klaus's turn the dust was so thick he could barely see a thing. Such was the power of the Sabre engine that the torque from the propeller caused the aircraft to veer violently to the right unless the pilot heavily corrected the yaw by pressing down hard on the port rudder. Klaus was well used to this foible by now, but even so, taking off, especially with such poor visibility, was a hazardous occupation at the best of times, and had to be done blind, using the gyro – the aircraft compass – to keep him straight.

They immediately climbed steeply and turned northwards, out to sea. Normally, Klaus could see the silver barrage balloons shielding the newly constructed Mulberry Harbour at Arromanches glinting in the sun, but not that morning: Normandy was still draped in soft, grey cloud. Norman took them to 8,000 feet then they turned back and flew inland once more. Circling over their patrol area, they soon spotted a cluster of scattered enemy transport – trucks, lorries and smaller vehicles – and so Norman led them down, the eight Typhoons, their engines screaming, plunging at nearly 600 miles per hour.

Each Typhoon hurtled over the enemy vehicles. Klaus released half his rockets, two at time, and pressed his thumb down on the gun button. Their efforts were clearly striking home. Balls of flame and columns of thick, black smoke erupted into the sky. All eight Typhoons managed to escape the fray and they climbed once more before attacking a wood they thought might be hiding more enemy equipment. Firing their remaining rockets, they left the wood in flames. Looking back, Klaus saw thick black smoke rising high into the sky. A little over ten minutes later, all eight aircraft were touching down back again at B.7.

It had been a good day for the squadron: three armed reconnaissance flights and targets hit on every one, and it marked the beginning of the destruction of the German Army in Normandy. Over the next week, the Allied Air Forces, including 609 Squadron, repeatedly flew over the remnants of the 7th and 5th Armies. On just one day – 18 August – 609 flew four separate missions, part of 1,471 individual sorties in which over a thousand enemy vehicles were destroyed, including ninety tanks. The Falaise Gap had become one of the greatest killing-grounds of the entire war.

On 22 August, Klaus saw the battlefield himself. 609 Squadron had been given the day off, so he and a number of other pilots drove over to the Falaise area. He soon wished he hadn't. Their truck became stuck among a long British armoured column moving at a snail's pace through the carnage. The road – or what was left of it – was choked with wreckage, swollen corpses and dead cattle and horses. 'The smell was terrible,' he says, and although they all put handkerchiefs over their faces, it did little to help; the sickly sweet smell of death stuck to their clothes for days to come. 'This was my first contact on the ground with the dead and what had been the enemy,' says Ken. In the air, most pilots were somewhat removed from the realities on the ground. Being so close to this horror came as a profound shock.

Strangely, however, Klaus felt more affected by the sight of bloated and rotting horses and cows than he did the many German dead; and it was particularly strange because the majority of the dead, although his enemy, were also his fellow countrymen.

However English it may have sounded, 'Adam' was the surname he had been born with. In the squadron he was known simply as 'Heinie', although because there had been another Adam in the squadron, he had taken to calling himself Adams to avoid any confusion. No one seemed to bat an eye that he was a German flying for the RAF. On the contrary, he was popular amongst the other pilots and they were proud to have him. They were also keenly aware that while they would be treated as prisoners of war were they to be shot down and captured, Heinie could expect no such clemency. As not only a traitor but also a Jew, he would be shot. 'To fly with this knowledge as well as the ordinary stresses,' the squadron medical officer said of him, 'must have taken immense courage.' And while all forms of aerial combat were dangerous, being a rocket-firing Typhoon pilot was particularly hazardous. Flying at such low altitudes, they were desperately vulnerable to being hit by the vast amounts of light flak that usually accompanied any attack. Unlike those fighting several miles high, there was little room in which to get out of trouble should they be hit. The Typhoon was robust, but although its wings and fuselage could take a fair amount of damage, the engine and the huge radiator slung beneath it were highly vulnerable. 'You only needed a stray bullet in there and you were in serious trouble,' says Ken. Diving into attack was also a dangerous manoeuvre. 'You went as low as you dared,' he says, 'but there were potentially two problems. First, you had to be careful not to be hit by explosions from your own rockets, and second, if you tried to pull up out of the dive too quickly, the Typhoon had a nasty habit of stalling at high speed, flipping over on its back and plunging into the ground.'

He was, he admits, sometimes 'shit-scared' but he was fortunate to be part of such a tightly knit squadron, a squadron that was infused with the particularly British traits of team spirit and understatement, but which was made up from young men from many of the Allied nations: Belgians, Dutch, French, Canadians, Americans, Australians, Norwegians, Poles. Klaus was no different from any of the other pilots speaking English with a thick accent. 'Everyone treated the job of combat flying as though it were a game of rugby or cricket,' says Ken – a defence mechanism, but an effective one, all the same. 'There would be very little outward emotion,' he says. Watching one of his comrades bursting into flames, his first thought would be relief that it was not him plunging to his death. Only later, back on the ground, would he think about these losses more deeply. He never saw anyone go to pieces, despite the many deaths the squadron suffered, although he admits 'there was a lot of vomiting going on behind the aircraft' – not that anyone ever made any comment.

Ken – or rather, Klaus – had been born in 1921, the third of three brothers and a sister. His had been an idyllic early childhood. His parents were upper-middle-class Berliners; his father ran a famous German sports store – S. Adam – which had been founded by Klaus's grandfather in the 1860s. 'It was very upmarket,' says Ken, 'more like Burberrys than Lillywhites.' His father financed a number of high-profile expeditions and projects, and Klaus met some well-known explorers and adventurers, including Amundsen, the conqueror of the South Pole. As well as the large house in Berlin, there was a holiday home on the Baltic coast, where the Adam family would go for Christmas and the summer. Practical and with a lively imagination, Klaus would spend his time building ever-faster sledges and sailing around the inlet on which their country farmhouse was built.

His parents were also exceptionally liberal. Although Jewish, they were not at all religious. Klaus was never made to go to a synagogue and nor was he sent to a Jewish school. Rather, he was educated at a highly prestigious French academy in Berlin. Neither of his parents seemed to sense what was coming, not even when the store went bust in 1932. 'The business failed partly because of the rise of anti-Semitism,' admits Ken, 'but also because its location had become unfashionable.' Undeterred, Herr Adam opened another store in a different part of town. 'He was an adventurer,' says Ken. 'A great German but not a very good businessman.' Having been a decorated cavalry officer in the First World War, Klaus's father had refused to believe that his future was in jeopardy from the Nazis and so ploughed all his remaining capital into the new – and doomed – venture.

Klaus was equally unaware that their lives would soon be thrown into turmoil. He was conscious that dramatic changes were taking place – he saw storm troopers in the streets, and witnessed a number of arrests – but did not realize how it might soon affect him; and although he heard plenty of anti-Semitic remarks, he barely understood what they meant. Only Klaus's older brother, Peter, older by seven years, seemed to sense which way the wind was blowing. 'He was the brightest in the family,' says Ken, 'and studying in France at the time. Living outside Germany, where the press was hostile to the Nazis, he could see what was happening.' Not until Herr Adam was arrested in 1933 did Klaus's father finally begin to understand that their lives were becoming threatened. On this occasion he was lucky – an employee high up in the Nazi Party secured his release after forty-eight hours. Soon after, Peter came back to Berlin. 'I remember on Sundays we children always had breakfast together with our parents in their gigantic double bed,' says Ken. 'One such Sunday, Peter came in and told my mother and father that they had to send us away.' It was Klaus's mother who supported Peter and finally persuaded Herr Adam that Klaus and his younger brother should be whisked abroad to safety.

Although the Adam children had all been brought up to speak French, it was to Britain that they were eventually sent. There was an English aunt – her part of the family had moved there the previous century – with whom Peter had a good relationship. She had links with a refugee organization in London called The Woburn House, and so in 1934, Klaus and his younger brother left Germany, sailing on a tramp steamer from Hamburg to Grimsby, and leaving behind their parents, friends and all that they had ever known. Klaus would not set foot again in the country of his birth for ten years – and when he did finally return to Berlin, the glittering city of his childhood lay in ruins.

After a brief period at a bleak public school outside Edinburgh, Klaus and his younger brother were joined in Britain by their parents and sister and the family moved to London. These were difficult times. His father was much changed, both emotionally and psychologically. He tried working as a salesman – a humiliating experience – but had aged terribly. Tragically, he died two years later, in 1936. It was left to Klaus's mother to hold the family together. Despite having never worked in her life, she proved to be an incredibly strong character. She bought a large house in Hampstead and opened a boarding-house, principally for refugees from all over Europe, while Peter became a successful chartered accountant in the city. By selling a couple of Renoirs and a Bechstein piano, as well as with help from Peter, she was able to send Klaus and his brother to St Paul's public school, while their sister, whose health was not good, was educated in Switzerland.

Klaus's time in Edinburgh had not been happy but St Paul's was a different matter. Slowly becoming accustomed to his new circumstances, he settled in well. 'Like most European immigrants, one wanted to be integrated into this country,' he says, 'to be more English than the English.' The educational system in England impressed him greatly – not so much the academic side of life, but rather, the emphasis on team sport. 'In Germany it was all gymnastics and so on – we didn't play soccer, cricket or rugby like we did at St Paul's.' A broken collar-bone soon ended his rugby career, but he loved cricket.

At seventeen he left St Paul's and went to University College, London, to study architecture. Although a student, he still had to be articled, and was taken on by C.W. Glover & Partners, where he was considered something of a rebel for his modernist tastes, influenced largely by the Bauhaus movement in Berlin. It was now 1938, and Glovers were designing air-raid shelters and bomb-proof buildings. Klaus found himself illustrating instruction manuals for them. Understandably, he felt the coming of war more keenly than many his age. He'd been outraged by the Anschluss in Austria and by the Nazi invasion of Czechoslovakia – he may have come from an apolitical family and been too young to fully comprehend what had been happening back in 1934, but at seventeen he had become fervently anti-Nazi, influenced not only by his own family's experiences but also by listening to the many refugees who boarded with them in Hampstead. 'Many of them were intellectuals and highly politically motivated,' he says. 'They all hated Hitler and Nazism.'

Klaus was determined to do his bit, and fully prepared to fight against his countrymen. He'd always been fascinated by aeroplanes and had often taken his model aircraft to fly in Regent's Park – so it was the RAF that he hoped to join. The attitude to German refugees had suddenly changed, however. First, he was refused entry into the University Air Squadron for being a German. Then he and his family were forced to face a tribunal to establish whether they should be considered as 'threatening aliens'. He passed this, but when, after war broke out, he tried to join the RAF, he was turned down. Instead, he was accepted into the Auxiliary Military Pioneer Corps. With his experience in the Cadet Force at St Paul's, he was made a corporal and sent to Ilfracombe in Devon, where he was told to organize the French legionnaires rescued from Narvik.

He persisted with the RAF, however, and much to his surprise, was finally accepted in early 1941, as the Blitz still raged over London. His medical showed up a defect in his eyes, however, and so it was not for a further six months, once the problem had been corrected, that he eventually began initial and elementary training in Yorkshire and Scotland. With all these obstacles overcome, he was, to his very great relief, selected for flying training, rather than as groundcrew, and sent to Canada. He reached Nova Scotia in the spring of 1942.

Once in Canada, a number of potential pilots were siphoned off to train in America at civilian flying schools as part of the Arnold Scheme. 'I had a girlfriend in New York,' says Ken. 'I'm not sure how I wangled it, but I was determined to be one of those sent to the US.' His girlfriend was soon forgotten, however, once he reached Georgia, where he learnt to fly with both British and American pilots. He soon met other girls anyway. 'I was quite a womanizer,' he admits, and celebrated his twenty-first birthday with his female navigation instructor. And he was a natural pilot. At one time, his class were stationed near an all-girl college. At the end of the course, Klaus flew low over the college giving an impromptu aerobatics display to impress the girls. His instructors were far from pleased, especially since a number of his fellow trainees had soon followed suit. Even so, it didn't stop him from gaining his US silver and RAF wings with an above-average rating and a likely commission in the RAF. Then came a setback. He was awaiting his first posting when his American commanding officer called him in and told him that 'pending further investigations', he was not to be commissioned after all, but to be sent back to England as a sergeant pilot. 'To this day, I have never found out why,' he says, although his nationality was almost certainly the reason for this sudden demotion.

It was disappointing, but he was pleased to be heading back to England and to be flying operationally. With his high marks, he had been half-expecting to be posted as an instructor, something he had most certainly not wanted. So it was that after flying Hurricanes at his Operational Training Unit in Scotland, he was posted, in October 1943, to 609 Squadron.

'I was amazed,' admits Ken. 'To have been viewed as somehow suspicious and then to be sent to one of the top-scoring fighter squadrons in the RAF seemed extraordinary.' He was also fortunate that although many RAF squadrons were filled with pilots from all around the world, this was particularly the case with 609. Made to feel at home immediately, Klaus was struck by the incredible sense of camaraderie and team spirit that pervaded the squadron. This was in part due to their current and highly inspirational commanding officer, Squadron Leader Pat Thornton-Brown. Loved dearly by all his men, he was utterly imperturbable and a high-class fighter pilot. New pilots like Klaus were not only welcomed warmly, but nurtured until their fighting skills were sufficiently honed. 'Charming!' was Thornton-Brown's usual response to anything unpleasant such as flying through intense flak. It was from him, as much as anyone, that Klaus learnt the benefits of understatement in a time of war.

Klaus had joined the squadron at Lympne, in Kent, on the day 609 celebrated its 200th aerial victory. At this time they were still operating independently rather than attached to a specific wing, although part of 11 Group. Although much of their time was spent protecting shipping, or carrying out sweeps in support of American bombers, they had begun flying 'ranger patrols' – low-level 'hedge-hopping' sweeps using auxiliary fuel tanks that enabled them to surprise and shoot up German airfields in France normally considered out of range to Allied fighters.

But it was on a supposed bomber escort that tragedy struck, just four days before Christmas. The squadron had been ordered to provide close support to a number of American Marauder bombers. Only six Typhoons were available, so the plan was for two Typhoons to escort each of the three formations of Marauders. Klaus was one of those due to be flying, but as soon as he reached his aircraft, he realized it hadn't been equipped with long-range auxiliary fuel tanks. 'I thought, "To hell with it,"' he says. 'Surely it wouldn't take long to escort a few bombers over to France?'

His youthful optimism soon proved to be misplaced. Having taken off, the Typhoons, led by Thornton-Brown, headed out over the coast, climbed to 20,000 feet then circled around Beachy Head waiting for the Marauders to appear. Only after twenty minutes burning precious fuel did they eventually spot the bombers and begin the mission, and by the time they reached the French coast, Klaus's aircraft was beginning to splutter. Although he was able to successfully switch over to his reserve tank, he was now acutely aware of how foolhardy he had been: the reserve tank would not last long and he was now flying over enemy territory. He called Thornton-Brown on the R/T and explained his predicament. 'You bloody fool,' the CO told him. 'Reduce your revs. Get a homing from Manston and try and glide as much as you can, and you might get back.'

Chastened, Klaus did as he was told, dropping out of formation and turning for home. Five minutes later, he heard panic on his radio. The Typhoons were under attack, not from the Luftwaffe, but from US P-47 Thunderbolts who had mistaken them for Focke-Wulfs. Recognition signals were hurriedly given, but to no avail. The American, Arty Ross, was hit by his countrymen, as were the Canadian, Chuck Miller and Thornton-Brown himself. Neither Miller nor the CO made it back – Thornton-Brown's wife had been due to join him for Christmas the following day. Klaus was more fortunate. His engine finally cut out just as he touched down at Manston. Even so, it was, he says, 'a terrible day'.

The Squadron's independent status changed early in 1944 after they had been retrained as a rocket-firing unit. By this time they were beginning to take part in active preparations for the Allied invasion. The 2nd Tactical Air Force had been formed and the squadron became attached to 123 Wing, part of 84 Group. Now based at Thorney Island, near Portsmouth on the south coast of England, they had become primarily aerial artillery, given the task of carrying out regular ground-attack 'shows' on targets in northern France. Early May began with a flurry of missions: an attack on a road bridge near Cherbourg on the second; the following day, nearly a hundred rockets were fired by the squadron at railway sheds near Amiens. On 7 May, targets included a shipping canal and another bridge.

Four days later – 11 May – Klaus was on a show to attack a radar station at Fécamp, near Le Havre. It was a big operation and their attack was preceded not only by American bombers, but other Typhoon squadrons as well. 'We were the last in,' says Ken. 'The

German flak was trained on us by the time our wave of Typhoons came in.' Moreover, they had been ordered to attack from inland and out to sea. The first four of 609's planes attacked in line astern, i.e., one behind the other, and two were promptly shot down, and a third badly hit. Flying behind, Klaus watched in horror as Flight Lieutenant Wood's Typhoon burst into flames, hit another Typhoon and then plunged to the ground. Realizing what sitting targets they were, he immediately fell out of the line astern formation, and made his attack from a different angle. This decision probably saved his life. 'Junior Soesman hit and bailed out but didn't get into dinghy,' Klaus noted in his logbook. 'Woody was also hit. Caught fire, collided with Adam and crashed into houses, exploding. Damned tough luck.' To lose three aircraft (and two pilots) out of eight was, as Klaus points out, 'a big hit'.

Losses were mounting. Five pilots were killed in May, four in June, five in July, and six in August – over 100 per cent casualty rates in under four months. In France, where precision was so important, a new system was introduced, copied from the Mediterranean Allied Tactical Air Force in Italy. This was 'VCP' – Visual Control Point – whereby an experienced RAF ground controller would travel about the front line in an army tank, and, equipped with a radio set tuned to the correct squadron frequency, would direct the Typhoons onto very precise targets. The pilots, working in flights of four, would operate a 'cab-rank' system: with the same maps as the controller on their knees, they would take it in turns to take off, climb to 8,000 feet, and circle around waiting to be directed onto a target. 'The controller would say, "Right, here's the grid reference, and in fifteen seconds you'll see red smoke. Go down and attack,"' says Ken, 'and then we'd find a Tiger tank or an 88mm gun and fire our rockets.' Flying so often and at such low altitudes, it was not surprising the squadron began to suffer.

'It was hard,' says Klaus of the number of losses. To avoid dwelling on such matters, there was a lot of drinking in the evenings, and much time spent gambling. If he woke up the following morning with a hangover, he usually found that flying at 10,000 feet with the oxygen on full would soon clear his head. By the middle of 1944, the RAF was struggling to recruit pilots for the rocket squadrons, so the Air Ministry decided that once a month, pilots could fly their aircraft back to England on a forty-eight-hour pass. On such occasions, Klaus would head straight for London, meeting up with girlfriends and doing his best to forget about the war for a couple of days. On the return trip, the pilots were expected to fly back with the gun bays crammed full of alcohol and whatever other goodies they could get their hands on. 'Then we would have a party,' says Ken.

In October, he lost his great friend Norman Merrett. 'He was always volunteering for the most ridiculous missions, which no one else would have done,' he says. Norman's luck finally ran out when, one day, he was asked to go on a weather reconnaissance flight. Spotting a train, he told his number two to stay at 8,000 feet, while he dived and attacked. His salvo of rockets missed, so he turned and attacked again. 'That was stupid – he should never have done that,' says Ken. On his second sweep over the train Norman's Typhoon was hit and he crash-landed. His number two watched him clamber out, and it was assumed he had become a prisoner of war. 'But he was so badly injured or beaten,' says Ken, 'he died at wherever it was they took him.'

Various squadron COs had repeatedly asked for Klaus to be given a commission but the request had been consistently refused. Around this time, he decided he had had enough and told his Wing Commander that he didn't mind risking his life from morning to evening, but wanted to be treated like everyone else, and so if he wasn't made an officer he would demand to be posted to Coastal Command. Wing Commander Scott immediately wrote to Anthony Eden, the Foreign Secretary – who had also been his tennis partner – and sure enough, soon after Klaus finally received his commission. The threat had worked, although he was glad he had not had to carry it out. Despite the fatigue, he still felt 'absolutely rooted' to the squadron.

In November, he suffered a severe hernia and was sent back to England for an operation. It was probably just as well, because although he refused to admit it to himself at the time, he now recognizes that he was beginning to feel considerably 'washed up' after thirteen months of almost continual active duty. Even so, three months later he was back, despite being scarcely fit to fly. 'I could barely walk,' he says.

With the war drawing to a close, he found himself back in Germany once more. It was an emotional experience for him. Soon after, he was asked to go into the nearest town and bring back as much drink as he could. Finding the mayor, he told him he was going to clear out the town hall's wine cellar. One woman watching him burst into tears. Klaus couldn't help feeling moved by her distress. Not until after the war, however, did he finally return to Berlin. 'It was October 1945,' he says. 'There was nothing left . . . our house wasn't there, just the ruins.'

Klaus stayed in the RAF on an extended commission until 1946. It had been his intention to continue flying, but his older brother, who had already been demobilized and had embarked on a successful career in London, talked him out of such a move. 'If you're lucky,' he'd told Klaus, 'you might make Group Captain in three years, but that'll be it. You'll never be properly accepted. It's not like America.' So Klaus began working for his brother, but only lasted a week; a career in the City was not for him. For a while he was doing nothing except wasting time and spending his money, but good fortune had spared him during the war, and it came to his rescue again now. His sister was working at the American Embassy, and one day a buyer on a film came in asking for help in supplying American props. In the course of their conversation, she told him about her brother and explained that he was looking for work. Klaus was taken on, and with his architectural background and artistic gifts soon began to do well. Before long he was making a name for himself as a production designer.

By the 1960s, Ken – as he had now become – was working on some of the most successful films of the period, responsible for set design on *Dr No, Goldfinger* and a number of other Bond films as well as *Dr Strangelove* and *Chitty Chitty Bang Bang*. 'They were fun,' he says, 'because I could let my imagination go. I am sure my childhood and wartime experience had a lot to do with it.' In his long career he has also earned two Oscars, the first for his work on Stanley Kubrick's *Barry Lyndon* and again for *The Madness of King George*. He was knighted in 2003. Curiously, he has never worked on a war film, despite being asked to be production designer on *The Battle of Britain*. 'I would have done it,' he says, 'but was working on *Chitty Chitty Bang Bang* at the time.'

He has found himself thinking more about his wartime experiences of late. Unearthed film footage of him flying his Typhoon in France and making an attack with his rockets brought a number of memories flooding back. Yet although many of these are painful, he remains enormously grateful for the friendships he made during those traumatic times. 'We established relationships back then,' he says, 'that just don't exist any more.'

SPORTING BLOOD

Tom Finney

Tom Finney has often been described as the most complete and versatile England footballer of all time. He showed technical mastery, and was a genuine two-footed player, capable of blasting a goalscoring shot with either foot. There was pace, too, and almost perfect balance, while his passing was famous for its judgement and accuracy. For England, he played left wing, right wing and centre forward. In seventy-six appearances, he scored thirty goals (fourth amongst the leading English goalscorers of all time), and set up many more. One newspaper claimed that, 'if all the brains in the game sat in committee to design the perfect player, they would come up with a reincarnation of Tom Finney,' while the legendary Bill Shankly once said that, 'Tom Finney would have been great in any team, in any match and in any age . . . even if he had been wearing an overcoat.' And yet Tom Finney did not start his first full League appearance for Preston North End until the age of twenty-four. For this he had the Second World War to thank. Like so many men his age, the war robbed him of his early years of adulthood, when he was in the prime of his life; a time when he could – and would – have been playing professional football for both Preston North End and England.

The Second World War affected the lives of every man, woman and child who lived through it, and that included footballers. Hard though it may be to imagine David Beckham or Wayne Rooney being packed off to war, that is exactly what happened to the vast majority of British footballers in 1939–1945. Conscription had been reinstated in May 1939 for men between the ages of twenty and twenty-one, and on the first day of the war, on 3 September 1939, Parliament passed the National Service Act, under which all men between eighteen and forty-one were made liable for conscription into the armed forces. There were, of course, exceptions – those with skills or jobs that would benefit the war effort, such as farmers, physicists, even trade union officials and lighthouse-keepers. But not footballers. Professional soccer players had to put away the studs and put on hob-nail boots instead, and like every other Tom, Dick, and Harry, go off and fight for King and Country.

Tom Finney had just turned twenty when his call-up papers arrived. By that time he was playing regularly for Preston North End in the unofficial Wartime League, but was also working as an apprentice plumber. 'I was twenty on 5 April 1942, and called up two weeks later,' he says. 'My papers came through the post and told me to report to Preston Barracks. I went up there and had a chat with the Army fellow who was on duty about what regiment I'd like to go in. I told him I wanted to join my brother in Burma. But I never heard another thing until I was told to report to some barracks down south and I ended up in the Royal Armoured Corps.'

Trooper T. Finney 7958274 was sent to Tidworth Barracks on Salisbury Plain for six weeks of square-bashing and initial training, then transferred back up north to Catterick, where he was told he was to become a driver-mechanic. 'Mostly I was in tanks,' he says. 'I never drove in my life before I went into the Army, but I could drive everything by the time I came out' – including a variety of British and American tanks. 'It was quite simple,' he says. 'They were controlled by sticks, as we called them. You pushed forward with the left stick and it held the track and you turned left, and vice versa.' He quite enjoyed the driving, had no trouble at all with the physical training, and even found the square-bashing quite rewarding. His fellows were of a similar age and background and he felt comfortable in their company. Tom was settling well into army life.

But after six months' training, he was posted overseas. A week's embarkation leave and a few days at home in Preston with his dad and his fiancée, Elsie, and then he was rumbling north on the night train to Glasgow to join the troopship, *Queen Mary*. Tom was one of 7,000 men packed like sardines onto the ship. Like so many others, he'd never left England before and had no idea how long he'd be gone or where they were heading. 'We knew it was going to be somewhere warm,' he says, 'because we were given tropical gear. But otherwise, we hadn't a clue.' He admits that he did feel a certain amount of apprehension about what might lie in store. 'When you were sent abroad, you knew you were likely to be going into action and your thoughts were on whether you'd ever come back – you know, would you get killed. But to be honest, I wasn't that worried. I think that because I'd lost my mother quite early on in life, I was quite good at looking after myself. I think it helped when it came to going off to war.'

Tom was just four when his mother died, aged only thirty-two. Misdiagnosed with appendicitis, her end was very sudden, and left Tom's father, Alf, with six children under the age of ten to look after: four girls, and Tom and his older brother, Joe. In the 1920s, it would not have been uncommon for the children to have been put into care in such circumstances, but Tom's father somehow managed to keep the family together. Financial necessity meant Alf Finney had to continue with his job with the Electricity Board, but he was fortunate to have support from the grandparents and from neighbours. Even so, to a certain degree, the children had to learn to fend for themselves, even when Tom's father remarried a few years later.

The Finneys were poor, like the majority of families in Preston. A typical Lancashire mill-town, Preston struggled like many other places in the Depression-hit twenties and thirties. Unemployment was high and wages low – Tom's father took home just fifty shillings (£2.50) a week. It was also a dirty place, with soot from the mills and rows of terraced houses filling the air and regularly causing thick smogs. But for Tom, Preston was his home and although they lived in a small house on a council estate, they were only a stone's throw from Deepdale, the home of Preston North End Football Club. As a boy, Tom could see the stands and terraces rising above the surrounding houses, a Mecca that from an early age became the focus of his dreams.

Two more brothers followed, so there were now eight children in the house. 'My father had a real struggle on his hands,' says Tom. He also admits he found having a step-mother in their lives difficult to come to terms with. But there was always football – the overriding passion for the men in the Finney family, and Alf did all he could to encourage Tom and Joe in their love of the game. Occasionally, when he could afford it, he even took them to Deepdale to watch Preston North End.

Although Tom proved himself to be good at most sports, nearly all his spare time was spent playing football, and he soon began to show a rare talent. When playing for Deepdale Modern's Under-12 team, they reached the final of the Dawson Cup, a local school tournament. The match was held at none other than Deepdale itself, and Tom scored the winning goal and was chaired from the field a hero. He continued doing well at school level, and at fourteen represented Preston Town in the All-England Schools' Shield. They even reached the final, drawing with West Ham to become joint champions. Shortly after, having left school, and still only fifteen and just four-foot-nine tall, Tom was given a trial with Preston North End, and impressed them enough to be offered a job on the groundstaff. He could hardly contain his excitement, but there was a cruel disappointment waiting for him. When he got home and told his father the good news, Alf told him to turn down the offer. Tom was devastated – but his father was adamant. His son had just started as an apprentice plumber and Alf felt he should learn a trade first before leaping headlong into a career in football.

Instead, he signed for North End as an amateur, which qualified him to play for the 'B' team and allowed him to join evening training sessions twice a week. This was a poor consolation, however. Few amateurs progressed to the first team, and Tom felt he had blown his chance to ever become a professional. No doubt he would have been an exception: his ball skills were unquestioned, and he practised hard – it was during this time that he taught himself to play with both feet with equal dexterity. But to a young teenager, full of burning desire for the sport he loved, life as a plumber was hardly the fulfilment of childhood ambition.

But with the outbreak of war, fate soon intervened. Just a few days after the beginning of hostilities, and under two weeks after the start of the new League season, the War Emergency Committee of the Football Association met to decide the course of action they should take with regard to the game now that war had been declared. The FA had already encouraged professional footballers to join the Territorial Army in a circular sent round the previous April, hoping that in the event of war, players would set a patriotic example. Tom's brother Joe, by then playing as an amateur with Blackburn Rovers, joined the TA along with a number of his team-mates. Some clubs joined wholesale, such as Liverpool FC's entire playing staff. Bolton Wanderers and West Ham United were two other teams who also joined the Territorials almost to a man. By the time war was declared, the majority of these footballers had either already been called up or soon would be – Joe Finney included.

This meant that when the War Emergency Committee met in September 1939, they had little hesitation in suspending the Football League until further notice. With clubs already decimated by war-time call-ups, and with the restrictions on travel already coming into place, it would have been impossible for the 1939–40 season to have continued. Initially, they prohibited all clubs from playing at all, allowing only Forces' matches. A few days later they relaxed some-what, approving 'friendly' fixtures between clubs instead, but the official FA Leagues were closed down for the duration of the war.

Tom Finney was still not quite seventeen and Britain was in the throes of the Phoney War when he was asked to go to Deepdale for a meeting with North End's Chairman, Jim Taylor. Arriving straight from work and still in his plumber's overalls, he found his father already there and Taylor ready with the paperwork that would make him a wartime professional on half-pay of ten shillings (50 pence) a week. He signed with a hand that was trembling with excitement.

It might not have been full League football, but for the time being a place in Preston's first team was good enough.

Wartime football was organized on a regional basis, and in Tom's first season they were Northern Section Champions. 'In my early days for Preston North End there were also a lot of guest players,' says Tom, 'players that were from other clubs but were stationed at camps nearby.' Even so, it was often a hit-and-miss affair as to whether clubs would be able to field a full side. But public demand was high and, on the whole, the new system seemed to work. Playing for Preston at that time was the legendary Bill Shankly, the man Tom claims was his footballing mentor, and a professional whom he looked up to with considerable awe. Indeed, in that first season, Tom found himself playing with and against a number of his childhood heroes, culminating in the final of the Wartime League Cup against Arsenal at Wembley in May 1941. 'That was a wonderful occasion for me,' says Tom. Opposite him was none other than the England captain, Eddie Hapgood; also playing for Arsenal were the two Compton brothers, Denis and Les. Because of the ongoing London Blitz, Preston arrived at Wembley on Final day itself, with the players having had little opportunity to prepare themselves. Tom was less worried about the bombs than the game, one which Arsenal were expected to cruise. But on the day, after early pressure from the Gunners, Tom helped set up a Preston goal. Preston had further chances but failed to make the most of them and Denis Compton later equalized. The match was a draw.

The rematch was to be held in the north, at Blackburn Rovers' ground at Ewood Park. Preston nearly lost one of their key strikers, Bobby Beattie, but at the last minute he was released by the RAF. With plenty of home support, Preston went a goal ahead early, but again, Arsenal equalized. Preston responded almost immediately, however, with Beattie scoring the winning goal and thus secured the Cup. Rather than being given Cup-Winner medals, however, each player was handed fifteen shillings' worth of wartime saving certificates, which most of them cashed right away.

*   *   *

Tom was enjoying the war. He was playing plenty of football – forty-one games for North End in the 1940–41 season – and had found the girl he intended to marry. He had first met Elsie Noblett at a dance organized by his local church, St Jude's, although it was some time before they got together. The occasion was a Greta Garbo film at the Rialto cinema in Preston. Tom was accompanying another girl, while his friend Alf Lorimer had taken Elsie. By the time they reached the cinema the film had started and as they fumbled to find seats in the dark, Tom ended up in a double seat with Elsie instead.

Love blossomed, and they began to see each other regularly, going to dances and films whenever they could, and Elsie watching him play football. They had been dating for about three years when Tom received his call-up papers, and he immediately decided it was time to take the relationship a step further. He wanted to get married right away, but Elsie was persuaded by her mother that they should wait. She did agree, however, that they should become engaged.

Tom found it hard to leave her and was sorry to call an end to his time with Preston North End, but he had known it was inevitable and that there was little he could do about it, except try to do his best and hope he came home again in one piece. 'I accepted it,' he says. 'You had no say in the matter at all, and there were plenty of other people who had to leave behind wives and girlfriends.'

In January 1943, he reached Egypt in the Middle East, and was sent to the base camp at Mena, close to Cairo and next to the pyramids. The British Eighth Army was by now over a thousand miles away, having broken out of Egypt at El Alamein the previous November, and then continued to chase Field Marshal Rommel's forces back across Libya. On 21 January, the Eighth Army captured Tripoli, and by March they were crossing the border into Tunisia. Back in Egypt, Tom took part in intensive training manoeuvres and fully expected to be sent along the North African coast and into action at any moment.

The order never came, however. In between exercises and manoeuvres, Tom had played a bit of football at Mena Camp. 'Word went round pretty quickly that I was a Preston North End player,' he says. Consequently, when Headquarters, Middle East Forces, decided to raise a football team to travel the Middle East entertaining the troops, Tom was asked to go to Cairo for a trial. He scored a hat-trick in the warm-up game and so was selected for the squad.

Playing Services XIs and national sides, the Wanderers, as they were called, toured Palestine, Syria and Egypt, travelling by train and lorry. 'We were pretty much all professional players,' says Tom. 'The pitches were sand and there was no grass, but it was a great experience and you learnt a lot about placing the ball and playing on hard surfaces.' Tom went on several such tours, playing against King Farouk's XI and the Egyptian Army team and other such sides. 'One time I played against Omar Sharif, the film star,' he says. 'I only found that out later, but it was all great fun.' They received no star treatment and were expected to 'rough it' just like any other servicemen, but the standard was pretty high and their matches were always watched by good crowds. And in between these tours, instead of being posted to Tunisia or Italy, he was sent on a cooking course. 'I think that was just to keep me at the Base Depot,' he says.

Nonetheless, he did feel pangs of guilt that others were getting themselves killed while he was on entertainment duties playing football for the troops. He needn't have worried, however. After two years in the Middle East, he was posted to Foggia in southern Italy in early 1945. 'I was interviewed by one of the base officers,' Tom recalls, 'and he said to me, "Have you seen any action yet?" I said, "No." And he said, "Well you bloody soon will." The following day I was off to join the 9th Queen's Royal Lancers.'

Throughout the long winter months, the Allies had been bogged down in a war of attrition, but with the onset of spring, they launched another assault to push the Germans back north beyond the River Po. This new offensive was known as Operation Grapeshot, and the 9th Lancers were in the thick of it, part of a mobile armoured force of Eighth Army's 78th Division, known as Kangaroo Force. Tom was made a tank driver in C Squadron, replacing a boy who had been killed the day before. C Squadron was the reconnaissance squadron, and used light, fast, Stuart tanks, known to the British troops as 'Honeys'. But despite the advantage of speed, Honeys were thinly armoured and lightly armed, and their crews were particularly vulnerable.

On 18 April, the 9th Lancers were involved in a particularly heavy attack when all three squadrons pushed north of the town of Argenta and captured a crucial railway bridge that had only been partially demolished by the retreating Germans. With the London Irish infantry in support, they attacked the gun lines of the German 42nd Jäger Division as daylight began to fade. As vehicles and ammunition dumps exploded, sending huge pyrotechnics high into the evening sky, the Lancers forged ahead, overwhelming the German position and capturing more than 450 prisoners. The cost to the Lancers was only two tanks damaged, but Tom readily admits that it was 'pretty scary'.

There was more fighting to come, however, as 78th Division pushed north towards the River Po and came across stubborn resistance from the German 29th Panzer Grenadier Division. 'The worst time I had,' says Tom, 'was going into action, surviving and coming back, only to have to go back in again and rescue some tanks that had been knocked out.'

He was also struck by the very large numbers of prisoners walking back through their lines. 'They were coming through in their hundreds,' he says. 'You felt they were just like you were: lads that had been called up and probably had no say in whether they went in the Army or not.'

They were on the muddy banks of the River Po when news arrived that the Germans had surrendered. 'We had a bit of a celebration,' he says, 'firing guns and so on, and then we all started wondering how long it would be before we were sent home.' He'd survived without a scratch, but many of his colleagues were not so fortunate. 'The sad part,' he says, 'was that you'd see someone in the morning when they were going out and then they'd be killed, so you never saw them again that evening. I didn't like fighting at all.'

With the war in Italy over, Tom began playing football once more, this time for the Eighth Army side, captained by his old Preston team-mate, Andy Beattie. They played all round Italy and in Austria, but there were other games as well. Tom was picked for a Central Mediterranean Forces XI against an FA Army XI. Again, the teams were made up almost entirely from pre-war professional players – the Army XI was captained by none other than Matt Busby. Played at Naples and watched by 30,000, the match was a fiercely competitive, hard-fought 2–2 draw.

The highlight of his wartime playing career came shortly after, however. One night Tom was woken at two in the morning by his commanding officer, who had received a telegram from the Football Association asking that Tom be released from service immediately to play for England in two unofficial internationals against Switzerland. Tom was over the moon, but his CO was not so happy. 'He wasn't very pleased about me being selected because we were in Austria,' he says, 'and he had to find transport to get me to Naples so that I could get an aircraft back to England.' Since Switzerland was a neutral country the players were not allowed to wear military uniforms, but Tom didn't have anything else. 'Stanley Rowse, who was then the Secretary of the FA, took me to London and bought me a suit,' he smiles. They lost the first game and won the second, but Tom had made his England debut.

Although the war was over, the Army had not finished with him. Apart from a few days' leave after the Switzerland games and a month home in November 1945 – when he finally married Elsie – he remained stuck in Italy. 'I wasn't doing much out there,' he says. 'Just passing the time of day really.' He used to take some of the men on training sessions and give them some football coaching. 'It was quite enjoyable,' he says, 'apart from the fact that I wanted to go home now the war was finished.' As it turned out, he was demobbed a few months early because he was a trained plumber and skilled workers were needed back in England, but even so it wasn't until the summer of 1946 that he finally made it home for good – just in time for the start of the first post-war League season.

*   *   *

So began his full professional career at last, in Preston's opening fixture, against Leeds United. 'I scored in that game,' he says, 'and then I was capped for England shortly after in September.' The match was against Northern Ireland, and both his father and brother Joe, now back from Burma, came to Belfast to watch him score in England's 7–2 victory.

He stayed with Preston North End until the end of his playing career in 1960, despite a lucrative offer to join Palermo in the 1950s. Football never made him rich – the FA still capped wages at that time – and he finally began to see the wisdom of his father's decision to make him learn a trade rather than rush into professional football. Tom set up Tom Finney Ltd with his brother, who was a qualified electrician, and it grew into a very successful plumbing and electrical business, one that kept him busy long after his playing days were over.

As a boy, his father had instilled into him values of decency, honesty and fair play, and in his long career, Tom was never once sent off or even booked. He was a shining example during the post-war Golden Age of Football, and although he never won any honours with Preston, and played in three unsuccessful England World Cup campaigns, he says he looks back on his career with no regrets at all.

Knighted in 1998, he remains one of the greats of the English game. His beloved wife Elsie passed away in November 2004, but since that blow he has tried to keep himself as busy as possible. 'I'm pretty tied up much of the time,' he says. 'I enjoy watching Preston and try and watch most of the home games. There're usually one or two engagements in the week. But it's best to keep active.'

And what of the war? 'I don't think back on the past a lot,' he says. 'The war was something you just accepted. I was lucky – I got to play some football, and to be honest, I think I came back a better player. But I was twenty-four when I came out of the forces, and I could have done without the experience.' He pauses, 'But it was the same for everyone. Everyone was in exactly the same boat.'

THE SHADOW WAR

Gianni Rossi

It was while returning from a raid on the Republican Army barracks in Tolé, in June 1944, that Gianni Rossi proved the worth of the Italian partisans. It had been his idea to linger by the road that ran beneath Monte Pastore – he had realized that the Germans and Fascists were already learning not to use the main valley roads for fear of the partisans' attacks. But Gianni, who had lived in the area all his life, knew that the road they were now on ran roughly parallel to the one that followed the River Reno away below them. It was, in fact, an alternative, albeit much twistier, narrower and slower route to Bologna.

Although their partisan band now numbered nearly a thousand men, Gianni had taken just four others with him on the raid to Tolé – they had discovered they could be more effective when operating in small hit-and-run guerrilla-style raids. And so, hiding behind a cemetery on the edge of a mountain village, they had sat and waited. There was only one other Italian amongst them – a young boy from Verona. The rest were former prisoners of war: Jock, a Scotsman; Herman, a South African; and Steve, a New Zealander. All had escaped from a train stopped by partisans a couple of months before which had been taking them to a new POW camp in the north.

Before long, a German staff car appeared, grinding its way slowly along the mountain road. As it drew near, the five partisans leapt

out from their hiding position and opened fire. The car, a
Kübelwagen staff car, crashed off the road, and Gianni and the
others cautiously approached. There had been just three in the car,
but Gianni could see all were dead. One was an officer, another a
doctor; the third was the driver. There was also a briefcase. Opening
it, they found a number of documents outlining the new fortifica-
tions along the Gothic Line, the defensive position the Germans
would shortly occupy.

Rome had recently fallen and the Germans were now retreating
northwards, holding off the advancing Allied forces in a series of
defensive stands between the capital and Florence. These were
just delaying actions, however, while the bulk of the German
forces in Italy fell back to their next line of defence: the Gothic
Line, a series of bunkers and gun positions that had been hastily
built across the width of Italy all the way from Rimini in the east
to Viareggio in the west, and making the most of the imposing
Apennine mountains that barred the way to the open plains of the
north.

Clearly, the documents they had now captured would be more
than worth their weight in gold to the Allies, but first they had to
make sure they got rid of any evidence of the attack – far better if
the car and its contents simply disappeared, spirited away somewhere in the mountains. Quickly rounding up some local men –
contadini farmers – they dug a large pit in a field by the road, then
rolled the car and the bodies into it and buried them. Then Gianni
and the others hurried back to Monte Sole, a mountain on the far
side of the Reno Valley and arranged for the documents to be taken
to Switzerland. Later, word reached the *Stella Rossa* that the Germans
had searched and searched for the missing men, and, presumably,
those vital documents, but with no success; they had vanished into
thin air. A week or so later, a British plane flew over Monte Sole and
dropped leaflets, thanking the partisans for capturing and deliver-
ing such vital information.

As Gianni finished his account of this episode, he lit another cigarette, the smoke curling around him in the sunshine of a spring-time afternoon. He smiled. 'Yes,' he said, 'that was a real coup.'

He had been a difficult man to track down. At the archives in Marzabotto, the principal town in the area, they had not even been sure whether he was still alive, yet as the former second-in-command of the *Stella Rossa* partisan band, they were certainly familiar with his name and wartime achievements. I was over there talking to a number of former partisans and civilians who had lived in the area during the war and it was eventually a lady now living in Bologna who told me she was certain he was still fit and well, although she couldn't help me with an address. 'But go to Gardaletto and ask in the bar there,' she suggested. 'They'll know.'

I left Bologna, and headed south. The mountains loom suddenly and before long I was driving down the valley road that ran along the River Reno – the very road where the *Stella Rossa* had made German and Fascist lives so difficult. Beyond Marzabotto, I crossed the river then began climbing into the mountains until I reached a kind of plateau nestling beneath the summit of several peaks, one of which was Monte Sole. There had been a number of villages and isolated farms up here once: this area had been lived on and farmed by sharecroppers – peasant farmers, or *contadini* – for centuries, although they had all gone now. It was here, with the help of these mountain people, that the *Stella Rossa* had begun their armed resistance; it was where they had ended their existence too.

Continuing down the other side, I reached another valley through which the River Setta ran. During the war, these two valleys, the Reno and the Setta, had offered vital routes from the south through the Apennines, leading to Bologna and the open plains beyond; no wonder Monte Sole had been such a strategi-cally important strong-point. From there, the partisans had been able to harass German troops and supplies heading to and from the front, which by the end of July 1944 had been some fifteen miles to the south.

I reached Quercia, a small hamlet, then turned left and after a mile came to Gardaletto. There was just one bar, so I stopped and asked them about Gianni. 'He used to live almost opposite,' smiled the old lady. 'His father built that house.' I followed her gaze. It was larger than most – a decent-sized family home.

'But he doesn't live there now?' I asked.

'No. I think he's in Vado. Go there and ask in the bar. They'll know where he is.'

From the way she had said it, I'd assumed that like Gardaletto, there was just the one bar in Vado. I was wrong: it was a small town, and had a number. The first one I went into suggested I try another; the next said, no, he didn't live in Vado anymore, but just outside. 'Go to Vado di Monzumo. They'll know him there.'

On I drove, past 'Via G. Rossi' and went into the fourth bar of my quest.

'You've just missed him,' the barman told me, my spirits rising. He gave me his address – it was only a few yards away – but added that Gianni was unlikely to talk. Then he suggested I take him some cigarettes. 'A few packets might persuade him.'

It was a good tip, for when I finally found myself face-to-face with the man himself, he showed no reluctance to talk at all; rather, only mild surprise. Perhaps the barman had merely been trying to get the old man a few free cigarettes.

Short and stocky, with a gentle voice and humorous eyes, Gianni spoke in a calm, measured tone. He struck me as a good man in a crisis: unflappable; a steady nerve, but tough as well. The attributes of any good soldier, even a partisan. Did he remember the first time he had opened fire on a fellow Italian, I asked him at one point. Yes, he replied. It was in March 1944, in the early days of the *Stella Rossa*. They attacked a truck of Republican troops. Any qualms or doubts about trying to kill your own countrymen? I asked. He merely shrugged. 'They had their dance,' he said, 'and we had ours.'

It is little known today that Italy found herself plunged into bitter civil war during the last years of the Second World War. It is also little known that there were more *partigiani* in Italy than there were *maquis* in France, or that there were more civilian atrocities in Italy than anywhere else in Western Europe outside the death camps – more than 700 separate cases, in which many thousands were shot, butchered, burnt alive and hanged. Women, children, the old and young. Whole communities were ruthlessly wiped out, usually part of reprisals – or *rastrellamenti* – inflicted in retaliation for the activities of the increasingly large numbers of partisans hiding in and operating from the mountains of northern Italy.

Any civil war is a messy, complicated affair, and Italy's was no exception. In July 1943, following the Allied invasion of Sicily, Italy's Fascist leader, Benito Mussolini, was deposed. The Fascist Party, which had reigned over Italy for twenty-one years, was finished, but the government that replaced it was weak and led by the ineffective Marshal Badoglio. Although it was obvious Italy was losing the war, for forty-five days Badoglio and King Victor Emmanuel III dithered and prevaricated, making peace overtures to the Allies on one hand and assuring Germany they would continue the fight on the other. In the meantime, German troops were pouring into Italy. It was not until 3 September that an armistice was finally signed, and not until the eighth that Italy's exit from the war was announced to her people.

Although some saw the armistice as a terrible betrayal, the majority of Italians were only too happy to be out of the war at last. Yet relief soon turned to despair. Chaos and confusion followed, with a meltdown of authority. Gianni Rossi had been serving in the Italian Navy, on the battleship *Alpino* based at Naples when the armistice was announced. He, along with most of his comrades, simply walked off the ship and headed home. After a week of walking and hitching rides, he arrived back at his family's apartment in Bologna. He was not alone: Italy was awash with troops heading home, but also escaped POWs too; when the guards had gone, hundreds of thousands had streamed out into the countryside.

Events moved rapidly. Mussolini was freed by the Germans and became head of a new Fascist state, the Republic of Salo. He was little more than a puppet: all Italy north of the front line was now occupied by Nazi Germany. Rome was also occupied, Badoglio and the King fleeing south to where the Allies had control.

Bologna and the mountainous region of Monte Sole where Gianni had been brought up, lay within the control of the Fascist regime. Those trapped in the part of Italy north of the front line were expected to fight for Mussolini and the Germans once more – all former servicemen, and also all those men born between the years 1923 and 1925. They would form the core of a new Fascist army, and were to report for duty on pain of death. Italy's young men were faced with a stark choice: join the Fascists, or flee and hide.

For Gianni, it was an easy decision. His family had always been vehemently anti-Fascist, even during the twenties and thirties when Mussolini had been basking in wide popular support. His father had continually found himself in trouble, refusing to carry a *tessera*, the Fascist Party card that every Italian was expected to keep. Harassed and taunted by the Blackshirts, he was also frequently flung in prison. 'If there was a Fascist dignitary due to be visiting the area,' Gianni said, 'he would be picked up beforehand and put in jail for a few days.' He remembered his father was flung in jail when Hitler visited in 1937.

Despite this, the Rossi family lived comfortably in their family home in the village of Gardaletto, along the banks of the River Setta. When not in trouble with the Fascists, Gianni's father, a decorated veteran of the Great War, was a successful builder and property developer. 'But all around us was poverty and misery,' Gianni told me.

At twelve, he left school and became an apprentice mechanic in Bologna. Soon, he moved there, living with an aunt, until just before the war the whole family moved into a large apartment in the city. Although they had kept the house in Gardaletto, Gianni's parents and younger brother continued living in Bologna throughout the war, and so it was to there that he returned after the armistice. And it was there that he met up again with his old childhood friend, Mario Musolesi, always known to everyone as *Il Lupo* – the Wolf.

Like Gianni, Lupo came from a family that had always been vehemently anti-Fascist. Several years older than Gianni, Lupo had also returned to Bologna, having walked out on the Army at the armistice. It was Lupo who suggested to Gianni and a few others that they should raid some of the army barracks that were now largely deserted. With arms, they could actively resist Germany and the new Fascist regime.

'We didn't have much of a plan,' Gianni explained. Having borrowed a lorry, they raided one of the barracks, took a stash of rifles and ammunition, then headed back to Gardaletto, where both Lupo and Gianni still had family homes, and hid their cache.

That first winter they did little, merely meeting up, gathering numbers and trying to carry on with their lives as best they could. The Fascist authorities were slow to react to the poor response to their call to arms. A deadline was imposed: all men called upon to fight had to report for duty by March 1944. It was this new deadline that proved the catalyst for Lupo and his embryonic band of partisans.

Leaving Bologna, they returned to Gardaletto and hid their cache of arms in a cave in the mountains. Soon after, they carried out their first attack. For Gianni, there was no crisis of conscience. 'I opened fire without emotion,' he told me. 'It was just something I had to do.' There were now about twenty of them and all had their own personal Rubicons. There could be no turning back.

There was also a price on their heads. 'They knew who we were,' Gianni explained, and so they took to the mountains, living in the barns of sympathetic *contadini*, or in caves, never in one place for long. Even his parents were forced to keep constantly on the move. The Fascists threatened to kill the families of 'deserters'.

In that spring of 1944, with the deadline for joining the new Fascist Army passing, the numbers of the *Stella Rossa,* as they now called themselves, began to grow rapidly. Most were frightened young men avoiding the draft. 'If they'd been caught, they'd have been arrested,' Gianni explained. 'And then shot.' Similar bands were forming elsewhere in Italy, as was a new political opposition. During the Fascist years there had been a number of clandestine opposition parties, although these were dominated by the Action Party and the Communists. These parties now decided to collaborate and form the Committee of National Liberation – or the CLN, as it was known. Although an underground organization, this became the unofficial opposition in Italy and the political wing of all armed resistance. It was through them, and with the help of undercover agents sent behind lines by the British Special Operations Executive (SOE) and American Office of Strategic Services (OSS), that these bands of partisans were given cohesion and also, crucially, supplies of arms, clothing and other equipment.

In April 1944, they were contacted by a former officer in the Italian Navy, whose girlfriend in Bologna was known to both Lupo and Gianni. The British first contacted them in April 1944, through a former Italian sailor who was working as an agent for SOE. It was this agent who helped arrange the *Stella Rossa*'s first arms drops. 'We just had an ordinary radio,' Gianni told me. 'We would tune into the BBC every evening waiting for the words, "Mario, get ready, Mario, get ready."' This was the signal for them to prepare a field ready for the drops. When they then heard the words, 'the birds are singing,' they would know the drop would arrive at 10 p.m. that night. They received three separate drops in May – canisters floating down on parachutes and filled with Sten light machineguns, rifles, ammunition, grenades, Bren heavy machineguns, as well as plenty of serge uniforms: trousers, battle-blouses and boots; most partisans reached the mountains with little more than the clothes they stood in.

By the middle of May, their numbers had grown to over 250 and with their new arms and equipment they began making raids into the valleys, attacking Fascists, blocking roads, and blowing up railway lines and bridges. They also destroyed an anti-aircraft battery at Vado, along the Setta Valley. It wasn't long before the Germans planned their first *rastrellamento* – or 'clean-up' – against them. On 24 May, German and Fascist troops began climbing the mountain in force, but lying in wait and hidden amongst the dense shrub on the upper reaches of the mountains, the partisans scored a notable victory. 'That was a good fight,' Gianni grinned, remembering. 'Really. We killed about 240 Germans – but only one of our men was wounded.' After that, the mountains became almost entirely off-limits to German and Republican troops – those who strayed out of the valleys, did so at extreme risk. Lupo was now king of Monte Sole.

As Gianni freely admitted, they would have got nowhere without the collaboration of the mountain people – the *contadini* and their families, who not only housed many of them, allowing partisans to sleep in barns and haylofts, but who also made many sacrifices in helping to feed increasingly large numbers of hungry young men. Rationing and taxes were brutal. Many *contadini* barely had enough food to eat themselves. For that reason alone it would have been entirely understandable if the *contadini* had tried to distance themselves from the partisans. Yet they also faced the threat of extremely harsh measures if they were either denounced or caught helping the partisans.

Both at the time and subsequently, the effectiveness of these growing partisan bands has often been questioned, yet there was no doubting Field Marshal Kesselring's view of them. By the summer of 1944, the German commander-in-chief in Italy saw them as a serious and highly disruptive menace and he was determined to stamp them out. Ten civilians would be executed for every one German killed by partisans, he announced; and civilians caught supplying partisans with food, shelter, or information – i.e., spying –

would also be shot. Hostages would be – and were – taken in areas where partisan bands were operating, while civilians captured during shoot-outs with partisans would be sent to the Reich as slave labourers.

Despite these very real threats, the mountain people continued to almost unequivocally support the *Stella Rossa*. A large number of civilians, many girls included, also helped by passing on crucial information. Known as *staffette,* they ensured a very effective bush telegraph operated on behalf of the partisans. It was because of fore-warning by these *staffette,* for example, that the *Stella Rossa* were ready and waiting for the German attack on 24 May.

Even so, not everyone could be trusted: the price on their head alone was enough to tempt some to spy for the Fascists. Gianni reckoned he never slept in the same place for more than a couple of nights at a time, and there would be sentries posted at all times. 'Twice we were nearly killed by spies,' Gianni admitted. The first time, Lupo's wine was poisoned, although he smelled the poison in time. The second time was when they were infiltrated by a young man known to them from before the war, called Amedeo Arcioni. The Italian SOE agent had even warned them against him, but Lupo had refused to believe it.

One night, they were sleeping in a cave – Gianni, Lupo and Amedeo. Lupo was on watch while Gianni slept. It was a cave they used regularly, and to make it more habitable, they had lined it with wood. Lupo had stuck his dagger into the wood above them and was watching at the edge of the cave when Amedeo went out to relieve himself. On his return, he snatched the knife and lunged at Lupo, catching him in the arm. Lupo's shouts for help woke Gianni instantly. Jumping up, he tried to pull off the traitor, but in the resulting tussle, Amedeo managed to get the better of him and was forcing the dagger ever closer to Gianni's head until the point pierced the skin on his forehead. Just at the moment when Gianni thought his time had come, Lupo managed to come to his rescue and between them they were able to pin Amedeo down.

So what did you do with him? I asked. Gianni smiled and made a pistol-shot movement with his hand. 'We took him outside,' he said.

By July and August 1944, the *Stella Rossa* were operating to the height of their effectiveness. They now had over a thousand men amongst them – mostly Italians, but also Russian deserters from the German Army, former Allied prisoners of war and escaped Todt workers, slave labourers from the Greater Reich. With the help of the SOE and OSS, as well as the former soldiers amongst them, Lupo and Gianni had organized the *Stella Rossa* along more conventional lines: their numbers were divided into companies, each of thirty or so men, and each with a leader. These were dispersed around the mountains of Monte Sole and beyond, the far side of the Setta and Reno Valleys. The *Stella Rossa* now operated in a wide area, although each company was still answerable to Lupo and the rest of his Headquarters Company. And although there were occasional large-scale fire fights, for the most part, the partisans followed guerrilla tactics only, hit-and-run attacks based on information passed to them by the *staffette*.

At the end of July, the Allies had reached the Gothic Line. On clear, still days, the sound of the guns could be heard, thudding dully over the mountains. More aircraft appeared in the skies, bombers and fighters. Lupo was confident that the Allies would soon break through and so had few qualms about following orders passed to them from the Allies. The *Stella Rossa*, they were told, had an important role to play, first in harassing the Germans when they began their retreat up the Setta and Reno Valleys, and second, by ensuring the Germans did not capture the high ground from which their guns could harass the Allied advance in turn. For these two reasons, Lupo was asked to concentrate his entire force in the Monte Sole area and await instructions. Lupo, flattered by the importance the Allies were giving them, and also conscious of wanting a role once the area was liberated, rigidly adhered to his instructions. 'Orders are orders,' he would say.

Gianni was quite clear that Lupo never once had his authority questioned, but there must have been those who wondered about the sense of following these directives. By August, the number of arms drops had fallen dramatically; the Allies had begun to concentrate their supply efforts on the Yugoslavian partisans, who were fighting alone without the help of any Allied army. As a result, the *Stella Rossa*'s ammunition supplies were now running dangerously low. Furthermore, by concentrating their numbers in such a small area, they were placing an even greater burden on the *contadini*. Most serious, however, was the threat of a renewed *rastrellamento* carried out in force. Short of ammunition and too numerous to hide effectively, they would be sitting ducks.

Several weeks passed. Repeated requests for more supplies were refused, yet there was still no sign of the Allies making a breakthrough. Then, towards the end of September, a would-be spy was caught trying to infiltrate them. Eventually he confessed that he'd been sent up to assess their strength and positions. A couple of days later, another partisan, Cacao, suddenly disappeared.

The mood amongst the *Stella Rossa* began to fluctuate wildly. Word reached them that the South Africans were just ten miles away and that the Germans were on the run. For a while it looked as though Lupo's gamble had paid off, but a day later it became clear that the disorganizing German columns 'fleeing' through the valleys below were doing no such thing. Rather, a counter-attack had forced back the Allies directly to the south, while new reports warned of large numbers of SS troops moving into the villages below. That meant one thing: a *rastrellamento* was being prepared.

By the last week of September, the rain had begun. Summer was dying and time was drastically running out if the Allies were to break through the Gothic Line before the onset of winter.

On the night of 28 September, Gianni and the headquarters company were staying at Cardotto, a farm on the slopes overlooking the River Setta. It had rained hard throughout the night, but by the time Gianni was urgently awoken early the next morning, a thick mist shrouded the mountains. The Germans are coming, he was told. Get up, quick. Grabbing his Sten gun, he hurried out of the house, ready to meet the oncoming SS troops. He could see very little – just spectral shapes ahead of him, and then he heard the sound of gunfire; the Germans were already behind their positions. Lupo was gunned down almost immediately, then Gianni was hit himself, in both arms and in the foot. 'We had been betrayed,' he told me. 'They had been led there by Cacao. He'd been with us since the very beginning.'

Despite his wounds, Gianni managed to escape, hiding in the mist and undergrowth and slowly working his way to the top of Monte Sole, one of two mountains, along with neighbouring Monte Caprata, that had been previously agreed would be an emergency rendezvous point, reached by hidden paths. Protected by sheer rock faces, dense undergrowth and thick woods, hundreds of partisans and *contadini* hid, while down below the Germans were continuing their brutal *rastrellamento*. Gianni was vague about just how he had managed the journey with such injuries. 'The wound in my foot was not too serious,' he told me, and having roughly bandaged his arms, he was able, with the help of others, to make reasonable progress.

Despite warnings to the contrary, it was widely believed that the Germans would not kill women or children. Whenever they had taken action in the area in the past, it had always been male civilians who had been taken hostage or shot. How wrong they were. Over the next three days, the Germans continued their *rastrellamento* with brutal efficiency. The farms, hamlets and villages of the mountains were burned, and any civilians found were rounded up and executed. Tragically, the mountains were awash with the elderly, women and children, who had ironically moved up to the mountains several days before hoping to avoid the clash of armies as the front moved northwards through the river valleys. Instead they found themselves trapped, herded into barns and churches and summarily shot; no one was spared. More than 1,800 people were executed in an orgy of death, their bodies left smouldering in piles in the ruins of a community that had barely changed in centuries. It was the biggest single atrocity in Italy during the entire war.

Gianni, hidden on the summit of Monte Sole, was one of the lucky ones, however, although his wounds were agony. When at last the Germans returned to the valleys, he crept away, moving carefully south with a handful of other partisans until they eventually managed to cross over the front line and into the hands of the Allies.

The *Stella Rossa* had been destroyed, but there was still a role for those partisans who had managed to escape, especially since the Allies had ultimately failed to break the Gothic Line: throughout the winter of 1944–45, the front barely moved. Amidst the Apennines a war of attrition developed, not dissimilar to that of the Western Front in the First World War.

After three weeks in an American military hospital, Gianni was recruited into the OSS under the command of Lieutenant Alessi, an American. Gianni joined a mixed squad of partisans and Americans who would regularly cross the front line and spend several days undercover spying on the Germans and noting troop movements and the strength of enemy forces. He was still with them when the mountains of Monte Sole were finally liberated at the end of April 1945. Only then was Lupo's body discovered – in the same ditch where he had fallen near the farm at Cardotto, seven months before.

With the war finally over, Gianni returned to Bologna and with a friend set up a company that ran local buses. He told me he still faced difficulties – not with the Fascists anymore, but with the Communists. 'They always had it in for me and Lupo,' he explained. 'They wanted the *Stella Rossa* to be Communist like some of the other bands, but we wouldn't have any of that. There were all sorts fighting with us – all sorts of political leanings. We weren't interested in allying ourselves to any particular party.' Yet although the Italian Communist Party was the largest in Western Europe, they did not prevail when the first post-war elections were held, something for which Gianni was very thankful.

He lit another cigarette and eyed me for a moment. 'I haven't spoken about all this for years,' he told me. 'It was a long time ago.'

Lise Graf

It was in June 1940, with France on her knees, that eighteen-year-old Lise Graf saw the German Army marching into Alsace. 'We were at our house in the country and I was standing on the balcony,' she told me, 'and far away on the road I saw them. I went to my step-father's room and I took his rifle because I wanted to shoot them. They were far away, but it was a hunting rifle. My step-father took it out of my hands. I said, "I don't want to see the Germans here." That was my first reaction. I said, "I must do something."' So began Lise's personal war against the Third Reich.

As Lise discovered to her horror, defeat meant not only occupation, but a change of national identity. Stretching down the eastern edge of France with the River Rhine as its border with Germany, Alsace had been fought over for many centuries and more recently had been a bone of contention between the two countries. After the Franco-Prussian War of 1870 it had become part of Germany, but returned to France half a century later at the end of the First World War. Following her defeat in June 1940, France was swiftly occupied by Germany in the north, while the south became a self-governed Fascist vassal state. Alsace, however, was absorbed into the Greater German Reich. Overnight, Lise had become a German citizen.

But she was headstrong, clever and talented, and while she recognized that opening fire on German troops would not get her very far, she knew she could not simply accept the situation. However, German citizenship had brought one small advantage: she was now entitled to travel freely throughout Germany. So when a friend of hers, Jacques Schneider, wrote to her from his prisoner of war camp in Germany, she decided she would try to visit him. 'I thought, OK, I really must do something,' she explained, 'so I asked the German government if I could visit him.' The pretext was to give him some food and clothing, and as she was now German in the eyes of the law, permission was granted. Seeing him merely stiffened her resolve. 'I told him that if he or any other prisoners wanted help escaping, I would do what I could. I would try and get them to Alsace and from Alsace into southern interior France, crossing over the mountains.'

There were also many Frenchmen now working in Germany as forced labour, and she realized that if she went to live in Germany, she would be better placed to try to help them escape back to France. A close friend of hers and her family, Doctor Koebele, was obliged to work in Germany in the area of Karlsruhe, as were three other friends working in Baden-Baden. After she had finished the second part of her baccalaureat, she told her parents she was leaving home. 'My excuse was that I wanted to study to be an actress,' she told me. She had already proved herself to be a talented performer on stage having won, at the age of sixteen, the Premier Prix de Comédie at the Conservatoire de Strasbourg, and so easily gained a place at the Conservatoire in Karlsruhe, in the Black Forest. 'It was true, I did want to be an actress, but I didn't tell my parents the real reason for going to Karlsruhe, and thank God I didn't because they would have been scared.' And so off she went, into the lion's den, with no real plan, acting entirely alone, and with little idea how she was actually going to help her fellow Frenchmen. 'But it was something I had to do,' she told me. 'I had to. If you cannot accept the situation you must do something against it. I said, "*Voilà*! I must enter the Resistance; I must fight the Germans." This was war!'

* * *

I met Lise Graf in Paris a few days before her eighty-third birthday. She had given me very clear instructions about how to find the Circle de Union Inter-Allié Club on the rue du Faubourg St-Honoré, and I arrived early and was waiting for her when she briskly entered the reception hall. Immaculately dressed, and looking many years younger than her true age, she cut a striking figure. Her hazel eyes were bright and intelligent and she spoke quickly and with enormous energy. First, she said, we would have lunch; then afterwards we would talk about the war. As we ate we chatted easily – about London and Paris, Britain and France, and also of politics, with which she is still quite involved; she is a personal friend of the President. She barely mentioned the past at all.

Our lunch finished, she gave me some cuttings and articles that she thought might be of interest. One was a note from the American Office of Strategic Services (OSS, and the forerunner of the CIA), confirming the invaluable work she had done for them in the war. Two press cuttings showed pictures of her as a young woman and as an actress in Paris after the war. She looked beautiful. One article referred to her decision to continue the fight against Germany. 'She began her shadow war not for glory, nor for adventure, but to avenge her country.'

We went into the bar, where it was quiet and all but empty. 'And so,' she said. 'What do you want to know?'

The whole story, I told her. But perhaps we could start at the beginning . . .

She was born in Strasbourg, an only child and the daughter of a successful surgeon. They lived in a house at the very heart of the city, right in front of the cathedral. Tragically, her father died young, at the age of forty, from tuberculosis; Lise was just twelve years old at the time. Not very long after, her mother remarried – the lawyer, Eugene Zilliox, who also happened to be an old friend of her father's. 'My father had known he was dying,' Lise said, 'and so he had asked my step-father to look after my mother.' Although devastated by the death of her father, she was glad her mother remarried. She liked her step-father very much.

I wondered if, as a teenager in the 1930s, she had been worried about the rise of Nazism; after all, Germany was just a few kilometres away across the River Rhine. 'Of course,' she said. 'We knew what was coming. Many German Jews came to Alsace.' And did you have an instinctive dislike of Nazism? 'Yes, you couldn't even think of it; it was impossible.' Both her father and step-father were vehemently anti-Nazi and she grew up in an environment where German ambition was deeply mistrusted, and Nazi policies despised. Unsurprisingly, this rubbed off onto Lise. She then told me about how, in 1938, her parents had sent her to Nuremberg to stay with a German family to improve her German. 'The family was very anti-Semitic,' she said, 'and very pro-Hitler. The man was a friend of Goebbels and they said to me, "You know, we will reconquer Alsace-Lorraine." I was very young. I called my parents and said, "I don't want to stay one minute more with this family." I took my luggage and I left them. Later, after we'd lost the war, the boy who had been in this family came to see my parents in Strasbourg and said to them, "You see? We reconquered. I told your daughter we would and we have."'

As soon as war was declared in September 1939, and with the French and German Armies squaring up to each other either side of the Rhine, Strasbourg was largely evacuated, and Lise and her family went to their house in the country, sixty kilometres south of the city. They only returned after the war was over. Once Alsace had been absorbed into the Reich, the Nazis wasted no time in Germanifying the region. The French language was banned; only German was permitted to be spoken. The area was renamed Elsass, and, incredibly, berets were also banned as a means of curbing any sense of French national identity. Nearly 200,000 Jews were rounded up and the region's young men were drafted to fight for Germany. Lise had to finish the second part of her baccalaureat in German.

She hated it – hated what had happened to France and to Alsace. So it was with a sense of relief that she moved to Karlsruhe; simply by making the move, she felt she was beginning to do something positive. Initially, she lived in Karlsruhe itself, but the town had armaments factories and a railway and soon came under aerial attack by the Allies, so she moved to nearby Baden-Baden, taking a room in the house of a German family and travelling by train to Karlsruhe to attend the Conservatoire.

All the while, however, she was helping French workers in Germany escape back to France. Then one day in late 1942, she was approached by Monsieur Dupont, an OSS agent working for the Americans. 'I was in Baden-Baden and he got in touch with me,' said Lise. 'I was a little suspicious, and I asked him what he was doing in Germany.' Dupont explained to her that when Germany occupied all of France in November 1942 after the Allied invasion of Northwest Africa, the American Embassy to Vichy France was shut down and the staff were sent to a hotel in Baden-Baden instead, where they effectively became prisoners in their own home. Dupont, however, as a former French Consul to the United States in Chicago, was asked to represent this newly located American Embassy, and so moved to Baden-Baden. He had, he told her, spoken to a number of French workers who had mentioned Lise and the work she had been doing helping them to escape Germany. Dupont wanted her to join the OSS. 'I was very excited,' Lise told me, 'and very pleased. To me it was like a gift from God, this man coming to see me.'

Dupont took her to see Thomas Cassady, the American Military Attaché at the Embassy. After gaining access by pretending to be Dupont's fiancée, Lise was given a brief to travel round Germany observing anti-aircraft defences and reporting back to Cassady – information that would be used for the Allies' bombing campaign. 'It was easy,' she said with a shrug. 'I could travel freely.' Perhaps, but it was also highly dangerous.

Then in early 1943, Dupont told her that Cassady wanted her to help him escape to Switzerland. She agreed, and immediately turned to the family friend of hers, Doctor Koebele, who was working in Germany against his wishes, but who had also been involved with Resistance activities. As a doctor, Koebele had a car, so he suggested they try to drive Cassady to the border. First, however, Cassady needed to get a coded message to the American Embassy in Geneva. To carry out this task, Koebele told Lise he had just the man – a Frenchman from Lorraine called Chavannes.

Koebele, along with two other Frenchmen, was also planning to escape Germany and Chavannes had already helped them by taking their papers safely to France. 'You can trust him,' Koebele told her, and arranged a meeting for her with Chavannes. 'Can you get papers to Switzerland?' Lise asked him when they met. 'No problem,' Chavannes told her, 'because my cousin lives near the border and he can get across in Switzerland.' Lise reported this back to Dupont and Cassady and was duly given the coded message to hand over. She was still a little suspicious, however, and so arranged to meet Chavannes at a café at the railway station in Heidelberg, a short distance from Baden-Baden. 'When I saw him,' Lise told me, 'I shook hands and I had the paper in my hand and he took it, and that moment I felt something – something in his eye. I said to myself, "Something is wrong, I must take it back." But when he declared everything was fine, I was stupid enough not to take it from him in spite of my bad impression. And so I gave it to him.'

Three days later, on 19 March 1943, she was at the Conservatoire in Karlsruhe when two Gestapo agents arrived and arrested her. Fourteen others were also arrested that day, including Dupont and Dr Koebele. Their Resistance activities were finished.

She was left alone in a bare prison cell. 'I was thinking maybe I would die,' she admitted, but although apprehensive and a little scared she was determined to keep calm and not think too many dark thoughts. 'I said to myself, I will meet the Gestapo and I shall see what will happen.'

After two days in the cell, she was taken to the Gestapo Headquarters in Karlsruhe and questioned by the director. Lise asked him why she had been arrested. 'He said, "You know exactly why you've been arrested." I said, "No, I don't. Because I speak French and meet with French people?" I thought maybe Chavannes could have been arrested. I was not sure he was a traitor. He said, "Then I will tell you. You have given a message to Monsieur Chavannes and he has been arrested at the border when he was trying to cross into Switzerland." I said, "No, I haven't given Chavannes any letter." So he said, "OK, let's ask Chavannes."'

Chavannes was brought in wearing handcuffs, and looking rough and unshaven, but otherwise all right. Lise flatly denied giving him any letter. When Chavannes insisted she had, Lise claimed he had made a pass at her and that he was telling lies about her because she had spurned him. She was pleased with her performance and her lie; it appeared to be working. Chavannes was taken away again but then the Gestapo chief told her that Chavannes had been working for them; that he was a double-agent. 'Maybe,' said Lise, 'but I didn't give him a letter.'

'You gave him a letter,' the Gestapo chief told her, 'because you have been followed by three different men.'

'OK,' she said, 'maybe I did give him a letter, but it was coded. I didn't know what it said.' After that she was taken back to prison, but she refused to be cowed. She even flatly refused to speak to one particular Gestapo agent. 'He tried to tell me my parents had been arrested,' Lise said, 'but I knew this was not true as my mother had brought some clothes to the prison for me the day before.' Incredibly, the commander agreed to send a different agent called Lehmann to question her in future. 'You know, with the Germans,' Lise said, 'you had to never show them you were frightened.'

She *was* frightened, however, and understandably so, expecting to be dragged out and tortured at any moment. One day, she was brought into a bare room, with nothing in it apart from a desk and a chair and a burning fireplace with some tongs beside it. For a while she was left alone in there and sensed that the time had come. She considered throwing herself out of the window. 'I had the biggest scare in my life,' she confessed. 'It was a horrible decision to have to take.' She was still racked with indecision when the door opened and she was led away. 'My legs were very weak,' she said, 'but I didn't show it.'

'One day you will talk,' an agent told her, but Lise told him she had nothing to say. 'In that case,' he said, 'you will go to court and you will be tried and found guilty, and your head will be cut off with an axe.'

After a while they gave up questioning her. Later, she discovered that M. Dupont had insisted she had known nothing about the contents of the letter. Had it not been for his intervention as a French diplomat, Lise is certain the Gestapo would have killed her. Instead she spent a year and a half languishing in solitary confinement in the *Frauengefängnis,* the women's prison in Karlsruhe. She was there when she turned twenty-one, in October 1943.

But she was determined not to be broken, and once more discovered that showing resilience and spirit could work in her favour. Soon after her arrival she was given a large sack of potatoes to peel. Lise refused, and left the sack untouched. Later that evening, Fräulein Becker, the principal wardress at the prison and independent of the Gestapo, came to see her. 'You didn't peel the potatoes,' she said.

'Fräulein,' Lise replied. 'I am a political prisoner. I will probably be condemned to death. Do you think I will peel potatoes for the German prisoners? No, I don't peel potatoes.'

When Becker threatened to fling her in the cellar, Lise still refused. Astonished by this reaction, the wardress let the matter drop; at any rate, Lise was never given potatoes to peel again. Instead, she would iron the altarcloths for the church, and would use the hot irons to warm her soup. 'Madame Becker was just an employee of the prison,' Lise explained. 'I think she had some sympathy for me because I was not a killer or a whore, but a political prisoner. And I think she could see that I wouldn't allow myself to be beaten. She liked that.'

Lise never allowed herself to give up hope. I wondered how she had kept herself sane; a year and a half is a long time to remain in a solitary cell. 'I could have books from the library, so I read a lot of books in German,' she told me. 'I saw the Gestapo nearly twice a week because they had to compile a case against me to bring it to court.' She shrugged again, then told me she felt sure a guardian angel had been watching over her. 'I could have been sent to a camp and killed, but they decided to take my case to court instead, so I was lucky to be in prison in Germany. It was chance.'

Then there was her Gestapo agent, Herr Lehmann. 'He was kind to me. To begin with, I did not understad why, but then one day a girl came into his office and I realized she looked a lot like me. She had the same face. I said to him, "Imagine, M. Lehmann, if it was your daughter in the same situation?"' Lise smiled at me. 'This is strange, *non*? If it was in a film no one would believe it but it is the truth and it's why the man was correct and polite with me.' One day she was very, very hungry and so she rang the bell in her cell and told the wardress she had something to tell the Gestapo. Shortly after, she was taken to see Herr Lehmann. 'So what can you tell me?' he asked her. 'I cannot tell you anything more,' Lise confessed, 'but I am so hungry and I would like to eat something.' She knew that her stepfather had permission to visit her in the office of the Gestapo and that he had left some food for her there. 'And M. Lehman let me eat,' Lise told me. 'He was not a bad man. One day he let me out of the prison and let me walk with him in the garden next door. I said to him, "M. Lehmann, you will lose the war. You are a very tall man, but in France we have a saying: often you need somebody who is shorter than you, and that is the case now. So if you need me, you can always write to me."' And after the war, she did write a letter in his defence, confirming he had treated her correctly.

Lise also became friends with the French girl in the cell next to her. This was Madeleine Damerment, an SOE agent for the British and known to Lise under her alias, Martine. Every night they would talk for hours via Morse code, tapping and scratching with a fork. I asked her what they talked about. 'Everything,' Lise told me. 'Her life, my life. What we had done in the war. It was a conversation – I had a friend, she had a friend.'

Lise also admitted to me that she had had some strange dreams while she was in prison in Karlsruhe. 'I had visions – real visions,' she said, then looked as though she regretted mentioning this. 'Nobody believes it but it's true,' she said. She explained that of the fifteen arrested at the same time as she was, twelve were later freed but three were imprisoned: herself, Dr Koebele and his wife. One day she had a vision of Madame Koebele leaving prison and her husband waiting for her. Lise called out to her and told her she would soon be freed. 'No, it's not true,' Madame Koebele replied. 'The Gestapo told me they would put me in the death camp of Struthof.' This was a notorious German extermination camp in Alsace. But Lise was adamant and sure enough, soon after, she was released just as Lise had predicted. In another vision she saw a man in black entering her cell. She couldn't understand what it meant because men were forbidden to enter their cells. Not long after, however, a priest came to see her. 'My step-father had asked the Apostolic Nuns of Germany to arrange for a priest to visit me,' she explained, 'because I could have been killed.'

She also foresaw her eventual trial in Berlin, so that when, in July 1944, Fräulein Becker came into her cell and told her she would be leaving the following day, Lise said, 'I know.'

'How do you know?' Becker asked.

'I know it,' Lise replied. And that night she also had a disturbing vision about Martine. It upset her greatly because she foresaw that her friend would also soon be leaving Karlsruhe, but that she would be killed. And indeed she was – shot in the back of the head along with three other agents at Dachau. 'I was crying for her when I left,' said Lise. After that she never had anymore such visions, and cannot really say why they happened. 'When you are alone in a cell for all that time, you have – how do you say? – the possibility to see outside yourself,' she said, by way of explanation. 'I had it then, for sure. *Voilà*.'

*　　*　　*

Lise was taken to Berlin, feeling scared and nervous about what lay in store. Her only cause for cheer was the terrible state the city was in after a night of Allied bombing, but her time in the open was brief. Taken to a large prison, she was locked up in a cell for those condemned to death. Desperately miserable and unable to stop crying, she suddenly noticed some graffiti on her cell wall. It was a message of victory saying, 'Even in Berlin you shall smile. If your morale is bad, let's smile,' and signed, 'Vicky – Condemned to Death with the Cross of de Gaulle.' Seeing this, Lise found her courage returning. Later, there was another air raid and the prisoners were conducted to the cellars to take shelter and there, amongst the crush of people, she found herself standing next to the same Vicky. While there, they agreed that they would whistle a song to each other every morning, so that they would know they were both still alive.

Her new friend Vicky was the first to be taken away. One morning, she whistled through the cells and told Lise she was going to be taken to Plötzensee that day. 'Plötzensee was where they executed prisoners,' Lise explained. 'I hoped Vicky did not know that. But I knew and my heart was badly broken when they took her away.' Sure enough, she was led out and duly beheaded. It was a fate Lise was becoming resigned to sharing.

Her trial took place on 19 July 1944. Her step-father had arranged for her to have a good lawyer, but her fate was in the hands of the widely feared and notorious Judge Freissler, later famous for presiding over the case of officers involved in the plot to kill Hitler. Lise told her lawyer that since her case was clearly hopeless, she would not appeal for clemency. Rather, when her time came to make her statement, and believing she had nothing to lose, she defiantly turned to Judge Freissler and said, 'We are in a war, Herr Judge, and I am not German, I am French. You cannot say to me that I was a traitor, Herr Judge, and if you had been in my place, you would have done the same.' A big silence followed her brave statement, but, miraculously, it seemed to have worked, because instead of demanding the death sentence, the prosecutor asked for only thirteen years' deportation instead. When she heard the verdict, Lise confessed that she 'jumped on my lawyer and kissed him'. She told me again about her guardian angel. 'The very next day,' she explained, 'the July plot to kill Hitler took place and after that, all political prisoners were automatically condemned to death and executed by Freissler. Had my trial been delayed, I would have been killed.'

She was sent to Waldheim Concentration Camp, near Dresden in southeast Germany. A number died of illness and hunger, she told me, but again, she was lucky – it was not a death camp. Even so, conditions were brutal. On arrival, Lise was taken before the camp commandant. 'What can you do?' the commandant asked her.

'I can do lots of things,' Lise replied. 'I can sew, I can . . . '

'We do not do these things here,' she told Lise and sentenced her to forty days in a punishment cell for showing impudence. There she had to separate feathers – the soft parts went into one sack, the harder quill into another.

One and a half months of that seemed bad enough but in many ways it was preferable to the *kommando* block she was put into afterwards. 'There were ten political prisoners there and fifty criminals,' Lise explained. 'One woman had killed her child and given the body to the pigs to eat.' Another woman there had murdered her husband by chopping off his penis. 'When I saw their faces,' she told me, 'I said to myself, this is hell.' She was given a rough wooden bunk to sleep on and a 'horrible, horrible' uniform – a black dress and wooden clogs. The guards called each of the prisoners by their number rather than a name – Lise's was 470.

She found some kind of solidarity, however, with a small gang of five other prisoners: four 'politicos' – another Frenchwoman called Susy, an Alsatian like herself; a Czech; a whore from Paris; a German (who had been forced to assist with the executions at Plötzensee); and one criminal – a German who had poisoned her fiancé. 'I was sympathetic towards her,' says Lise of the German girl, 'because her fiancé had been a German soldier and her family had forced her to accept his proposal against her wishes. Also, her real father had been a French prisoner who had fought in the First World War.' The rougher criminals made their lives difficult, however. 'They stole our bread and didn't like us,' said Lise. She tried to keep out of their way as much as possible, but one time she was denounced by one of the criminal prisoners, who told the guards Lise had been planning to escape. Despite her protestations of innocence, Lise was put in a cellar with nothing on but her underclothes. It was winter and freezing. 'I don't know how we survived that cold. Sometimes it was thirty degrees below,' she said. In the cellar, she was so cold she used to run around most of the night trying to keep warm. Unsurprisingly, she became ill – the only time during her entire incarceration – and was in hospital for four days.

By day they worked in a nearby armaments factory where they made parts for the V2 rockets. There, Lise and her friend Susy risked their lives by sabotaging the parts as much as she could. 'We had to fight the Germans in whatever way we could,' she said. Then, in January 1945, they heard the Russian guns firing in the distance. It gave Lise heart. For so long she had kept faith that she would survive and that Germany would lose the war – now, at long last, that moment seemed to be drawing near. Then, in February, they saw Dresden being destroyed by one of the most notorious Allied bombing raids of the war. 'It burned for a week,' she told me. 'We could see it from the camp.'

Weeks passed. The noise of the canons seemed to be getting closer. Then one day, some men came to the camp and began digging a huge hole in the ground. Lise said to her friend, Susy: 'They will kill the politicos and throw them in this hole. We are in a bad situation.' Yet that very night, at midnight, the Russians arrived at the camp; by dawn, the Americans had reached them as well. For Lise, the war was finally over. It had come not a moment too soon. 'Thanks to my guardian angel,' Lise adds, 'who I always believed in.'

After being debriefed by the Americans, she was flown to Paris and eventually made it home to Strasbourg where she was reunited with her parents. She did not stay in Alsace, however, even though it was part of France once more. Instead, she took up a place at the Conservatoire in Paris and became an actress – and quite well known as well. 'I did a lot of television, but *malheureusement*, I met a man and fell in love with him and I married him,' she told me. 'And it was the biggest mistake I made in my life. My parents didn't like him and it caused great problems with my family. I had my son and stopped being an actress for three years to take care of him, but then I divorced my husband, and when you stop in this job, it's hard to get back.' Instead, she entered the well-known Ecole du Louvre, where after three years of study she got her degree in art history. At the same time, she set up an antiques business which proved very successful and which she enjoyed well enough. '*C'est tout*,' she said, 'but I still have a knife in my heart because I could not live my passion – being an actress.'

She was – and is – obviously a very strong character. I wondered where she found her resilience and tremendous reserves of mental strength. She shrugged again then told me a story about her father. 'One time he was slicing *jambon*,' she told me, 'and the knife slipped and he cut his hand badly. He went into his office and I heard him whistling as he sewed his hand by himself. He came back with a bandage but acted like nothing had happened. *Voilà*. So maybe I got it from him.'

And the word 'acting' was, I thought, telling. Confronting the Gestapo, trying to keep her head above water in prison; the ability to put on an act when necessary must have helped her.

What about some of the others, I asked. M. Dupont? Dr Koebele? And Chavannes, the man who had betrayed her? She smiled at me. 'You ask more questions than the Gestapo.' Dupont survived, she then told me, and so did the doctor. 'He had been condemned to death but was sent to a camp and survived. He was very ill, but he recovered and later became a very well-known surgeon.' Chavannes, however, had his comeuppance. Her step-father had put the word around that Chavannes was a traitor and he was shot by the

Resistance. '*Voilà*,' she said. 'He was killed.'

After the war, she visited the families of the friends she had made in prison, telling the parents of both Martine and Vicky all she knew and could remember about their time together. She also took her son to Dachau and saw the plaque there for the six women agents who were executed, including the name of her dear friend Martine. 'Such a horror,' she said. She has also received considerable recognition for her work in the Resistance and OSS. General König, the Military Governor of Paris, presented her with the Médaille Militaire in 1945, but other honours followed: the Médaille de la Résistance, and the Croix de Guerre avec Palmes, as well as being made a Commander de la Légion d'Honneur. Yet although she sometimes goes back to Dachau and Berlin to pay her respects, and despite becoming very involved with the Combattants Volontaires de la Résistance, she told me she does not spend much time thinking about the war. Nor has she ever once had a bad dream about her experiences, or suffered any kind of post-traumatic stress. 'No,' she told me. 'When the curtain is closed, it's closed. You cannot dwell on the past.'

BENEATH THE WAVES

Michael 'Tubby' Crawford

Although it would probably embarrass him to read this, Tubby Crawford is one of the most distinguished British submariners from the Second World War still alive. Serving on submarines throughout the war, he not only commanded his own boat, but was also second-in-command of the most successful Allied submarine ever. In terms of tonnage of ships sunk, no other submarine can beat HMS *Upholder*'s record.

And yet it is probably fair to say that when the words 'submarine' and the 'Second World War' are put together, most people think of the German U-boats, and the Wolf-Pack menace in the Battle of the Atlantic, rather than those of the Royal Navy. There is a reason for this. Britain and the Allies were far more dependent on the world's sea-routes – and especially the Atlantic – for their war effort than was Germany, and it was as an anti-shipping weapon that submarines were most effective during the war.

Yet although most of Germany's war material was either home-grown or came from their conquered continental territories, there was one theatre of war where Germany and her Axis partner, Italy, were entirely dependent on the ocean waves for supplying their war effort: the Mediterranean. The battle for North Africa was as much a war of logistics as it was of the men who fought their way back and forth along that two-thousand-mile coastline. As one air commander quite correctly predicted, whoever won the battle for logistics would win the campaign.

Between 1940 and 1942, with much of the Mediterranean in Axis hands, Britain was only able to supply her forces by a long steamship haul around Africa, via the Cape and then up through the Suez Canal, an extremely long journey and one that typically took three months. The Axis, on the other hand, had a far shorter sea-voyage, across the Mediterranean from southern Italy and later from Greece. Fortunately for them, by the time Germany joined in the North African campaign in the spring of 1941 most of the Mediterranean coastline, and especially the crucial central section, lay in Axis hands.

Most, but not all. One tiny island held out against the odds, the indomitable British fortress of Malta. Lying smack in the middle of the Mediterranean, it was more than nine hundred miles away from Alexandria at one end and Gibraltar at the other, and lay directly in the path of the Axis shipping routes feeding Rommel's forces in North Africa. Consequently, it was a place of enormous strategic importance and one that had the potential to prove a major thorn in the Axis's side.

Malta is now chiefly remembered for the long and brutal siege it endured, for the somewhat dubious honour – by 1943 – of being the most bombed place on earth, and, as an island, for the unprecedented award of the George Cross, the highest civilian medal for valour in the British honours system. Malta's *offensive* role, rather than her ability to withstand sustained aerial bombardment, is often overlooked, and it is in this particular aspect of the Mediterranean theatre that the Royal Navy's tiny submarine force played such a devastating and critical part.

The Royal Navy, despite having rather too many outdated ships, still excelled in terms of seamanship. Its submarine branch, however, was still seriously underdeveloped. Despite the success of the German U-boats during the First World War, Britain had remained deeply mistrustful of submarines and had twice, in 1922 and again in the thirties, called for an international ban on submarines alto-gether. Unsurprisingly, she had not got her way, but it didn't stop the Navy from woefully neglecting this arm of the service. By 1940 there were just twelve British submarines in the entire Mediterranean, all of which were out of date, and on Malta, proposed plans to build a series of protective submarine pens were dismissed out of hand – a decision that would be rued later.

Nonetheless, by the autumn of 1940, and with the Mediterranean now a live theatre of war, the Admiralty finally decided to act, appointing a new and highly able submariner, Commander George 'Shrimp' Simpson, to take charge and develop the embryonic Malta submarine base. His brief was a simple one: to attack and sink as many Axis convoys bound for North Africa as possible.

One of the first submarines to be sent to Malta as part of Simpson's new force was the Unity-class boat, HMS *Upholder*. The Unity-class was smaller than both the German and Italian U-boats and other British varieties, and had been originally designed as a training vessel, but it had two big advantages: first, it was comparatively easy – and inexpensive – to build, and second, it had a particularly fast diving speed, which, it was hoped, would prove useful in the clear Mediterranean waters. A brand-new boat, *Upholder* had carried out a number of tests in home waters, then finally left Portsmouth for Malta on 10 December 1940.

Although the crew had been together only a couple of months, the second-in-command – or 'No 1' as he was known – had been with them just a few days after the original holder of the post had been selected for Perisher, the commanders' course. Pleased to be given an active posting, twenty-three-year-old Lieutenant 'Tubby' Crawford was nonetheless understandably apprehensive. After all, he did not know his new skipper, Lieutenant-Commander David Wanklyn, had never set foot on a Unity-class submarine before, had no idea where they were headed, and furthermore, it was his first posting as a No 1.

It was not until they were at sea that he discovered they were bound for Malta, although Tubby was not at all unhappy about this: it was an island he had come to know well before the war. Moreover, although long journeys could be monotonous and horribly cramped, there was something to be said for a month-long voyage which would enable him to thoroughly familiarize himself with both the new submarine and the crew.

It did not pay to be either tall or of large build when serving on submarines, and fortunately Tubby was neither, despite the moniker. Admittedly, he had been a hefty baby but had grown into a slight frame, albeit one with a rounded, smiling face. Precisely how he was given the nickname, he is unsure, but it was whilst still a boy and for some reason it stuck. From childhood to old age, he has never been known as anything else.

Although a product of Dartmouth Naval College and a career sailor, Tubby did not come from a naval background. Rather, his father had been in the Army, and after the First World War, had been demobbed and had decided to try his luck farming in East Africa. As was the way with the sons of colonial officers, Tubby was sent to boarding school in England at the age of seven. Tragically, his father died two years later and his mother then came back, set-tling on the Isle of Wight. It was being surrounded by water and boats of all sizes that Tubby believes first drew him to the sea. 'I did a lot of sailing in the Solent,' he explains. 'I just seemed to like the sea.' At thirteen, his mother agreed he could go to Dartmouth. The naval college was, Tubby admits, 'quite rugged' but did not put him off a life in the senior service. In 1934, aged seventeen, he passed out of the college and began his midshipman's apprenticeship and a career in the Navy. That this might take him off to war never really crossed his mind. 'I don't think one joined with a view to fighting,' he says.

Nor had he originally thought of serving on submarines, but had discovered that being a midshipman on a large battleship was slightly frustrating: one of many, there was always much to do but little responsibility. Not so on a submarine, where each officer had a clearly defined role. Unperturbed about living a claustrophobic underwater existence, he volunteered to be transferred to submarines as soon as he had completed his sub-lieutenant's courses. And having gone through submarine training in 1938, he was posted to the Mediterranean to join HMS *Sealion* under Commander Ben Bryant, one of the most respected and experienced submariners in the service.

That had been in January 1939. By 1940, *Sealion* was back in home waters, patrolling the Dutch coast and Scandinavia, until in August she was rammed and had her periscopes knocked off. With *Sealion* undergoing repairs, Tubby was promoted and sent up to Scapa Flow in Scotland as first lieutenant on a training submarine, *L23*. Three months later he was being sent to join *Upholder*. Little did he realize then what a life-changing experience that would prove to be.

Upholder inched into Malta for the first time on 10 January 1941. It was also the first day the German Luftwaffe made their presence felt over Malta's waters. Until then, that task had been left entirely to the Italian Air Force, and as the islanders were soon to discover, the intensity and ferocity with which the Luftwaffe dropped their bombs made the Italians seem positively harmless in comparison. The Germans' principal target was the British aircraft carrier, HMS *Illustrious*. Badly damaged, she made for Malta, limping into Grand Harbour for repairs.

By the time *Illustrious* arrived, her neighbour in Grand Harbour was none other than *Upholder*, who after her long voyage needed some minor repairs and adjustments before heading out on her first operational patrol. The newly arrived submarine was still there when the Axis began their first aerial blitz of the now-berthed *Illustrious* on 16 January. Most of *Upholder*'s crew were sent to take shelter on shore, but Tubby, along with two ratings, stayed on board, manning the twin Lewis machineguns and firing for all they were worth at the German bombers. 'That was our first real experience of being bombed,' says Tubby, who remembers the soaking they got from the enormous fountains of spray erupting all around them and the devastating number of German bombers screaming overhead. 'It was quite shattering to see so many,' he admits.

Despite this first brush with the enemy, and despite the fact that the submarine base on Manoel Island in neighbouring Marsamxett Harbour was still far from functioning properly, morale was high when they finally set off on their first combat patrol on 24 January. On 26 January, at one-thirty in the morning, *Upholder* was patrolling northwest of Tripoli in North Africa when they sighted an Axis convoy of three merchant ships, escorted by a lone destroyer. Although they quickly manoeuvred for attack, they could not get closer than 2,500 yards. The captain, David Wanklyn, faced a dilemma. Because of the shortage of torpedoes on Malta, Shrimp Simpson had told his COs not to open fire from distances of more than 2,000 yards, but Wanklyn was reluctant to miss such a potentially rich opportunity just because they were 500 yards long on range. He gave the order to attack, but having overestimated the speed of the convoy, the first two torpedoes missed. By the time the next two were fired, the distance was 3,000 yards; these also went wide of their mark. The Unity-class had only four torpedo tubes and could carry just eight torpedoes in total. Half her armament for the patrol had now gone with no result.

Talk to a sailor about being stalked by a submarine and he will tell you the attacker holds all the cards, but in fact it was extremely difficult to successfully hit another vessel. Submarines were very slow – and the Unity-class especially so. When properly submerged, they could travel at speeds of eight knots (about nine miles an hour) for a limited period. On the surface a speed of ten knots was possible, but heavy seas would reduce this. Most merchant vessels, on the other hand, sailed at between eight and fourteen knots, while the fastest destroyers exceeded thirty knots. In other words, a submarine could not simply latch onto a ship, follow it, and fire a torpedo into its stern. Rather, the only way to get into a decent firing position was to anticipate where a ship was likely to be passing and then position the submarine as close as possible – and with the help of only limited intelligence and only a basic form of sonar, known as an asdic, this was no easy task.

Attacks needed to be made at periscope depth – i.e., twelve feet or so below the surface – but this caused further difficulties. As Tubby had discovered on the journey to Malta, the Unity-class suffered particularly sensitive trim – or balance – and so unless the water was flat calm, it was hard to keep her steady; firing a torpedo, or the wake of another vessel, could also affect trim. During an attack, control of the submarine was Tubby's job – a task that took skill and patience. For a torpedo to actually hit, a number of calculations had to be made: speed of the submarine, speed of the target, speed of the torpedo, and distance from the submarine to the target. There was a primitive computer known as a 'fruit machine' but most calculations had to be made quickly – and essentially mentally – by the CO.

The successful COs were those who developed 'the knack' – but many never mastered it, which was why ninety per cent of all successes were achieved by just twenty per cent of skippers. And although two nights after this failed attack *Upholder* managed to open her score, sinking a merchant vessel and then another on 30 January, her next four patrols were a disaster. None of the Malta submarines seemed to be doing particularly well, but if anything, *Upholder*'s crew were getting worse. Captain Raw, commander of the First Submarine Flotilla in Alexandria, wrote to Simpson after their fifth patrol. 'Eight torpedoes were fired without scoring a single hit,' he noted, 'a result which can only be considered extremely disappointing.'

'There is no doubt Simpson was getting worried,' admits Tubby, who, like the rest of the crew, was disappointed by their lack of success. If they had ever had the knack, they seemed to have lost it, and Simpson was beginning to wonder whether he should relieve Wanklyn of his command. When they set sail again on 21 April, they had just one more chance to prove themselves.

Tubby, however, had no cause to doubt the abilities of his CO, someone he had come to like and respect enormously. Tall, hawkish, with intense eyes and a patriarchal beard, 'Wanks', as he was known, also remained highly popular with the rest of the crew. 'Whatever his personal feelings might have been,' says Tubby, 'he always went about his business with confidence and determination and the morale of the ship's company remained at a high level.'

Even so, there was a palpable sense of tension, when, shortly after noon on the 24th, an enemy ship was sighted off the coast of the tiny Italian island of Lampedusa. Calm as ever, Wanklyn gave the order to start the attack. The waters were choppy and there was a heavy swell; Tubby needed all the concentration he could muster to maintain a near-perfect trim.

In the cramped control room was the CO, Tubby, the torpedo officer, the navigation officer and the two hydroplane operators, who, on Tubby's orders, controlled the trim. Just 700 yards from the target, Wanklyn gave the order to fire. As the torpedoes shot out of the prow, Tubby felt the pressure on his ears and steadied himself as the boat lurched backwards. Everyone held their breath. Seconds passed: ten, fifteen, twenty, twenty-five – then at last an explosion, the blast rocking *Upholder*. The lights flickered and forward some bulbs even smashed. Tubby was busy trying to steady the submarine, but noticed his CO smile with satisfaction.

The next day, they finished off a supply ship off the Tunisian coast that had been attacked and had run aground, then a few days later ran into a convoy of five ships. The weather was terrible and Tubby had great difficulty keeping her steady. Trying to make calculations through a spray-washed periscope was ever trickier, but their confidence had grown and so Wanklyn ordered a full salvo of four torpedoes, and soon after they heard three explosions. Two had struck a German ship of 7,000 tons, which sank immediately, while a third hit a second, smaller vessel. Although the escort of destroyers launched a counter-attack, *Upholder* managed to make good their escape.

When they returned, on 1 May, they slid into Marsamxett with a Jolly Roger hoisted above the conning tower. It was a tradition begun during the First World War as a signal that a patrol had been successful. And already sewn next to the skull and crossbones were four white bars – one for each of the ships sunk.

'Naturally, the whole ship's company were elated,' says Tubby of this sudden change of fortunes. He is unsure precisely why Wanklyn rediscovered his 'knack', but points out that during the first few patrols, many of their attacks took place at night, when estimations of enemy course and speed were harder to make, and not helped by the rudimentary night-sight on the bridge. 'But who can tell?' he adds, and admits that when they set off for their next patrol in the middle of May, confidence was extremely high.

Nonetheless, the pressure was still on, for it was important to prove that this new-found success was no flash in the pan. And to begin with, it seemed as though luck was against them: one of the torpedoes developed a leak and had to be changed, and then their asdic broke down. Although a pretty basic piece of equipment, without it they had no listening device, making detection almost impossible.

Despite this, they were warned on 19 May that an enemy convoy was heading their way and the next day managed to spot it, and although they were quite a long way away, tried their best to intercept. Wanklyn gave the order to open fire at a staggering 7,000 yards – nearly four miles – and incredibly, they sank a tanker, which for Rommel's forces in North Africa was the most precious cargo of all. Three days later they sank another ship. *Upholder* had suddenly become unstoppable.

On the 24th, they were preparing to head back to Malta, satisfied with their bag. On watch in the control room, peering through the periscope just as the light was fading, Tubby suddenly noticed something on the horizon. At first, he could make out nothing but a dark shape, but slowly he realized he was looking at an enormous troopship headed to North Africa and surrounded by a screen of destroyers. Soon, three further troopships revealed themselves – an entire convoy zigzagging to their west. Initially, Tubby didn't think an attack would be possible. They had just two torpedoes left, there was a considerable swell, and their asdic was still out of order. The odds of success were hugely stacked against them.

Unperturbed, however, Wanklyn decided to press home the attack. It was getting dark, he argued, which would make it harder for the destroyers to spot them. If they could just get close enough, they wouldn't need the asdic: they could fire at almost point-blank range. But it was still a high-risk strategy, and escaping from the inevitable counter-attack would be hazardous in the extreme.

With *Upholder* bobbing up and down on the swell, they manoeuvred into position until they were so close they were nearly rammed by one of the escorting destroyers. Frantically diving, they avoided collision by a hair's breadth, but when they rose again to periscope depth, they were inside the destroyer screen. While Tubby was desperately trying to keep the submarine steady and below surface, he was all too aware that they were now in a perilous position. Destroyers circling submarines was how many of the U-boats were eventually sunk in the Atlantic – once trapped inside the screen, their chances of escape were almost nil.

But the point-blank range that Wanklyn had hoped for was theirs, and opening fire with their final two torpedoes, one ripped into the largest troopship, which, after a massive explosion, began to sink. Meanwhile, *Upholder* immediately dived, but avoiding the depth charges of five irate destroyers steaming after them at ten times their own speed required nerves of steel and no shortage of skill.

Getting them out of there was almost entirely the skipper's responsibility and his alone. In the control room, there was complete silence apart from a few orders from Wanklyn. Even then, Tubby remembers, he exuded calm, gently stroking his beard and changing the course, speed and depth constantly. Whenever they came under attack, Tubby tried to console himself by thinking how hard it was for a depth charge to hit – it needed to be accurate on three planes: forward, sideways and vertically. But as they heard the swish of a destroyer's propellers increasing with intensity as it passed overhead, Tubby found himself gripping tightly on to the chair of the hydroplane operator and ducking involuntarily. Then the explosions would start, rocking the submarine, causing lights to flicker out and pieces of corking from the deckhead to drop over their heads. One simply had to hope and pray they did not explode close enough to cause any serious damage.

The counter-attack lasted twenty minutes, in which time no less than thirty-seven depth charges were dropped. One crewman lost his nerve entirely and dashed to the conning tower and tried to unclip the hatch until he was grabbed and forcibly held down. The last four charges seemed to be particularly close, then the crew heard a curious creaking and groaning, like wire being scraped along the hull. 'It's the enemy ship breaking up,' Wanklyn assured them.

Eventually surfacing at 11 p.m., the sea was now deserted: the destroyers and the rest of the convoy had gone. An oily smell drifted over the surface. None of them knew it at the time, but they had just sunk the *Conte Rosso,* an 18,000-ton troopship that went down with 1,300 Axis soldiers on board.

The winning streak continued throughout the summer of 1941 and into the autumn, but while *Upholder* continued to make it safely back to Malta after every patrol, losses were mounting. 'If three submarines were ever sailing at one time,' says Tubby, 'we knew pretty certainly that one of those wouldn't be returning.' Those still at base would keep tabs on who was due back and when. When a crew was more than two days late returning, it was usually accepted that they were lost, and rarely would any of them be heard of again. 'But you just got on with life,' says Tubby. 'You had to. If you started thinking it might be me next time, you'd never get anywhere.'

Getting on with life meant absolute dedication to one's duty when at sea, but letting one's hair down as much as possible when back from patrol. The submariners on Malta lived in the Lazzaretto, a former quarantine hospital on Manoel Island, a stone's throw from the island's capital, Valletta. Amenities were pretty basic but Shrimp Simpson was keenly aware of the importance of R&R between patrols. Being away at sea for ten days to a fortnight was stressful – partly because of the tension and anxiety caused by any action, but also because of the cramped conditions on board. As many as thirty-one men would be squeezed into a Unity-class submarine like *Upholder*. During the day, when they would be submerged almost constantly, there would be no fresh air, and the atmosphere soon became pretty rank, smelling of sweat, diesel fumes and increasingly rancid food. 'The cook on *Upholder* was supposed to have come from the Savoy before the war,' says Tubby, 'but it was an absolute farce because he was no good at all.'

The quality of food was hardly good on Malta either, so Simpson encouraged them to grow some vegetables and they also kept a couple of pigs. A makeshift cinema was set up in one of the workshops. From passing naval ships, they managed to get hold of a number of films – *Dumbo* was a particular favourite.

'In between patrols one used to go ashore and have a pretty riotous time,' says Tubby, who remembers going on bar crawls, drinking the full range of Pimm's Numbers 1 to 7, and horse and cart races around Valletta. 'It could get a bit raucous,' he admits, with what sounds suspiciously like understatement. Still, this was hardly surprising. In the summer of 1941, Tubby turned twenty-four; most of the officers were under twenty-five, incredibly young when considering the enormous stress and responsibility that lay on their shoulders.

In November, Tubby finally parted company with his celebrated crew and with a Distinguished Service Cross (DSC) to his name, returned to England to take his Perisher – the CO's course – and a just desert after his achievements with *Upholder*. Soon after his arrival back in Portsmouth, he learned that Wanklyn had been awarded a Victoria Cross for the attack on the *Conte Rosso* back in May. Tubby was, he admits, surprised. 'A VC is usually given for personal heroism in the immediate face of the enemy and so doesn't normally go to the Navy. But it was a very skilful attack, and he certainly showed a lot of courage.'

He was not so surprised, however, when five months later, in April 1942, he heard that *Upholder* had failed to return from a patrol. By that time, Malta was at the height of the siege, the Germans had discovered the submarine base and life for the submariners was becoming intolerable. Rest between patrols was, as Simpson had recognized, essential, but by the spring of 1942, his crews were being depth-charged at sea and bombed on land. In any case, *Upholder* had been overdue a rest: most tours of duty were for a year, but most of her crew had been out there for eighteen months by that time. 'I think there is no doubt that the strain was beginning to show,' says Tubby, adding, 'the news of the loss of Wanklyn and a very fine ship's company caused me great sadness.' He points out that, ironically, *Upholder* had been finally due to return home at the end of that patrol. Indeed, at the end of April 1942, conditions were so bad on the island that the entire Tenth Flotilla – as the Malta submarines were now called – temporarily moved to Beirut.

Yet with the tide turned in the air battle for Malta, by the end of July the Tenth Flotilla was beginning to return to its old base on the island. At the same time back in England, Tubby was taking command of his first boat, the brand-new Unity-class, *P.51*. And after six weeks of acclimatizing and testing in home waters, Tubby found himself once more setting off on the long voyage to Malta.

Reaching Gibraltar on 4 October, they pulled into port for some minor repairs necessitated by bad weather on the way. By the time they were ready to set sail again, the Allies were about to launch the joint British and American invasion of Northwest Africa, and so *P.51* was ordered to carry out her first combat patrol as part of the naval operation for the landings.

It was a traumatic first trip. On 6 November, just a few days before the Allied invasion, Tubby spotted a destroyer entering Toulon in the south of France. Having been told to report the movement of any Vichy French vessel seen, Tubby signalled his sighting. Unfortunately, in doing so he revealed his presence and the following day a number of Vichy French anti-submarine vessels were looking for him. *P.51* was detected and summarily depth-charged, with five explosions horribly close and causing the quick-diving emergency tank – the Q tank – to flood. Suddenly, the submarine was sinking rapidly, and at a speed and to a depth that was hard to control. To suffer this kind of attack was as stiff a test of Tubby's resolve and leadership as he was ever likely to get.

All eyes were now on him. As captain it was his responsibility and his alone to resolve this crisis. By quickly ordering numbers one and two main ballast tanks to be blown – the normal procedure for rising to the surface – he hoped he could stop their terrifying descent. His plan worked, but the submarine did not finally steady until they were 345 feet below the surface, some 145 feet below the designed safe diving depth of the U-class. Solving one crisis potentially created another, however. With the two ballast tanks blown, *P.51* began rising to the surface once again, and with it the worry that they would pop up like a cork. The only course of action was to open the vents and pray that the escaping air would not cause too much disturbance on the surface and give their position away.

Fortunately, luck was with them and they were able to make good their escape without being further spotted. 'It wasn't very pleasant,' admits Tubby, although it gave him confidence to know the submarine could safely dive to such a depth. Already, he was discovering that there was a big leap between being first lieutenant and commander, a task that because of the war had come to him much sooner than would have been the case in peacetime. 'Of course it was a great thrill to get a command,' he says, 'but a fairly awesome responsibility too.' Absolutely.

After further repairs in Gibraltar, they finally set off for Malta at the beginning of December, their submarine sailing under its new name, HMS *Unseen* – an irony lost on no one. They arrived, laden with stores, nine days later. Tubby had mixed feelings about being back. He was pleased to see Shrimp Simpson again, and also to renew his friendship with Margaret Lewis, one of the few British girls to have remained on the island throughout the siege. But life on Malta was still pretty grim, despite the lifting of the siege. There was bomb damage everywhere, the harbours were still full of half-sunken ships, and there were shortages of absolutely everything. 'Glasses in the mess were sawn-off beer bottles,' he says. 'It was pretty basic, and it certainly wasn't much fun ashore anymore.'

Having sunk a couple of enemy ships in their first patrols with the Tenth Flotilla, *Unseen* was, in May 1943, assigned to a different role. With the North African campaign drawing to a close, the Allies began preparing for the invasion of Sicily, and *Unseen* helped with top-secret reconnaissance work along the beaches. Tubby and his crew spent four months in this role. The usual practice was to carry out a periscope reconnaissance of the area by day and select a launching position. After dark they would head to the launching position and send in a Chariot, a two-man underwater human torpedo. Tubby would then give the order to dive and they would sit on the bottom, until, at an agreed time, they would surface again and flash an infra-red torch towards the beach. 'This was the uncomfortable period,' says Tubby, 'sitting on the surface stopped, while waiting for the Chariot to return. They were not operations that submariners enjoyed.'

With her now intimate knowledge of the Sicilian coast, *Unseen* was also sent to act as a beach-marker for the invasion. They dropped sonar beacons, flashed an infra-red lamp out to sea for the incoming ships to home in on, and landed a beach-marker team. 'That was our contribution to Sicily,' says Tubby, although he admits he missed the actual invasion itself. Having been on the surface and overseen all the dropping of the beacons and infra-red flashes, he had looked out to sea and had seen the invasion fleet miles away. Still feeling a bit fragile after a bout of sandfly fever, he said to his No 1, 'Let me know when they start getting close,' then had gone to his berth, had a cup of cocoa, and had fallen soundly asleep. 'The next thing I knew, the invasion was well under way.'

Tubby remained with *Unseen* for a year before finally heading back to England again in December 1943 to take up a post as an instructor. Before he left, however, he became engaged to Margaret Lewis, although they had to wait a further eight months to get married, as Margaret was unable to get away from Malta until after the D-Day invasion of France. On a September day of grey skies and heavy rain, they married in Blyth, Northumberland, where Tubby was serving with the submarine school.

With the war in Europe won, Tubby took command of a larger submarine, HMS *Tireless* and set off for the Far East. 'Fortunately, the Japanese surrendered before we got there,' he says. He stayed in the Navy, however, commanding surface ships once more and, in the 1960s, returning to Malta. 'It was my last job on the active list,' says Tubby. 'It had changed quite a bit, but there were a lot of old friends still out there.'

Tubby last went back to Malta in 1975. He and Margaret had gone for the dedication of the Tenth Flotilla plaque and stained-glass window in St Paul's Cathedral, Valletta. Accompanying them were a number of former Malta submariners and also Wanklyn's widow, Betty. 'Betty did the actual dedication,' he says.

He's kept busy ever since, with his family and with helping the Submarine Museum in Gosport, and by working tirelessly for the RNLI. He's not a man prone to sentimentality, and when talking of those days, does so with enormous modesty and understatement. And yet his achievements – shown by his two Distinguished Service

Crosses and Mention in Dispatches – are considerable. Wanklyn was once asked what was most needed in submarine warfare for success, and after thinking a moment, replied, 'Imperturbability.' It was clearly a quality shared by his right-hand man, Captain Tubby Crawford.

THE HEROIC ALLY

Wladek Rubnikowicz

Britain and America were lucky. They did not have the traumatic experience of enemy armies marching through their country. And although Britain suffered her fair share of bombing and rocket attacks, the devastation and upheaval were slight compared with much of continental Europe. In Poland, for example, the wholesale and systematic destruction of a nation and its pre-war way of life is almost beyond comprehension.

It is easy to forget that Germany's invasion of Poland on 1 September 1939 was the reason Britain declared war two days later. Poland was her ally, but as Germany was invading from the west, and Russia from the east, Britain and France barely lifted a finger to help. And yet which was the top-scoring squadron in the Battle of Britain? 303 Polish Squadron. And which forces finally captured Monte Cassino after six bloody months of attrition? II Polish Corps. In fact, despite no longer having a nation they could inhabit, Polish forces fought on all fronts in the war against Germany: in Norway and France in 1940; in the air offensive against Germany; in North Africa; throughout much of the Italian campaign; on the Eastern Front with the Russians; and also at sea, from the Baltic to the Mediterranean.

Few people realize the enormous sacrifice so many of these Poles made, or the enormous courage they showed in their quest to help the Allied cause. The tragedy is that even while they were still fighting their way towards victory, their future was being decided by the most powerful men in the world. Just months before the end of the war, at the Yalta Conference in February 1945, Churchill and President Roosevelt agreed with Stalin that Poland should remain part of the Soviet Union once the war was over. Admittedly, short of declaring war again – which Britain was in no position to do – there was little Churchill could do about it, yet it was a tragic irony that when the end in Europe finally came, the country for which Britain had gone to war in the first place remained shrouded by a dark cloud of oppression, cut off from the free world.

There are countless tales that could be told of the incredible courage displayed by Polish patriots, yet the story of Wladek Rubnikowicz shows something not only of the agony and suffering they experienced, but also the pride, determination and strength of human spirit that helped keep so many fighting from the very begin- ning to the very end of the war.

The Battle for Poland lasted just twenty-eight days, and on 29 September, the country was carved in two by the month-old allies, Germany and Russia. What had been a beacon of democracy was now subjugated under Nazism in one half, and Stalinist Communism in the other. Its cities and towns lay in ruins, while its stunned people wondered how this apocalypse could have happened in such a very short space of time.

Soon after the end of the 'Blitz War', Wladek Rubnikowicz managed to make his way home to the small country town of Glebokie, in what just a few weeks before had been northeast Poland. A cadet in the Polish Army, he had been wounded in the back in the final days of the war. Left behind by his regiment in a disused schoolhouse with only his pistol to protect him, he had slowly recovered, helped by the kindness of a few local girls who brought him food and water. But by the time he was fit enough to walk again, the war was over and he was on the wrong side of the German–Russian border.

Fortunately, in those first few weeks, the border had not been properly stabilized and Wladek had been able to make his way into Russian Poland and finally back to Glebokie. It was a traumatic homecoming. His older brother, Gracjan, had already been killed. Married with two small boys, Gracjan had died in the fighting around Warsaw. His body had not been found. Already grieving the loss of his brother, Wladek now saw, in the early hours of that October morning, what had become of his home. Glebokie had been a bustling and thriving country town, surrounded by beautiful countryside. It had been an idyllic place to grow up. Wladek had lived in a large, comfortable house, near to a lake where children swam and went canoeing. There were woods in which to build camps, and close by were mountains where they could ski. But the war had passed through Glebokie and Wladek was shocked by how much the place had changed. 'I could see everything that made life worthwhile had come to a standstill,' he says. Walking on through deserted streets, he approached his house and saw his mother already standing outside the gate. With tears in her eyes, she came towards her surviving son. 'When I asked her why she was standing outside so early in the day,' says Wladek, 'she simply replied, "I was waiting for you." I have never mocked intuition since that day.'

But although Wladek had made it safely home, he could not stay. Russian troops were everywhere. There was little food and most shops remained permanently closed. Queuing for what paltry supplies there were in the freezing early morning cold was the principal daily occupation. It was a demoralizing and heart-breaking exercise – all too often a sign would go up saying, 'No more left', before a fraction of the queue had reached the counter. Soon the Russians started arresting people: first, the police, taken away never to be seen or heard of again; then civil servants and local dignitaries. Fear and mistrust spread. Before long, people were being arrested at the slightest provocation. 'Once accused they simply disappeared,' says Wladek. 'Justice had died.'

A Jewish friend of his who had joined the local Communist Party warned Wladek he should leave. 'Your turn is next,' he told him, and so at the end of December 1939, Wladek decided he should try and reach Warsaw, on the German side, where, he hoped, he might have a better chance of survival. With a heavy heart, he bade his parents farewell, and set off, although getting to Warsaw was no easy matter. Travelling by train was the only option – there were no cars left – but fortunately, a childhood friend who worked at the station agreed to give him a ticket without the necessary documentation. Later, this friend was arrested, tortured and killed. 'All because he had in his possession a photograph of me,' says Wladek.

His ticket got him as far as Bialystok in the north of Poland, where he joined a number of others trying to reach the new frontier. Wladek and several others were already sitting on the train when Russian guards entered their carriage and asked to see their tickets. When they could not produce one, they were pushed off, but they crawled under the carriage and as the train began to start, jumped onto the buffers. Temperatures were well below freezing. 'It was an ordeal,' he admits. 'We grew stiff holding onto the wagon and standing motionless – we became frozen statues.' As the train finally neared the border, they jumped off – leaving skin stuck to the buffers – and fell into four feet of snow. Wading through the drifts, they neared the border wire only to hear a commotion breaking out. Suddenly a soldier with an Alsatian dog ran towards them, ordering them to stop, and firing a warning shot. It was a heart-stopping moment. Wladek froze, his hands in the air. 'If we'd made a run for it, we'd have been shot,' he says. Arrested on the spot, they were all taken a short way from the border and locked in a barn. Incredibly, they were left unguarded, however, and so managed to escape, and the next day reached the frontier once more. This time, luck was with Wladek. As he was about to make a dash across the border, a guard dog approached him, but instead of barking and snarling as he was trained to do, he simply nuzzled Wladek, licked him, then turned and ran in a different direction.

Warsaw was even more unrecognizable than his home town had been. The once elegant and beautiful city now lay in ruins after sustained bombing and fighting in its streets. He made contact with a friend, but soon realized life in Warsaw was hardly better under the Germans than it had been at home under the Russians. With no job and no money, he wondered what he was going to do until, through another friend, he was recruited into the Underground Resistance movement.

Wladek's task was to help prepare and distribute information and bulletins. Armed with a forged identity card, he would often travel into the country to hand out leaflets and pass on information to other Resistance groups. In April 1940, however, he was given a more important task. Near Kovel, in Russian-occupied Poland, a large stash of weapons and ammunition had been buried, and it was Wladek's job to tell the local Resistance commander the exact location of this hidden hoard. It meant travelling back over the border, but this time he knew the ropes and where best to cross, and made it into the Russian zone without difficulty. The mission was a success. He kept his rendezvous and passed on the relevant information, but now faced the daunting task of getting back to Warsaw. It was considerably easier to cross the border to the east than vice versa, and once more, Wladek found himself travelling on the buffers of a train heading west. But the good fortune that had seen him cross into German-occupied Poland a few months before had deserted him. Arrested at the border for a second time, he was taken back to Bialystok and flung in prison.

For thirteen long months, Wladek remained in Bialystok prison. He was one of fifty-six prisoners crammed into an eight-man cell. There were no beds, so they slept on a concrete floor. Space was so tight, they had to lie closely to one another, all facing the same direction. 'We had an agreement amongst ourselves,' says Wladek, 'that until midnight, say, we slept on our right side, and then we all turned on our left.'

Periodically, he was interrogated. 'They called us spies,' he says, 'and later they told me the court in Moscow, without seeing me, had sentenced me to three years in the labour camps of Siberia.' Humiliated and degraded, they had to queue for the toilet and shave with a piece of broken glass. Wladek admits he sometimes considered killing himself with the glass. 'But part of one's will was still to defy the horrors of this life which had engulfed us,' he says, 'and fight on.'

In June 1941, he was suddenly called out of his cell and along with five hundred others, taken to the railway station. They all knew this could mean only one thing – they were heading for the gulags. 'We all knew about the labour camps,' he says, 'and the terrible conditions.' With mounting despair, he wondered whether he would be able to withstand the ordeal ahead, and whether he would ever see his parents and his home again. His chances, he knew, were not good.

First, however, he had to survive the journey. Fifty prisoners at a time were shoved into a goods wagon. In each were rows of narrow wooden shelves. Wladek squeezed himself onto one and watched the doors being closed and locked. Ventilation for the wagon came from a small, barred hole and there was a further hole in the floor for the toilet. There was not enough air and they all struggled to breathe properly. They were given 400 grammes of bread and one herring each as they began the journey, but the salty herring just made them thirsty. They were eventually given a small cup of water each, which, they were told, had to last until the following day. Dysentery soon gripped many of them, and most had fever. A number died, their bodies remaining where they lay amongst the living. 'Can you imagine?' says Wladek. 'We didn't realize then that of course the Soviets hoped these conditions would kill off many of us on the way.'

The journey lasted two weeks, and the further they travelled the more bleak and desolate the surrounding country became. Eventually, they halted at Kozhva, the railhead on the Pechora River. Staggering off their wagon, they were herded towards a transit camp before continuing their journey by paddle steamer. This took them a further 700 hundred miles north, and when they disembarked a week later at Naryan-Mar Gulag, in the Balshezemelskaya Tundra, they were in one of the most northern parts of Russia and had broken through into the Arctic Circle. It was now late June and although it was not as cold as it would get in winter, it was far from warm. The days were endless – literally, with the sun rising again before it touched the horizon. 'At first we couldn't get used to it,' says Wladek, 'and confused day with night.'

Conditions had been bad at Bialystok, but Naryan-Mar reached new depths of deprivation. There were a couple of thousand at the camp, and all were housed in large marquee-like summer tents, each holding around 180 men. Although they were given a rough wooden bunk to sleep on, there were neither mattresses nor blankets and the prisoners slept fully clothed at all times. These they lined with cotton wool and although they just about managed to keep warm, they soon became full of lice. 'The lice and the dirt,' sighs Wladek. 'Lice, lice, all the time.' Every fortnight, they would be allowed to wash and as they did so their clothes would be treated. But the lice soon returned, another discomfort in their already miserable existence.

Every day they were put to work at the nearby port on the mouth of the Pechora. They rose at six in the morning. At breakfast they were given a bowl of tea and 500 grammes of bread. The lump of bread would be divided into three: one lump for breakfast, one with their soup at lunchtime and the last bit with their soup in the evening. The soup was watery, made with barley or flour and occasionally with pieces of fish floating in it, and they were constantly hungry. Every day, they were marched to the port by armed guards, starting physically demanding work loading and unloading goods at seven in the morning and finishing at seven at night. As Wladek points out, 'We worked as slaves.'

The camp was surrounded by barbed wire and watchtowers, but there was nowhere a prisoner could go even if they did escape: they were miles from anywhere and the surrounding forests and marshes were home to wolves. Even so, Wladek did make one bid for freedom. A Swedish vessel came into port and thinking the crew seemed friendly and sympathetic, he managed to slip away and hide in the hold. He misjudged them, however. Soon discovered, he was handed back to the Russians. 'The punishment I received I shall never forget,' he says. Beaten to within an inch of his life, he still has back problems as a result to this day. He also still feels bitter towards the Swedes who betrayed him, and since then has made a point of neither visiting Sweden nor making friends with any Swedes. 'I might forgive – one day,' he says, 'but I will never forget.'

Inevitably, many succumbed to disease. 'The general condition of people was very bad,' says Wladek. 'Poor food and long hours of work made them weaker every day.' Illness, however, was no excuse not to work. Despite high fevers and crippling dysentery, prisoners *had* to keep going. 'The alternative to working,' he says, 'was death.' Wladek did not suffer from dysentery like many, but he did start going blind. His affliction was worse in the evening. Malnutrition and the total absence of a balanced diet of any kind were the causes, but he could not afford to step out of line. To ensure he made it safely back to camp each night, he had to depend on others to guide him.

They had heard about the German invasion of Russia in June 1941, but it wasn't until some months later that Wladek's work gang happened to be thrown a newspaper at the port. Reading it,

RIGHT Trooper Tom Finney of the Royal Armoured Corps. Tom may have been a football star in the making, but he still had to go and fight just like everyone else, and saw action as a tank driver in Italy.

BELOW Tom playing for England in the 1950s. Although the war cut six years from his professional playing career, he recognised that the non-league and forces football he played during the war years helped him hone his skills and become a better player. He went on to play seventy-six times for England, scored thirty goals, and was later knighted for his services to the game.

RIGHT Gianni Rossi (left) in 1942, when he was still serving in the Italian Navy. After the armistice in September 1943, he returned home to Bologna, but by spring had started a partisan band, the *Stella Rossa*, with his friend Mario Musolesi, better known as 'Il Lupo' – the Wolf.

ABOVE A British military photograph of Monte Sole from the Setta Valley, an area of great strategic importance. Through the summer of 1944, the *Stella Rossa* made life very difficult for the German and Fascist forces, moving back and forth from the front through the two river valleys below. The summit of Monte Sole is denoted by the number seven. Lupo was killed and Gianni wounded near the area marked number two.

LEFT Gardaletta, Gianni Rossi's hometown in the Setta Valley, south of Bologna.

RIGHT A group of Italian partisans. Under-nourished, poorly equipped and mostly very young men and boys, they were often, like the *Stella Rossa,* sorely let down by the Allies, whose resources were often siphoned elsewhere, such as France and the Balkans.

ABOVE Lise Graf as a young student in 1941.

ABOVE Tea-time in Lise Graf's room in Baden-Baden. On the left is Pierre Dupont, the French consul; next to him is Lise's friend, Marguerite; Lise is standing behind, while to the right is the American attaché, Thomas Cassady. It was whilst trying to help smuggle Cassady out of Germany that Lise was betrayed and arrested by the Gestapo.

ABOVE A publicity shot of Lise taken in Paris soon after the war, when she was starting to make a name for herself as an actress.

ABOVE Receiving her Médaille Militaire from General Koenig at the Invalides in 1945. This was not long after Lise was finally liberated from Waldheim concentration camp in Germany.

ABOVE The crew of HMS *Upholder*, the most successful Allied submarine of the war, in 1941. Her commander, David Wanklyn, was also the first British submariner to win the Victoria Cross. Wanklyn is to the right of centre, with his trademark beard. To his right is his second-in-command, Tubby Crawford.

ABOVE HMS *Unseen* slips out of Malta for another Mediterranean patrol. *Unseen* reached Malta in December 1942. It was her commander Tubby Crawford's second wartime posting to the island.

LEFT A Polish prisoner at a Russian labour camp, or Gulag. Many prisoners, like Wladek Rubnikowicz, were sent to camps within the Arctic Circle, where they were expected to work twelve-hour days with little to eat but watery soup and a few other scraps. Theirs was an utterly degrading and wretched existence, and most were guilty of nothing more than being Polish.

ABOVE RIGHT With the German invasion of Russia in June 1941, the Polish prisoners were gradually released and with little help were expected to travel thousands of miles south to the Persian border, where they began mustering to form a new Polish Army. It would take time, however, before men like these were fit enough to fight once more.

ABOVE Monte Cassino was widely accepted as one of the most bitter battles in the west. The Poles were given, in their first action since reforming in Uzbekistan, the task of taking the monastery in the Fourth Battle of Cassino. They succeeded, raising a Polish pennant above the monastery on 18 May 1944.

RIGHT Polish troops at Cassino. The Polish Corps fought tenaciously right up through Italy, even after they discovered, in February 1945, that there would be no free Poland to go home to when the war was finally over.

LEFT Jimmy James with a friend in Egypt. Badly wounded when his plane carrying General 'Strafer' Gott was shot down in August 1942, he had only just rejoined the squadron some months later when this picture was taken. Awarded a Distinguished Flying Medal for his outstanding bravery during the attack and for his efforts to help the survivors, Jimmy had been unable to save the General. Only recently appointed commander of the Eighth Army when he was killed, Gott was replaced by General Bernard Montgomery.

ABOVE The Bristol Bombay. Before Jimmy achieved the feat, it had not been thought possible to land a Bombay with neither engine operating.

RIGHT Jimmy with Emil Clade in March 2005, more than sixty years after Herr Clade had shot him down in the Egyptian Desert. It was an emotional experience for both men.

LEFT Heinz Puschmann as a young paratrooper, or *Fallschirmjäger*. After surviving Cassino, Heinz was severely wounded at Carentan shortly after D-Day. He later witnessed the bombing of Dresden and was fighting in Italy once more when the war finally came to an end.

RIGHT A recruitment poster. All *Fallschirmjägers* were volunteers.

BELOW German paratroopers waiting to go into action at Cassino. The 1st Parachute Division almost single-handedly defended Cassino and the monastery throughout the four battles, gaining the lifelong respect of their opponents.

RIGHT Although part of the Luftwaffe, the *Fallschirmjägers* were elite troops amongst the German armed forces, and lived by a different creed to most German fighting troops. The photograph of this man shows the different uniform and equipment that marked out the *Fallschirmjäger*.

LEFT Bill Pierce of the United States Marine Corps after his return from the Pacific.

BELOW The heaviest fighting took place in May 1945, coinciding with the rainy season. The battleground in the south became a quagmire, adding to the misery of the combatants. Here, an American 37mm crew struggle to push their gun into position.

LEFT A Marine cautiously approaches a Japanese bunker on Okinawa, with dead civilians at its entrance. More than 150,000 Okinawans lost their lives during this brutal last battle of the war, more than were killed at Hiroshima or, for that matter, died at Dresden.

RIGHT American casualties on Okinawa were the highest of the entire war, greater even than those suffered at Iwo Jima. Eighty per cent of Bill's Marine division were killed or wounded during the battle, Bill included. Here Marines carry a dead comrade away. Many of the fallen remained where they died for weeks on end, littering the ground and adding to the stench that hung heavily over the battleground.

they learnt that the head of the Polish Government in exile, General Sikorski, had negotiated with Stalin for the release of all Polish prisoners. They were now allies of sorts, and in his fight against Germany, the Soviet leader needed every man he could lay his hands on.

The news soon spread around the camp and although several weeks followed without any further news of their release, finally one morning the guards woke them and told them they were being freed. 'It was a wonderful moment,' says Wladek. Each man was given a piece of paper stating they had been released from their gulag and entitling them to free rail travel. They were also handed a loaf of bread, a lump of rancid butter, and two dry herring – food that was supposed to last a month as they made their way 3,000 miles south to Uzbekistan, where the Polish General Wladyslaw Anders was beginning to muster a Polish Army once more.

By the end of 1941, more than 850,000 former Polish soldiers and civilians had been released, a mass exodus that the Soviets had neither properly organized nor prepared for. An estimated 93,000 – more than the total number of civilians killed in Britain during the entire war – died as they journeyed south after their liberation, most from a combination of disease and exhaustion. Wladek had, like most of his colleagues, eaten his meagre rations within two days. The trains travelled so slowly, however, that he was often able to jump off, snatch a few potatoes from a field, and leap back on again. But when they eventually reached southern Russia, the Polish authorities who they had been told would be there to meet them were nowhere to be seen. Instead, there were Russian officials directing them onto a river barge.

Unbeknown to Wladek and his fellows, the Russians were already reneging on their agreements. The Poles were taken down-river to a small town and put to work on a collective farm separating sacks of cotton. Wladek loathed the work and felt angry and frustrated that they had been prevented from joining the Army.

'We all still had tremendous national pride,' he says, 'and we wanted to join General Anders and fight for our country.' Instead, they were effectively prisoners once more. Furthermore, the conditions were little better than the gulag. They were already severely undernourished, and their insufficient rations lacked the calories they needed for the work and gave them all terrible diarrhoea. They were so hungry, they even killed and ate a dog. For an animal lover such as Wladek, who had always kept pet dogs as a boy, this was literally hard to swallow. 'But,' he says, 'we had to do this to survive.'

They became more adept at stealing, and soon after pilfered and cooked a chicken. Their thoughts were now of escape, but to do so, they needed more food to take on a journey of unknown length and duration. The collective farm had a flock of sheep and so one evening they managed to grab and bind a ram without the shepherd noticing. Later, under the cover of darkness, they killed and skinned it and took it back to their shack. A couple of hours later, in the early hours of the morning, and now armed with a couple of knives, an axe, and plenty of meat, seven of them set off, walking by the stars, and hoping that before long they would reach a railway.

Days passed. Another sheep was stolen and killed. Their shoes disintegrated. Footsore and bleeding, they had no real idea where they were heading, but one night, walking under a bright moon, they reached a fork in the road. Instinctively, Wladek felt they should turn right towards a village, and there they at last found a railway station. They caught a train that took them to Bukhara, then boarded another to Guzar, one of the most southerly towns in the Soviet Union, lying not far north of the Afghan border in Uzbekistan. There was a large Polish camp there, set up as a mustering point where freed prisoners could register for the Army.

It had been an extraordinarily long journey from the Arctic Circle to the edge of Persia. Even by the time Wladek had left the gulag at Naryan-Mar, he had been in a weakened physical state and a fraction of his normal body weight. Several thousand miles later, having travelled by rail, boat, and on sore and bloody feet, he was seriously ill. Struggling with a high fever, he staggered to the register office and then was promptly sent to the first aid station, where they told him he had contracted typhoid. 'Guzar has the doubtful distinction of having the largest Polish cemetery in the Soviet Union,' he says, and had it not been for the two sheep they had eaten along the way, he is sure his body would have been too weak to survive such a serious illness.

As it was, he was now close to death. With his body entirely shaved and treated, and slipping in and out of consciousness, he was taken to a hospital near Tashkent, the capital of Uzbekistan. 'I was lucky,' he says. 'There was a Russian nurse there who took a fancy to me and used to hide a couple of crusts of bread under her arm and give them to me, and also tobacco.' The fever passed and with the help from the Russian nurse, he began to recover his strength. 'I used to make dates with her,' he says. 'She had a good heart.'

Meanwhile, General Anders in the southern Soviet Union, and General Sikorski in London, had been having a difficult time with the Soviet leaders. It had been the Poles' hope and intention that the reconstituted Polish Army should fight as a whole against Germany on the Eastern Front, which would send out a strong signal to the world about Polish solidarity and their fighting spirit. Stalin, however, who had designs on Poland if and when Germany was beaten, had no intention of allowing this to happen, and so had been making life as difficult as possible, giving the Poles mustering areas and camps in inhospitable parts of the Soviet Union where disease – such as typhoid – was rife, and waylaying potential Polish troops on collective farms.

Eventually, however, the Soviet leader decided he wanted to free himself of any obligations to arm and provide for the Polish Army, no matter how useful they might have been. Churchill had let it be known that he wanted Polish forces fighting alongside the Allies in the Middle East, and so under pressure from both Britain and America, Sikorski agreed that Anders's Polish Army should be evacuated to Persia, from where they would train under British guidance.

Wladek Rubnikowicz arrived back at Guzar too late to join the first evacuation in March 1942. Another was being planned, however, and so he remained at camp, now dressed in British army uniform and spending his time training and slowly building up strength. It was while he was stuck at Guzar that he heard word of his parents. One evening he was sitting by a camp fire when he saw a familiar-looking girl from the women's detachment. With her shaved head and emaciated frame, she, too, had clearly recently recovered from typhoid. On seeing Wladek she rushed over to him. 'You are Wladek, Wladek Rubnikowicz,' she said. 'Yes, I am,' he replied, but still could not place her. She then told him her name – she was the sister of one his oldest friends from home. Wladek could hardly believe it. The last time he had seen her she had been a plump and happy girl with long, full hair. The change was shocking.

She told him that his parents had been deported to Siberia, not as prisoners as such, but as 'transplants' to a collective farm. Both saddened and elated at the same time, Wladek was determined to try and get them out of the Soviet Union. One of the agreements with Russia was that liberated Poles now heading to Persia were entitled to take their next of kin with them, who in Wladek's case were his parents. The following morning, armed with the name of the collective where his parents now were, he went to his commanding officer and asked permission to go and find them and bring them back. Wladek was due to be part of the second evacuation which was leaving imminently, and so his request was turned down. However, his CO did obtain from the Russians the necessary documents asserting that Wladek was, indeed, his parents' next of kin. 'I then took them to a KGB officer along with a note telling my parents to quietly leave the farm, go to the nearest station, and get themselves to the Persian border,' says Wladek. 'He gave his word that he would send the papers to them. Sometimes you find a man with some heart. Not all Russians were horrible.'

Many months passed. Wladek left the Soviet Union, and was sent to a camp at Pahlevi in Persia (now Iran), on the Caspian Sea. Finally off Russian soil, he felt safe at last, although his troubles were not over. Although getting stronger, he had been unable to rid himself of constant stomach gripes and still far from fully fit, he now succumbed to malaria. Although after a couple of weeks the fever had subsided, he now faced recurrences of the disease plaguing him for some time to come. In the meantime, however, Wladek began yet another long journey, on this occasion by truck over the mountains into Iraq, first to a transit camp and then on to a training camp at Quisil Ribat Oasis, where General Anders had established his headquarters.

In Iraq, training began in earnest. Now attached to a reconnaissance regiment, the 12th Polish Lancers, Wladek was sent on a driving instructor's course. 'It was easy,' he says, 'as the only real hazard in the desert would be if one collided with a camel.' He was at Quisil Ribat for several months and it was whilst there that an incredible piece of serendipity occurred. One day Wladek was travelling in a lorry along with twenty or so other troops. One of the soldiers was passing a photograph around. He had just come from Tehran in Persia, where an elderly Polish couple had approached him and given him a picture of their son. They were looking for him and asked the soldier to keep a lookout when he reached Iraq. 'When it was passed to me I could hardly believe it,' says Wladek. 'It was a picture of myself. It was a miracle!'

This time his commanding officer granted his request for leave. 'Pack your bags and go for three weeks,' his CO told him. A week later, Wladek reached Tehran and made his way to Camp No 3, where he had been told his parents were staying. A guide led him to their small, two-man tent. 'I went inside and there are no words yet invented to describe that moment,' he says. 'We had been through so much. We had lost so much, and we had feared we would never see each other again. We were never a demonstrative family, but that day we hugged each other and cried and cried.'

After a week with his parents, he returned to Iraq. The regiment was transferred to the Kirkuk region in the Kurdish north where they trained some more and carried out border patrols. With plentiful rations and a moderately balanced diet, Wladek and the rest of the Polish Army gradually began building up their strength. The bedraggled, malnourished, disease-ridden skeletons that had staggered into Guzar now looked liked the fighting-fit Army they were supposed to be. But in July 1943, as they were about to be posted to Palestine, another blow befell the Poles when news reached them that General Sikorski, their universally adored leader, had been killed in an air crash at Gibraltar. 'It was a tragedy,' says Wladek, who thought very highly of the general and had been present at a parade attended by Sikorski just a few weeks before. If anything, though, Sikorski's death only spurred them on further. 'We all felt anxious to get to the front,' he says, 'and begin fighting for the liberation of Poland. That may sound strange, but it's true.'

That moment was drawing closer. Despite another bout of malaria, Wladek continued training in Palestine until late in 1943, when they moved south to Egypt and the Suez Canal ready to sail for Italy.

The 12th Lancers, part of the 3rd Carpathian Division, reached Italy in December 1943 at a difficult time for the Allies. After their successes in North Africa and Sicily, the joint Anglo–US campaign in Italy had been going less well. The landings at Salerno in September 1943 had seen them almost knocked back into the sea, and despite recovering and beginning the push north, in September 1943, the Allies had come unstuck along the German defences known as the Gustav Line – and specifically in the mountains and flooded valley around Cassino.

Anders's force, now called II Polish Corps, spent several months carrying out final training and acclimatizing, at the end of which time the Allies had failed no less than three times to break the stalemate at Cassino, already one of the bloodiest and most brutal battles of the war. A new offensive was being planned for the beginning of May 1944. This time, it was hoped, with new, fresh troops, and improved weather, the Allies would prevail and at long last push on north and capture Rome. The Poles were given the task of capturing Monastery Hill and the now ruined monastery of St Benedict, the focus of nearly six months' bitter fighting. This was an extraordinary directive. The taking of Monastery Hill would undoubtedly be the toughest assignment in the forthcoming battle, yet after their epic journey from the wilds of Russia and their subsequent reconstitution, it was also to be their first time in action. At Monte Cassino, the Poles were being thrown in at the deep end.

Wladek points out that they were all proud to have been given such a formidable task. 'We all wanted to be able to fight for our country,' he says. 'All of us, a hundred per cent and a hundred per cent more, felt a sense of honour at going into battle for Poland.' They began moving into position on 3 May. While most of the 3rd Carpathian Division was to attack over Snake's Head Ridge, a long hill overlooking the monastery, the 12th Lancers were to approach from the slightly lower ground directly below. Wladek was in the 2nd Squadron of the 12th Lancers and would normally have been operating in an armoured car, but there was little opportunity for vehicles on Monte Cassino. 'Most of our supplies came up by mule,' he says. 'Not until we were much further north were we able to use our armoured cars with ease.'

Launch day for the new offensive was 11 May and that night, the Poles began their attack. By bad luck, the Germans had chosen the same night to relieve many of their troops, so in the cross-over there were many more enemy forces opposing them than there might have been. The extra German fire-power meant that although the Poles reached their first objectives, they were soon pinned down and by the following afternoon were forced to retreat. The attack had cost them 4,000 casualties, nearly half their attacking strength.

Undeterred, for the next few days the Poles dug in and patrolled aggressively by night. 'We were in what is now a lovely meadow below Snake's Head Ridge,' says Wladek. 'You couldn't move by day. If you got up out of position you would be shot.' The monastery was heavily mined, and Wladek remembers watching a number of them exploding, detonated by Polish shellfire. This made their night-time patrolling marginally less fraught. Shells and mortars rained over the narrow battlefield day and night. 'One time I was behind three men all sitting in front of me,' he says. 'A shell came over and exploded right on top of them. Two of the men disappeared into thin air. There was nothing left. But on a bush nearby I saw the ammunition belt and the stomach of the third. That was all that was left.' On another occasion, Wladek remembers seeing a soldier sitting down staring into space. The man was covered in dust and had a glazed expression on his face. Wladek bent over and touched his back and saw that it was covered in blood. 'He was,' he says, 'quite dead.'

They attacked again on 16 May. The fighting was brutal. 'It was often a case of kill or be killed,' he says. 'Bullets were flying everywhere. One simply had to pray the angels made those bullets go around you.' This second attack was more successful, however, and in the early morning of 18 May, a battered white flag was hoisted above the monastery. A dozen men from the 1st Squadron of the 12th Lancers cautiously picked their way through the minefield and approached the ruins. They found only a handful of German paratroopers left, who all surrendered without firing a shot. The Poles, unable to find a Polish flag, attached a 12th Lancers pennant to a branch and stuck that into the rubble instead. In their first battle, the Poles had won a victory that none of the Allies before them had been able to achieve. Monte Cassino was theirs. 'Of course we were thrilled to have taken Monte Cassino,' says Wladek. 'When we captured it we all felt as though we had shown everyone what we were capable of. But a lot of people died. It's difficult to talk about – I get very emotional thinking about it.'

Afterwards there followed 'fighting, fighting and more fighting'. The Poles were incorporated into the British Eighth Army, taking the easternmost flank on the Italian coast as they tried to break the next major German system of defence, the Gothic Line. Another stalemate occurred as a particularly vicious winter set in. 'It was cold and there was endless rain and mud and snow,' says Wladek. 'There was often a frost and we had no anti-freeze for our armoured cars, so we had to constantly check the sump and the radiator and make sure it hadn't frozen.' One time he forgot to check the top of the engine and the head subsequently cracked. 'I got seven days' detention for this,' he says.

But they kept going, battling on in the belief that they would soon be marching back victorious to a liberated Poland. A shattering blow was awaiting them, however. Early in 1945, they heard the news from Yalta that when the war was over, Poland would be absorbed permanently into the Soviet Union. 'You cannot imagine what it was like to hear that,' says Wladek. 'We all felt betrayed, that we'd been sold out by the very Allies in whom we had placed so much trust. I loved my country. To know that all we had fought for had been for nothing was completely devastating.'

When the war finally came to an end, Wladek was at Casarano in southern Italy training Polish cadets. In 1939, he had been fighting in Poland. Six years later, having been wounded, flung in jail, sent to a labour camp, crossed continents, been struck down by two life-threatening diseases, and survived some of the most vicious fighting seen in the West, he was still alive, but the country for which he had suffered so much was not. Poland was no more. With no home for him to go to, he remained in the Army, watching his people's further humiliations from afar. Out of 'sensitivity' to the Russians, the Polish Forces were excluded from any of the victory parades in London that followed the end of the war. Polish troops were also asked not to talk publicly about their experiences in Russia. It was as though their sacrifices counted for nothing.

By the time he was demobilized in 1946, he had risen to the rank of Lieutenant-Colonel and was Second-in-Command of the Polish Cadet Officer School near Lecce in southern Italy. Poles had been offered asylum in Britain and so that was where he settled. 'People would ask me why I did not go home to Poland,' says Wladek, 'but I could not. As soon as I did, I would have been arrested.'

He has lived in England ever since, marrying an English girl and settling in London. His parents, who had moved to India after leaving Tehran, also joined him in London, although, sadly, his father died soon after. But although he was happily married and had a daughter he adored, his dream of one day going back home was never far from his thoughts.

The years passed, then decades, but with the emergence of the perestroika reforms in the later 1980s, there came a flicker of hope. Then Poland gained its independence and democracy returned. Despite Wladek's joy for Poland, however, the country now had very different borders; Glebokie was in Belarus. In 1991, the Soviet Union collapsed and at last it seemed that one day it might be possible to return, but even two years later when Wladek, accompanied by his wife and daughter, finally made the trip to his old home, their journey was frustrated by Soviet-era red tape at every turn.

Nonetheless, they did finally make it. Glebokie had changed greatly. No one spoke Polish anymore, only Russian. The streets looked grey and neglected. His family home had gone as had many other buildings he remembered. But there was much that was familiar too: the old schoolroom he had attended as a small boy, and the lake where he had once canoed with his brother and childhood friends.

And there was a surprise waiting for him. Wladek had hoped he might find someone he had known as a boy still living there, but was astounded to discover that not only was his sister, Zosia, still in Glebokie, but also his brother's two sons, Josef and Jurek. 'It was a very emotional homecoming,' he says. 'When I left home at the end of 1939, I never thought it would be fifty-three years before I was back again.' More than half a century on, Wladek's long, long exile was over.

BOY TO MAN

Hugh 'Jimmy' James

On 7 August 1942, just after half-past-two in the afternoon, Sergeant Pilot Jimmy James was approaching the roughly cleared landing strip at Burg el Arab, thirty-five miles west of Alexandria on the Egyptian coast, and headquarters of the British Eighth Army and RAF's Desert Air Force. It had been a difficult flight. Turbulence over the Western Desert was always considerable, but always worse in the middle of the day, especially when it was sizzlingly hot and humid, as it was that day, and particularly when you were flying at only fifty feet above the ground in an ageing Bristol Bombay transport plane, as Jimmy was doing. Still, it was better to risk a sudden lurch and drop of twenty feet courtesy of swirling thermals than be shot down by marauding German fighters – and at Burg el Arab, just a few miles behind the front line, that was an ever-present and very real danger.

After a tight circuit over the landing strip, Jimmy brought the Bombay in to land, then hurriedly taxied to the few tents at the far end of the strip. Turning the aircraft ready to take off again, Jimmy braked, and with the twin engines still running, left the cockpit and hurried over to the tents. That was a golden rule: never switch off your engines; keep them running for a quick departure. It was too dangerous to do otherwise.

As Jimmy strode over to the operations tent to report to the Duty Ops Officer, Flying Officer 'Jonah' Whale, lorries and ambulances were already hurrying out to the stationary Bombay. Everything was done at the quickest speed possible: cargo unloaded, then mail bags, personnel, and, if there was room, wounded men hoisted into the back, then off again. With luck, the turn-around would take no more than five minutes.

Whenever he could, Jimmy would bring Jonah a bottle of beer and a newspaper from Cairo. And more often than not, Jonah would tell Jimmy how lucky he'd been the last time he'd flown into Burg el Arab. 'Just after you left the other day, we were bombed to hell,' he would say, or, 'You were lucky yesterday – five minutes after you left the whole place was strafed!'

Jimmy liked him well enough but that kind of talk made him feel edgy and so he never wasted time, getting back into the cockpit as quickly as he could. But on this occasion, Jimmy had walked fifteen yards back towards the Bombay when he heard the field telephone ring and a moment later, Jonah was calling out to him to stop. 'Switch off!' Jonah shouted.

'What?' said Jimmy, incredulously. 'No, we're not allowed.'

'I'm ordering you to,' Jonah told him. 'That's straight from Air Headquarters. Stop the engines and wait. You've got somebody coming with you, somebody important.'

Reluctantly, Jimmy signalled to his second pilot to switch off. This in itself was a worry – when engines became overheated, as they did very quickly when stationary, they could be difficult to start up again. Cursing and pacing anxiously, Jimmy scanned the skies, then, because of the intense heat in the belly of the plane, ordered the wounded to be taken off again and put back into the ambulances and driven around so they might have some cooler air.

It had already been a strange day. 216 Transport Squadron tended to carry out most flights of this nature first thing in the morning, before the heat of the day made flying – and life – so difficult, but when Jimmy reported to the Flight Commander's tent at 6 a.m., he was told he would not be flying until eleven o'clock. But eleven o'clock came and went. At noon he and his crew were told to go and have a quick lunch. By one they still hadn't left. Not until two was the Bombay ready, by which time Jimmy was sweating profusely and wondering why on earth they had to fly at such an unusual hour. Inevitably, the plane lurched all over the place, and as they entered the battle zone and dropped to fifty feet, the Bombay suddenly fell so sharply they almost touched the ground before rearing into the sky again.

Jimmy was still only nineteen. From a typical coal-mining village in South Wales, he had developed an obsession with aircraft at an early age. 'No one could understand it,' he says, 'because there were only five cars in the village and we never saw any aeroplanes.' Rather, the brass bands, choirs and rugby team were where the mining community found their entertainment. 'There was great poverty at times – coal mining was the only industry there – but also terrific pride,' he admits. 'There were two choirs and eight different chapels.' Jimmy's father played the organ at the Welsh Wesleyan Chapel, and Jimmy and his five older brothers and sisters were expected to attend three services every Sunday, always in their best clothes. 'It was a three-line whip,' he says. 'There was no way we could get out of it.'

Much to his family's surprise, Jimmy passed his matriculation at school, and having done so his parents were determined he would go to university no matter what the sacrifices they needed to make. But then the war began. In 1940, Jimmy was still studying for his Higher School Certificate when one day the headmaster asked for volunteers to suspend their studies for a short while and go to Gloucestershire to become temporary civil servants. The Air Ministry had been evacuated there from London but because so many of their employees had already joined up, they were badly short-staffed.

Jimmy volunteered and found himself in England for the first time in his life. 'I was so naïve,' he admits. 'The world's most naïve little boy.' On his first Sunday there, he cycled past an RAF recruiting office and fifteen minutes later, having lied about his age – he was still seventeen – had signed up.

It was, he confesses, the fulfilment of a childhood dream. 'I'd never even seen a real aeroplane before. I remember touching the wingtip of the Tiger Moth and thinking it was the most wonderful moment in my life.' Nor was he disappointed. 'Very few moments have ever surpassed the thrill of that first flight,' he confesses.

And he was a good pilot, passing his wings with an 'above average' score. Like most young pilots, he hoped to join a fighter squadron and was disappointed to find himself posted to an Operational Training Unit (OTU) to be converted to fly cumbersome Wellington bombers. 'I didn't want to be a bus driver so much,' he admits. 'The Wellington was funny-looking and I thought of all the nice pictures I'd seen of other aircraft.' But no sooner had he reached his OTU than he was told to pack his bags once more. Jimmy was being posted overseas.

It was a rough sea journey into the Atlantic and around the Cape. They were part of a huge, heavily escorted convoy, and the voyage was dogged by frequent enemy attacks and terrible storms. Their ship was filled with one thousand aircrew – five hundred Australians, 480 Canadians and twenty RAF and New Zealanders, of which Jimmy was one. All the way from Durban in South Africa to the Suez Canal they were given lectures and briefings, told that they were the crème de la crème of a new bomber force that was being assembled to fly the latest light American bombers. 'What we didn't know about Mitchells and Marauders by the time we got there wasn't worth knowing,' says Jimmy.

They arrived in a state of great excitement and enthusiasm, but rather than disembark, they were kept stuck on the ship for three days. By then the specially selected 1,000 were beginning to ask questions; the high spirits were starting to dampen. Eventually, on the evening of the third day, they were finally disembarked and marched to a cramped holding camp where there were not enough tents to go round. 'They weren't expecting us,' says Jimmy;

something was clearly wrong. Then word got around: there had been a cock-up at the Air Ministry. RAF Middle East – using American terminology for the American aircraft to which they were referring – had asked for 'one thousand air screws'. Propellers, not aircrew.

Incredibly, this was no rumour: RAF Middle East had a thousand trained bomber pilots and aircrew they had not asked for.

Ten days later a lumbering Bristol Bombay flew over their camp, amidst shouts of derision from below. Soon after, the commanding officer of 216 Transport Squadron began interviewing new crew. Jimmy volunteered immediately. 'I was so fed up by this time,' he says, 'I didn't care what I flew.' An hour later he was wallowing across the sky in the same fixed-wheel Bombay, feeling very depressed and wondering whether he'd made the right decision.

That had been in February 1942, and very soon his doubts had been cast aside. Although 216 was a transport squadron, the flying was challenging, and often both dangerous and exciting. Designed to carry between three and four tonnes, the Bombay was a workhorse – 'the mother duck of the Middle East' – but appreciated by the troops, because they ferried to the front any number of much-needed supplies: fuel and ammunition, even minefield marker tape, and, most important of all, the mail bags.

To begin with, Jimmy was a second, or co-pilot, but he became captain of his own aircraft in June 1942, shortly after the new offensive in Libya had begun. This was a hectic time for anyone involved with the RAF in the Middle East. During the battles, 216 Squadron were constantly bringing supplies forward and taking back the wounded. Then in June, once Tobruk had fallen and Eighth Army was in retreat, 'all hell broke loose'.

It was the RAF that effectively saved Eighth Army, fighter squadrons covering the backs of the retreating army below, and leap-frogging backwards. Jimmy's squadron was given the job of not only supplying these forward units but helping move the groundcrew and equipment when the moment came for them to fall back. On one occasion, Jimmy was taking off and to his right, just a quarter of a mile away, were a number of trucks with black swastikas on the side. 'We'd come in to help bring out some groundcrew and equipment,' Jimmy explains, 'but they'd already gone – and the Germans had arrived. It was a wild time.' On other occasions, Jimmy would fly across the Mediterranean to the besieged island of Malta. 'That was pretty hair-raising too,' he admits. 'It was bloody dangerous with lots of Germans swarming about and bomb craters all over the place.' He was there on 8 April, the day after Malta's world-famous opera house had been destroyed by the Luftwaffe. 'I had my first haircut in a very long time,' he recalls. 'There were huge amounts of rubble strewn down the street. And in the middle of all this wreckage, the barber continued to work.'

Flying over the desert could also cause problems, and not just from the turbulence. At the low heights they operated, the desert became a much harder place in which to navigate. At fifty feet off the ground, Jimmy found it difficult to get a proper perspective – there were often no features on which to get a bearing. 'The most important person was the navigator – for me, it was essential he could still navigate even in sandstorms and thick haze.' Fortunately, his regular navigator was superb; as Jimmy puts it, 'He could read the desert like Braille.'

Despite the frequently fraught missions, Jimmy was enjoying himself enormously. It was, he says, 'the most wonderful schoolboy dream come true'. He relished the gypsy life, constantly on the move and feeling like a buccaneer of old. Furthermore, there was a great sense of camaraderie and fellowship within the squadron. Jimmy had made good friends and enjoyed the company of his fellows. And despite the limited food and water rations and shortage of both amenities and alcohol, they still found ways to amuse themselves. 'We entertained ourselves all sorts of ways. One of our navigators would lay out a nine-hole golf course,' says Jimmy, 'and we'd play with a walking stick and a tennis ball. We all had sheets of paper with our scores.' Good company and plenty of exhilarating flying ensured that Jimmy had had no regrets about volunteering to join the squadron.

But on that baking hot afternoon in early August 1942, events were soon about to take a catastrophic turn. Having ordered the wounded back off the plane, Jimmy walked over again to the ops tent. 'They're on their way,' Jonah told him. 'They'll be here in a short while. It's Gott. You know, "Strafer" Gott, that brilliant general – he's going to be the new commander of Eighth Army.'

Jimmy had no sooner ordered the wounded back on board than two Humber staff cars drove up. He watched a number of people get out and immediately noticed the general – he was tall, smart and very alert and had remarkable presence. The others were shaking his hand, wishing him good luck at his meetings in Cairo and telling him they would see him the following day. Then he strode over. Jimmy suddenly felt conspicuously scruffy.

'Are you the captain?' the General asked.

'Yes sir,' Jimmy replied. 'I'm terribly sorry, sir, I don't have a hat. I can't salute you.'

'My boy, don't worry about that,' Gott smiled. 'Are you ready to go?'

'Yes, sir, we're starting the engines up now.' And just as he said that, Jimmy heard the engines catch and whirr into life. With relief surging over him, he showed the General to his seat, apologizing for the squash and lack of comfort. Again, Gott reassured him. 'Don't worry about me, I'll sit anywhere,' he said.

Jimmy was impressed. 'He looked enormously fit and had such presence. Every inch the general,' he says, 'although he had the smallest general's pips I've ever seen. No large tabs like some generals wore.'

'Strafer' Gott, as he was known, was one of the most popular British generals of the North African campaign. Beloved of his men, he was one of the few commanders whose reputation remained intact during the defeat and retreat of May and June 1942. At the beginning of August, the Prime Minister, Winston Churchill and the chief of the imperial general staff, General Sir Alan Brooke, visited the Middle East to see for themselves what was going so terribly wrong with the campaign. The Commander-in-Chief Middle East, General Auchinleck, had himself taken over direct command of Eighth Army after the fall of Tobruk in June, but the PM had decided to relieve him of both jobs. General Alexander was to take over as C-in-C Middle East, and Gott was to be the new commander of Eighth Army. It would be Gott's job to defeat Rommel when battle was inevitably rejoined at El Alamein.

Jimmy had never flown such an important person before, let alone an army commander, and by now extremely anxious about the time they'd spent on the ground, and the even greater responsibility now resting on his very young shoulders, he hastily opened up the throttles and took off as quickly as he could. Flying at just fifty feet over the dunes, he warned his Canadian second pilot to keep a sharp watch on the engines, because if one were to seize due to over-heating, he wanted to be able to quickly climb and gain height in order to get a better view of where he might try and make an emergency landing. 'The engines were so hot they were in the danger zone,' Jimmy explains. 'I was desperately hoping to get out of the battle zone where it would be safe to climb and find some cooler air.'

And then there was a loud bang and a whip-lashing noise and the starboard engine stopped dead.

'You fool!' Jimmy shouted at his Number Two.

'But look!' the second pilot shouted back.

Jimmy looked and to his horror saw cannon and machinegun tracers whooshing past him and into and all over the plane. The starboard engine was now on fire, smoke billowing from it as it came to a dead stop. Jimmy felt utterly cornered. 'I've never felt tension like it,' he says. 'I thought, what are you doing? You're in charge!' He then experienced a very strange sensation. He felt a yellow streak go from the back of his head, and run all the way down his body. 'It was a greenish-yellow. The most peculiar feeling. I've no idea what it was, but that is the best way I can describe it.' Frantically searching for somewhere to land, and praying to God, he felt momentarily paralysed. All sound had gone – he couldn't hear any screams, or the noise of the cannon shells exploding. 'At that moment,' says Jimmy, 'I changed from being a small, naïve, little schoolboy on his adventures, into an aggressive man.'

A sense of resolve and determination suddenly gripped him. Shouting at the second pilot to duck down and get the Medical Orderly from the back, he suddenly saw the other engine stop dead. Although the cockpit was now rapidly filling with smoke, Jimmy used what remaining speed there was to climb to about a hundred and twenty feet. Conscious of one enemy fighter hurtling past his wing, he saw another roar through the smoke until two more opened fire. On this second pass, the enemy punctured his main fuel tanks in the high wing. Fuel began pouring into the stricken aircraft between the cockpit and the passenger area. Enemy aircraft – Messerschmitt 109s – were now swarming all over him. As he looked back momentarily he could see that his Wireless Operator had had his arm badly shot up. His second pilot had also been wounded but managed to bring back the Medical Orderly, jumping through the flames that were burning between the cockpit and the main body of the plane.

'Get all the wounded off the stretcher hooks and lie them on the floor,' Jimmy ordered. The two men disappeared and a short while later came back again. 'Everything's fine,' the Medical Orderly told him. 'Everyone's on the floor and alive and no one's injured.' Most of the hits had been on the front half and on the wings of the Bombay.

By now, Jimmy had absolutely no power at all. He was merely gliding. Ahead the desert sloped slightly downwards in a long and very gradual descent. It was also uneven and there was a small but significant crosswind. By a fine piece of flying, he managed to glide the heavy old Bombay down gradually so that they touched down quite gently. But although the front two wheels were now on the ground, he couldn't get the tail to lower as he was landing in a cross-wind. 'It just wouldn't drop and so I dared not use my brakes without risking a turnover.' There were other problems: the desert was strewn with rocks, which he tried to swerve around by kicking his rudders one way and then the other; and in between the sand was very soft. If the wheels had dug themselves in at any point, the Bombay would have been beyond control and crashed. Concentrating as hard as he possibly could, he had to manhandle the control column and rudders as the Bombay continued to rumble forwards. 'On and on and on,' says Jimmy. 'It was extremely hard – like driving a ten-ton truck over sand.'

Eventually, however, the tail came down, but when Jimmy then finally applied the brakes he discovered they no longer worked, so still the Bombay sped forwards down the long desert incline. Only when they had slowed to about forty miles per hour did he tell his second pilot to warn the passengers to stand by to evacuate. 'Get the door off and make sure it's right off its hinge,' he told him, 'and then when I give the word, drop them out onto the sand.'

By now, the flames had spread into the cockpit. Jimmy was in a bad way: his face, and particularly his hands, were badly burned. Smoke choked his lungs. And at that moment, he saw through the windscreen his attackers circling low down in the distance. 'The bastards,' he thought with horror, 'they're going to come back!' This was unusual. The Bombay was clearly never going to fly again and normally after an attack of this kind the 109s would have disappeared as quickly as possible in case there were any British fighters about. 'Stand by!' he yelled at his co-pilot and Medical Orderly, who had come back through the flames and smoke for more instructions. 'Open the hatch on the cockpit floor,' Jimmy told him, conscious that his wireless operator would not be able to get to the back of the plane with only one arm. The Medical Orderly did so, then the second pilot confirmed. 'Right. All set in the back,' he told Jimmy.

'And I actually looked back,' says Jimmy, 'and through the smoke I could see some of them and they were giving me a thumbs-up.' Hitting some softer sand, the aircraft slowed and by keeping the control column drawn tightly towards him, the Bombay slowed down to about 20 mph. 'Now!' shouted Jimmy, and suddenly he was alone in the cockpit.

Desperately hoping he'd done everything he could, he slid sideways off his seat to go back and help the evacuation, and as he did so, the 109s unleashed their second attack. Bullets and cannon shells tore through the cockpit and blew up the instrument panel; had they come just a second earlier, Jimmy would have been torn to shreds. 'That shattered me,' he admits. 'There were bits of shrapnel whistling and crashing all over the place – the smoke and noise was dreadful.' Glancing at his feet, he noticed the heels of his desert boots were on fire. In front of him, the Perspex of the canopy was melting. Somehow, however, he pulled himself together and tried to get to the back to check that everyone was safely off the aircraft before finally making his own leap for his life. As the 109s made another pass, their guns broke up the Bombay's fuel tanks completely. A surge of flame blew Jimmy back into the cockpit and although he tried twice more to get to the back, the flames were now so thick he could not get through.

The plane had finally come to a halt and deciding it was at last time make his escape, Jimmy lowered himself through the hatch. Instead of falling six feet, however, the drop was little more than a foot – on the last pass, the Bombay's landing gear had finally buckled. Crawling blindly underneath the aircraft with great difficulty, amidst the thick clouds of smoke, Jimmy passed one of the blazing main tyres and immediately knew that the moment it burst he would be crushed to death. Scrambling out, he emerged through the smoke into brilliant, blinding sunshine. As he stumbled clear, there was a loud bang and a grinding crash as the Bombay collapsed completely.

Staggering around the wing to the rear of the plane, he expected
to see twenty-one people waiting there. Instead there were just four.
Utterly stunned, he could scarcely believe it. 'What the hell have you
done with all the passengers? Where are they? Where are they?' he
asked incredulously.

'In there,' they told him, pointing to the plane. Jimmy looked. The
entire aircraft was now a ball of fire, and changing shape with the
heat; melting before his eyes. It had been the job of the two groundcrew who always came on every desert flight to take the door off its
hinges. Unbeknown to Jimmy, one of these experienced men had
been taken off at the last minute and replaced at base just before
take-off by a new boy. 'Had we gone at 11 a.m., as we were supposed
to,' says Jimmy, 'we would have had two very experienced groundcrew on that flight.' But it was not to be. Instead of taking the door
off its hinges in accordance with standard emergency procedures as
Jimmy had ordered, it had merely been latched backwards and
during the long, wild, landing run, the latch had disastrously broken
and the door jammed shut. It was only a matter of a few minutes
before the second attack started, and the passengers at the back,
with General Gott nearest the door, were trapped and unable to get
out. The only survivors had been those who had escaped out of the
front floor hatch: the badly wounded Wireless Operator, the Second
Pilot, a very sick and disorientated soldier, and the Medical Orderly,
who had been helping them and had accidentally fallen out during
the mayhem.

Jimmy tried to approach the jammed doors of the burning aircraft several times but at each attempt was forced back by the billowing flames and heat. Eventually, the Medical Orderly grabbed
him and held him, and finally seeing sense, Jimmy stood back,
aghast, and looked at the survivors. 'Most were in a state near to
death,' he says. With nothing but open desert in all directions,
Jimmy instinctively decided to go for help. He told the Medical
Orderly to do his best for the others, and placed him in charge
with orders not to move under any circumstances. Then having

taken some swigs of water, he left the rest of the water bottles behind for the others, and set off to the northwest in an effort to try and get help.

In a numbed state of shock, Jimmy had not really considered how badly wounded he was. His shoes and socks were burned, his shorts frayed and his shirt in shreds. Alternating between walking and jogging, he covered at least three miles until he looked down and saw that one of his boots was full of blood. Although he felt no pain, he stumbled as he clambered over a sandhill and fainted.

Just ahead of him, however, was a Bedouin, resting in a shallow hollow with his camels. Jimmy came to as the Arab ran towards him. 'Inglese, Inglese,' Jimmy told him, pointing to the northwest. Having given him some water, the Bedouin helped him onto a camel and together they set off at a wild pace, Jimmy passing in and out of consciousness.

He was unsure how far they travelled, but after a while they stopped and the Bedouin took off his turban and excitedly began waving it and pointing to movement in the distance. Following suit, Jimmy took off his shirt and began waving it too. He couldn't understand how he could have been wearing a red shirt. 'And then,' says Jimmy, 'I realized for the first time that I must have been shot in the back.'

A truck came towards them. By good fortune, it was men of the Royal Army Service Corps, testing a repaired fifteen-hundredweight truck. Jimmy was picked up and put in the front. 'Christ, you've got no hair,' said the horrified driver. 'Your face is burned, look at your hands! Look at your hands!' And Jimmy looked and saw that they were blackened with bone standing out.

Back at their RASC camp, Jimmy was placed on a stretcher and an ambulance called, but as soon as he saw the commanding officer there, he said, 'Sir, telephone Army Headquarters and tell them General Gott has been killed. Bristol Bombay shot down.'

'What was that?' said the major.

'Telephone bloody Headquarters – it's an emergency. Now! Quickly!'

The major hurried off to make the call then organized a search party for the survivors. Jimmy insisted on coming with them. 'I promised my crew I'd be back,' he told the major, 'and only I know the way.'

'Don't be a damn fool,' said the major, but Jimmy was adamant. He dragged himself into the lead jeep as the pain now began to hit him, but clutching the bar with a deathlike grip, he refused to be moved and led the convoy up a tortuous route over the escarpment and on to the open desert back towards the wreckage of the Bombay. 'I had a sense of duty to the others that was entirely instinctive,' he explains. 'I don't know where it came from, but I did feel it – very strongly.' Not until they spotted the column of smoke rising into the sky dead ahead did Jimmy finally pass out.

Initially treated in a field hospital, he was operated on several times and for a while was inches away from death. But after four days, Jimmy was stable enough to be flown back to a main base hospital. It was a Bombay from his own squadron that came to fly him and a number of other wounded back to Cairo. Jimmy was barely conscious when the captain came through to the back to check on his cargo, but he immediately recognized the pilot's voice as one of his tent-mates. As the captain passed him, Jimmy reached out and touched his foot. When his friend pulled it away, Jimmy grabbed his foot again.

'I called out his name,' says Jimmy. '"Ron!" I called, and he said, "How do you know my name?" and when he realized who I was he nearly died on the spot.' Jimmy had shared a tent with Ron and two others. Some time before, they'd agreed to each hide two pounds under the tent posts; the idea was that if one of them died, the other three were to use the eight pounds to have a party in Cairo in their friend's honour. Ron and the other two had been toasting Jimmy just the night before.

He was in hospital for four long months. During that time, he was told he'd been awarded the Distinguished Flying Medal, the second highest award in the RAF to be given for valour – after the Victoria Cross. Eventually passing his medical, he was then, to his surprise, sent straight back to 216 Squadron, where he had a great welcome. 'They were all delighted about the DFM,' he admits. 'It was an honour for the whole squadron, not just for me.'

Although still only twenty years old, Jimmy seems to have had only a few qualms nor any kind of trauma about getting back into another plane and flying once more. In fact, he stayed with the squadron until the very end of the war and beyond, amassing a staggering three thousand hours, and serving throughout the remainder of the North African campaign, as well as in Sicily, Italy, the Dodecanese and the invasion of Greece. Eventually commissioned, he became the squadron's principal training pilot and having been converted to flying American Dakotas, helped oversee the conversion of the rest of the squadron as the old Bombays were finally being phased out.

At the end of the war, he finally left the squadron having been with them for nearly four years. For this and for his involvement in the Berlin Airlift, he was twice awarded the Air Force Cross to add to his DFM. He was then posted to VIP flying, taking Prime Minister Clement Attlee, numerous generals, ambassadors and even members of the Royal family around the world. 'But,' he confesses, 'I never flew Churchill – much to my regret.'

One of the few pilots to be chosen for a permanent commission in the RAF after the war, Jimmy held a number of interesting posts, becoming senior flight commander in the first night-fighter squadron of Vampire jets, then later seconded to the US Air Force in Alaska where he was responsible for the operations and training of a three-squadron all-weather fighter group. Two and a half years later, he returned to England to command a squadron of Javelins, an aircraft then still very much in development. 'It was a wonderful time,' he says, 'and the Javelin was a fantastic and brilliant night-fighter.' And he relished the chance to have his own squadron too.

Not until 1966 did he finally retire from the service, working in the family business for four years before taking a post in an electronics company until he retired for good. Not that he's been idle since then. 'I'm the sort of person that has to be active and be involved all the time,' he confesses, and so he still plays an enthusiastic part in local ex-service organizations, and church and community affairs.

It's been a full and varied life, yet he has always been dogged by the events of that August day in 1942. Churchill was still in Cairo at the time of Gott's death and on hearing the news, wept quite openly, both for personal reasons and because he'd lost the man he had hoped would help bring victory in North Africa. Gott's replacement was none other than General Montgomery – and as it happened, working alongside General Alexander, Monty did achieve the emphatic battlefield victory the Prime Minister – and all of Britain – had so craved.

Yet in the aftermath of Gott's death, an immediate news clampdown was put in place, supposedly until the truth about precisely what had happened was discovered. But in doing so, the facts were never widely revealed. 'I kept getting fed up hearing I was dead from various people,' says Jimmy. Historians would make the same mistake. He lost count of the different versions of what was supposed to have happened, none of which were ever close to the real truth. He made several efforts to persuade the RAF Air Historical Branch that the official history had got it all wrong, but his version of events was routinely ignored.

In 1958, he'd gone to visit Gott's widow, who had been relieved to see him. She was, she told him, sick and tired of the letters she had had from the War Office, Air Ministry and elsewhere, all containing contradictory information about what had happened to her husband, and was frustrated that no one had made a proper investigation into her husband's death. Having been asked to tell her everything he knew, sparing no detail, Jimmy had readily done so, although he wished he could find proof to back up what he remembered so very vividly – his second pilot had died later in the war and he had been unable to discover either the fate or whereabouts of the other three survivors.

Then incredibly, sixty years later, Jimmy finally found the witness he had needed for so long. In a book about wartime fighter tactics, Herr Emil Clade recounted shooting down the Bombay exactly as Jimmy had remembered. 'I was flabbergasted,' he admits, 'because many years before I'd been told that none of the pilots that had been in that particular unit at that time had survived the war.'

It took him a further two years, but eventually he tracked down Herr Clade, and in March 2005, they met at Bonn airport in Germany, sixty-two and a half years after the events of that fateful August afternoon. Herr Clade could scarcely have been more hospitable or pleased to see Jimmy, greeting him with the emotion normally reserved for an old friend. Although over ninety, he was happy to talk about his wartime experiences and remembered well what had happened that August day.

He told Jimmy he had been leading a *schwarm* of fighters, i.e., four aircraft. At the last minute two more had joined them, which was unusual, and then the ground controller told them to keep absolute radio silence at all times – and that, he told Jimmy, had been even more unusual. They had spotted the Bombay, and, as leader, Herr Clade had made the first attack. 'I shot out your starboard engine,' he told him – again, exactly as Jimmy had remembered, and also confirmed that the Bombay had only been about fifty feet off the ground.

Normally when behind enemy lines, the German fighters would expect to be attacked by RAF fighters, so once the three pairs of Messerschmitts had made their first attacks over the plane, they circled a short distance away to the southwest while Herr Clade flew a quick recce flight over the burning and badly damaged Bombay and decided that a further attack was necessary to ensure the aircraft would not fly again. At that time, a degree of chivalry existed

towards downed aircraft in the Western Desert, so a second attack
would normally have been considered unnecessary. 'It was never-
theless a brilliant interception by the Me 109s,' admits Jimmy, 'in
what was, for them, a very dangerous area.' When there was no sign
of any British fighters, the German pilots flew back to the Bombay
and made their second attack, after which they finally headed back
to their landing ground.

Herr Clade then told Jimmy something else. After they had
landed, they were reporting to the Intelligence Officer when the flap
of the tent was pulled back and in strode a senior officer – a 'kom-
mandant' – who said, 'Congratulations, gentlemen! You have just
shot down a transport aircraft and have killed General "Strafer" Gott,
the new Commander of Eighth Army!'

Jimmy reckoned that must have been at about five o'clock at
the very latest. He knew neither he nor anyone else in the Bombay
had sent a radio signal about the catastrophe, and also knew for a
fact that at that time he was still stumbling across the desert. In
other words, it was clear the Germans had known Gott was killed
some time *before* the British. 'Even if I had sent a signal,' says
Jimmy, 'my radio never worked at fifty feet – you needed to be
much higher than that.' The Germans must have found out that
Gott was going to be on board. A throw-away comment, a careless
radio signal – whatever; the news had been intercepted, and Gott
had been assassinated.

'How many were killed?' Herr Clade asked. 'Five?'

No, Jimmy told him. Eighteen. And all had died because of the
second strafing attack. 'When I told him that,' says Jimmy, 'he burst
into tears and could not be consoled.'

Despite this, Jimmy assured him he bore him no grudge and
they embraced as friends. Herr Clade's family had arranged for
them to then fly together, so up they went, over Germany, two
former enemies now taking to the skies side by side. 'He was a good
man, I must say,' says Jimmy, 'and he had done his duty and done it
well.' Their meeting was, Jimmy admits, 'a staggeringly emotional

experience'. But at last he feels he has learnt the truth about what happened that day – a day that changed his life for ever, and possibly even the course of the war.

PARATROOPER

Heinz Puschmann

Heinz Puschmann remembers the evening of 5 June 1944 very well. 'The sun went down dark blood-red,' he says. 'It was a nice sunset.' Sitting in his tent on the edge of Carentan, he turned to one of his comrades and wondered whether it would be one of the last sunsets they would ever see. 'Here the conversation came to an abrupt stop,' he says. 'Each of us followed our own thoughts.'

They knew the Allied invasion was coming. Indeed, the 6th *Fallschirmjäger* – Paratroop – Regiment had been sent to the Cotentin Peninsula in Normandy a little over a month before for precisely that reason, part of the German defences along the Atlantic Wall. The only paratroop regiment in the area, the three battalions had been split up – the 1st Battalion to Ste Marie du Mont, the 2nd to Ste Mère-Eglise, and the 3rd, to which Heinz was attached, to Carentan. They had spent several weeks making a thorough investigation of the surrounding countryside, which was largely reclaimed marshland criss-crossed with a close network of hedgerows, or *bocages*. These, they realized, were often high earthen walls, thickly woven with dense tree and bush roots. And so they trained hard, carrying out regular exercises that made the most of these natural defences, and waiting for the day the Allied armada arrived off the coast of France – as they knew it surely would.

Heinz was in the Signals Unit. Their teams had been divided

amongst the various companies, but Heinz had remained based at Battalion Headquarters – it was their job to make sure the battalion companies remained in touch with one another, and for his battalion to be communicating with the other battalions in the regiment. No one knew when the Allies would come or even where, but rapid and co-ordinated response would be essential if they were to have any chance of repulsing the invaders.

By 5 June, however, Heinz was pretty sure the Allies would be landing somewhere in Normandy. For the past few days, they had been bombed both heavily and regularly. And once the bombers disappeared, before the dust had hardly begun to settle, fighter planes had roared over, especially, Heinz had noted, American Mustangs and Thunderbolts. On the fifth, these fighters had been over the Carentan area continually since before dawn, dropping bombs, strafing and patrolling. Not surprisingly, everyone at Battalion HQ felt tense, sensing the invasion must surely now arrive at any moment.

The night of 5/6 June was initially, Heinz clearly recalls, 'bright, clear and moonlit'. In the early hours of the morning, they heard the sound of large formations of aircraft flying over and to begin with thought it must be another bombing raid. But then at around 2.30 a.m., the alarm was raised – thousands of enemy paratroopers were raining down from the skies around Carentan. As a signaller, Heinz was busy. Reports were coming in from the Company Commanders, while orders were being sent out from Battalion HQ. So this was it, Heinz realized: the invasion had begun. He could hear single shots being fired but not much more. There was an air of confusion – no one quite knew where the enemy were or what would happen next.

The invaders landing in 6th *Fallschirmjäger*'s section were the American 101st Airborne Division, and as the grey dawn crept over Carentan, Heinz and his comrades saw the land round about covered in silk parachutes of various colours. The Germans wondered whether these colours represented different units, but certainly the mass of silk was put to good use. 'We went and cut them and used them as scarves,' says Heinz.

The American drop had not been particularly successful and the 101st Airborne, especially, were spread far and wide. It took them a while to regroup, but eventually they began heading towards the coast to secure the exit routes off 'Utah' and 'Omaha', the beaches where American ground troops had already begun landing. Pushed northwards to battle against their American counterparts were the 1st and 2nd Battalions who soon found themselves in the thick of heavy fighting. At Carentan, Heinz saw his first American prisoners later in the day. 'They were tall and heavily built,' he says. 'We joked that they looked as though they were from Sing Sing, the famous prison in America.'

There was little opportunity for further levity, however. Although the German paratroopers fought tenaciously, they could not match the massive fire-power of the Allies. During the first two days of the invasion, the 1st Battalion was annihilated – almost entirely wiped out. Falling back to Carentan, the regiment established a new defence line around the town, but they were now almost surrounded and were cut off from their neighbouring German units. Allied fighter aircraft seemed to be constantly buzzing overhead. 'We wondered where our fighter planes were,' says Heinz. But the Luftwaffe were almost entirely absent from the air; the Allies had learnt their lessons during five long years of war. Victory on the ground, they had discovered, could only be achieved once command of the skies had been secured.

The intensity of the fighting grew with every passing day and with every passing hour. Casualties were mounting further, including Heinz's best friend, Theo Keilholz. They had got to know one another back in February, when the 6th Regiment had been formed in Cologne. Until May, when they were posted to Normandy, they had trained hard, and during that time Heinz and Theo had not only been in the same battalion, but had also shared a room together. 'My friend died,' says Heinz. 'At least, I assume he died. I was talking to him on the radio then heard him scream and then there was silence. I never heard from him again.'

On Sunday, 11 June, the Allied Navy began bombarding Carentan, an assault that lasted for twelve hours. Shells screamed through the air constantly, exploding and causing the ground to shake. 'When the bombardment stopped,' says Heinz, 'the fighters were in the air again.' Soon after, the Americans launched their final attack on the town. Major von der Heydte, commander of the 6th *Fallschirmjäger* Regiment, asked for urgent reinforcements from their command division, the 17th Panzer Grenadier, but his request was refused. With their situation now hopeless, Major von der Heydte ordered the paratroopers to begin withdrawing south towards Périers.

Carentan fell the following day and it was during their retreat that Heinz was badly wounded. 'I was on patrol and lying on the ground,' he says, 'when all of a sudden I was hit.' He had been shot below the ear, and the bullet had gone through the lower part of his head, through his mouth and had become lodged in his neck. 'Blood was pouring out of my mouth,' he says. 'That was pretty alarming, and when I touched my forehead, it was ice-cold. I thought of my mother and father and sister. It was very frightening.' He wasn't sure if he would die, but knew his wound was very serious. A medic hurried over to him and helped get him back to the regimental dressing station, and from there he was taken to Paris, where the bullet was removed. 'I couldn't eat,' he says, 'because the bullet had gone through my nose and they had to pin my jaw so I couldn't move it sideways.'

As the Allies advanced out of Normandy and began to push through France, Heinz was transferred to several different hospitals in Germany, until finally ending up at a hospital in Hanau, near Frankfurt, where they specialized in dealing with such injuries. 'I was out of the war for several months,' he says matter-of-factly. He was lucky to be alive at all. In the fighting around Carentan, the 6th *Fallschirmjäger* were almost entirely wiped out. 'Before D-Day, we had 1,800 men in the regiment,' says Heinz, 'and when they assembled again after Carentan, there were only forty men left.'

* * *

Heinz had known from an early age that he wanted to join the Luftwaffe. As a boy, he enjoyed the outdoor life and had a taste for adventure. At ten he had joined the Boy Scouts and greatly enjoyed the camps they would go on; at thirteen, he was in the Hitler Youth. 'It was good fun,' he says, and points out that at the time, Hitler seemed to have dragged Germany out of the Depression and brought prosperity and a return of national pride. The Hitler Youth was part of that. Although the organization was, to a certain degree, a glorified version of the Boy Scouts, there was also a military emphasis, and in Heinz's group, boys could decide what area of the military they were interested in and gain some experience in that field. Heinz chose the Luftwaffe and learnt to fly gliders. He was also given tuition in how to build and repair his own plane. 'But I wasn't very good with my hands, so I switched to signals instead,' he says. 'I learnt Morse Code and how to read signals. I had to do about two hours a week evening signal duty, and then I could fly at the weekend. We didn't have to pay for it.' Little wonder, then, that boys like Heinz enjoyed it so much.

Little wonder, too, that when his father asked him what he would like to do in life, Heinz told him he wanted a career in the Air Force. Just fourteen at the time, Heinz had been due to start high school. 'All right,' his father told his son, 'there's no high school for you, boy. You go and learn a trade.' Heinz became an apprentice fitter and turner.

Born and brought up in Hindenburg, in Silesia, just six miles from the Polish border and still only fifteen when the war began, Heinz remembers the German Army massing along the frontier before the invasion in September 1939. 'The police needed runners because there were soldiers up in church towers watching for Polish troops and aircraft,' he says. Heinz was one of the boys chosen for such a task and spent the opening days of the war sleeping at the Police HQ and taking messages to the church towers and other lookout posts. 'One night the sky was lit up with flares,' he says. 'A Polish plane came over – we thought it had been shot down but a few minutes later it came back again and dropped bombs.'

His apprenticeship should have lasted three and a half years, but he never completed it because when he was seventeen and a half, he applied to become an officer cadet in the Luftwaffe's paratroop wing. 'To begin,' he says, 'I really wanted to be a pilot. But then they started the Paratroopers, and it seemed more adventurous and I liked the idea of doing jumps.'

From the outset, the *Fallschirmjäger* were intended to be an elite body, set apart from the rest of the German armed forces – even the Luftwaffe, of which they were a part. Their role was to be shock assault troops – *Fallschirmjäger* literally means 'paratrooper hunter' – and as they proved when they almost single-handedly took Rotterdam during the Blitzkrieg in May 1940, and again in Crete a year later, they could be very effective. Most, like Heinz, were volunteers. Enormous emphasis was placed on physical and mental preparation and the would-be paratroopers faced increasingly difficult tests throughout their training. If at any point they failed one of these tests, they would be thrown off the course. 'For example,' says Heinz, 'you had to jump off a five-metre-high tower. If you didn't jump, they saw you didn't have the will or courage to be a paratrooper.' Even when they were finally taken for their first jump from an aeroplane, they were given no more than ten seconds at the hatch in which to make the leap.

But Heinz had no such problems. He found that jumping from aeroplanes was every bit as exciting as he'd hoped, and having completed his six day-jumps and one night-jump, was awarded his paratrooper wings. It was a proud moment, and it was only then that he confessed to his parents that he had joined the *Fallschirmjäger*. Heinz smiles. 'My father believed I had gone into the Air Force.'

Having completed his parachute training he was sent to Officer Training School. 'I had to do a course for three months and then I was accepted and promoted and had to go to the front to prove myself.' He was posted to Italy, still as an ordinary paratrooper, and then after a stint in the front line, where he volunteered for as many patrols as he possibly could, he was sent back to Officer Training

School to complete the second part of the course. Even then, cadet officers were not promoted – not until they had earned it by front-line duty a second time. Ability in training was one thing; proving it in battle, with men being killed and wounded, bullets whizzing past, and shells exploding all around, was quite another. 'I was sent back to Italy – to Cassino,' says Heinz. 'It was horrendous.' He fought with the 1st *Fallschirmjäger* Division through much of the Second Battle of Cassino, witness to particularly brutal fighting on and around Monastery Hill. 'We were fighting against the New Zealanders,' he says. With many veteran troops from North Africa and Crete, the New Zealanders were among the most tenacious and experienced men the Allies had.

It was after this experience that Heinz was finally promoted and sent to Cologne for the formation of the 6th *Fallschirmjäger* Regiment. There were certainly compelling reasons for making officer training in the *Fallschirmjäger* so tough – after all, they were elite troops and needed to be led by highly trained, battle-experienced officers. Heinz was proud to be a part of such a force and enjoyed the intense camaraderie and sense of honour and discipline that came with it. 'We were taught to fight fairly and squarely,' he says, 'and to treat our enemies properly when taken as POWs. Never harm the defenceless. We fought hard but fair.' Most who found themselves opposite the German paratroopers at Cassino, for example, would vouch for this. Heinz cites examples: they were not allowed to open fire on an enemy paratrooper until he had touched the ground. To do otherwise was a court-martial offence. Nor were they allowed to loot or steal, no matter how hungry they might have been. 'If we had stolen something and were caught, we would be finished. Court-martialled and kicked out,' he says, then adds, 'I'm talking about paratroopers – I'm not speaking for any other units.'

After his horrific wound in Normandy, Heinz spent six months in hospital and was finally released from Hanau in December 1944. 'The doctor told me I could go home and have some leave, but I asked if he could postpone it for a week – it was the beginning of December and I really wanted to have one last Christmas at home with my parents.' The doctor agreed. As Heinz was well aware, Germany was losing the war and when he finally made it home to Hindenburg, his worst fears were confirmed. 'I could hear the rumble of the cannons,' he says, 'and when you stood outside at night, you could see the flashing lights from the explosions. The Russians were coming.' The town was also busy with refugees. Heinz saw their worried faces as they pulled carts piled high with their belongings. Often there were small children sitting on top, too cold and too weary to walk. 'Those people did not care if it was Christmas,' says Heinz. 'Their only thoughts were to get away from the Russians. It was very sad to see.'

A Home Defence Unit was being formed in Hindenburg and Heinz asked if he could join and help. 'I wanted to defend my home town,' he explains, but his request was turned down: he was an experienced paratrooper and the *Fallschirmjäger* still needed him. And so, his leave over, he left home on 30 December with a heavy heart. 'My father didn't want to move from Hindenburg,' says Heinz. Nor did he try to persuade him otherwise. 'I never talked to my father about politics, and never about the Third Reich because I knew he was not in favour of it. He was not happy about what had happened.'

With his father at work, his mother accompanied him to the train station to see him off. She was understandably upset. Sending a son away to war must be horrendous for any parent, but many times worse when both mother and son know they will probably never see each other again, and that the home they love will soon be swept aside by the juggernaut of war.

Heinz reported back to the *Fallschirmjäger* garrison town of Stendal, where he met up with a number of former comrades and together they were sent on a month-long 'tank distraction' course. Once the course was completed, they were given orders to journey by train to

Italy, where they were to join the 4th Division. On 13 February, their train reached Dresden, and overnight was standing on some sidings in the marshalling yard when the air-raid sirens began wailing. Next to them was a train full of Russian prisoners, so Heinz agreed to stay and guard their own train while the others took shelter in case the Russians managed to escape. 'Our train was full of gear and equipment,' Heinz explains. 'We couldn't just leave it.'

Around ten o'clock that evening, the first bombs began falling. 'The Russian prisoners started screaming,' says Heinz. 'It was just about the worst thing I heard in the entire war. If the bombs had started coming too close, we could have jumped off and run for cover. But those Russians couldn't jump. It was cruel.' Locked in their cattle wagons, they became increasingly hysterical. 'I have to say,' he adds, 'that really upset me. I can still hear them now.'

But fortune was with them. Although less than half a mile from the centre of the attack, few bombs hit the railway. Even so, once the raiders had passed, they could see Dresden had taken a terrible pounding. 'After the raid we went to the station master and ordered him to move our transport train out of Dresden immediately,' says Heinz. 'We didn't want our equipment destroyed by another raid.' The station master promised to do his best, but finding an engine driver on such a night was no easy task. As they feared, the bombers returned. Three hours later, the air-raid warning sounded again and this time it was Heinz's turn to take shelter in a nearby cellar. By this time a fire storm had developed and was sweeping through the heart of the city. 'The change of air pressure from the fire storm was so intense,' says Heinz, 'that suddenly the cellar door blew open.'

They were still stuck on the marshalling yards the following morning when a third attack arrived. Rather than shelter in the cellar, they ran into fields instead, taking cover in a small wooden hut. Bombs started falling again, this time uncomfortably close. 'I said, "I'm not staying here,"' says Heinz, and they ran a short way and took shelter in a bomb crater. Suddenly they heard the whistling of falling bombs, followed by an enormous explosion. Earth clattered down onto their helmets. 'When we looked up,' says Heinz, 'the hut was gone – completely vanished.'

Finally leaving the burning city behind, they continued their journey to Italy, through the Brenner Pass and down onto the plains of the north. Just before they reached Verona they stopped. Once more they heard the sound of air-raid sirens droning. Another Allied bombing raid was soon in progress. When they later passed through, the town was still burning.

Soon after joining the 4th Division near Bologna, Heinz found himself retreating back northwards towards the River Po. Free of the mountains at last, the Allies were now able to make the most of their enormous advantage in fire-power. As at Normandy, fighter planes dogged their every move. 'And when the planes were not in the air,' he says, 'the tanks and flame-thrower tanks arrived.' These, he adds, had a demoralizing effect; they wished they could call on their own air forces, but the Luftwaffe as a fighting force had already been destroyed. 'The anger and frustration grew,' he admits.

When they reached the River Po, there was no bridge left, and so they were given the order to destroy most of their equipment. Heinz was fortunate to get a ride on one of the last ferries going across before the Allies caught up with them, but others, in their desperation not to be captured, tried swimming to safety. 'But the Po is dangerous,' says Heinz. 'Many of our boys lost their lives trying to swim across.'

After regrouping, they headed north, passing lines of burnt-out cars and guns, dead soldiers and mules. They had little equipment left, but as Heinz explains, 'the enemy infantry was no longer in close combat with us – it was now more a war from the air.' Fighter planes, bombing and machinegunning them, harassed them all the way to Ala, in the foothills of the Alps, where they took over positions from the SS. Here, they prepared for the final showdown. But strangely, for several days it was quiet; there was no sign of the American troops they were expecting.

They were still there on 1 May, when their commander assembled them in a cave above Ala. 'I can remember like it was yesterday,' says Heinz. 'He told us that Hitler had been killed in the fighting for Berlin. We didn't know then that he had shot himself.' They held a few minutes' silence then moved on again, ten miles north to Rovoreto. The next day, having reached Rovoreto, they heard that the war in Italy was over.

A surreal atmosphere hung over the band of paratroopers. Most were agreed that they should try and get over the Alps. 'We wanted to get into Austria and fight the Russians,' Heinz explains, 'but every time we set off, we were fired upon by the partisans.' A few days later, after some tense moments with the local partisans in Rovoreto, the Americans arrived; there would be no fighting the Russians. Instead, they were told they were now officially prisoners of war.

Heinz remained a prisoner of war in Italy until December 1946, and although he moved camp several times, he spent some time helping to rebuild Cassino. 'They said, "You destroyed the monastery, you rebuild it,"' he says, although, in fact, it had been the Allies who had bombed and destroyed it, in February 1944. 'We had to shift a lot of heavy stones. It was quite dangerous work because there were still many unexploded bombs and mines about.'

Even once he was freed he could still not return home, however. Hindenburg was no longer in Germany. Renamed Zabrze, it had been ceded into the new Polish boundaries and was now in the Soviet East. His mother, he knew, was dead, just as he had feared. Not long after Heinz departed for Italy, the Soviet troops had reached Hindenburg. Their house had been ransacked, and the Russians had stolen anything of value, both actual and sentimental. His father, an engineer working in Hindenburg, had been out at work at the time. On his way home, the Russians were transporting a number of German POWs and swept him up too. Heinz's mother only later found out what had happened to him. 'They took him to Siberia to work in the mines,' says Heinz, 'and six months later my mother was dead.' She had died of a broken heart.

With neither home nor family to turn to, he made his way to
Alzenau, near Frankfurt. He had met Lydia, his future wife, in
Cologne before being posted to Normandy. At the time she had been
working at a Luftwaffe night-fighter base. A few months before being
released as a POW, Heinz had written to her. 'I had lost contact with
her,' he says, 'and wasn't sure if she was even still alive.' But to his
great relief, Lydia replied, and told him to come and see her as soon
as he was freed. Ten months after his release, in September 1947, they
were married.

He had hoped to study engineering, but could not afford to and
so was considering entering the priesthood instead. His father-in-law
came to the rescue, however, agreeing to pay for him to go through
university. 'So I majored in engineering at Frankfurt University,' says
Heinz, 'and it was while I was there that we decided to go to New
Zealand.' During his time as a POW, Heinz had become friends with
a New Zealand Army major. 'He came to visit us in Alzenau,' recalls
Heinz, 'and he said, "Why don't you come and see New Zealand
for yourself?"' Heinz had always had great respect for the New
Zealanders as soldiers and had liked the ones he had met after the
war, and so after graduating in 1952, he and his wife emigrated to
Auckland.

By that time his father had been released from prison and was
living back in Hindenburg – or rather, Zabrze – as was his sister. But
Heinz still couldn't go there because of the political situation and
later the Iron Curtain. 'We wrote to each other,' says Heinz, 'but what
is a letter when you can't have personal contact?' Not until 1972 did
he finally manage to get a visa to visit them both. It was the first time
he had returned home since that December night in the last winter
of the war, and the first time his wife had ever met his family. His
father died three years later.

Looking back on his war years, he says, 'You forget the bad times and
remember the good.' He was glad he had been a paratrooper, and is
still proud to have been part of such an elite force. But the bad times

have not gone from his memory entirely. He mentions, for example, that after his friend Theo Keilholz was killed in Normandy, he made a point of not becoming good friends with any more of his comrades. 'My attitude was this,' he says: 'be friendly, and rely on them because they'll rely on you, but don't get too close because you never know when it will end. Otherwise you get too upset.' Nor can he stand the sight of blood. 'I can't bear it,' he admits. 'I can't even look at raw meat.'

And there is also the trauma of defeat. 'The hopes of victory faded away at Carentan,' he admits. 'When Carentan was attacked and there was only about forty of us left around our commander – well, when you're put in that position as a soldier, it is devastating.'

But still he fought on, even after recovering from a life-threatening wound. 'I always felt that what I was doing was right because I wasn't doing it for myself,' he explains. 'I was doing it for the Fatherland. I was protecting my home, my family, and many other families because it is my duty. I am not glorifying war, and please don't think I am – war is terrible. It should be outlawed.'

Heinz mentions a time after the war, when he was clearing Cassino as a prisoner of war. There were still plenty of corpses about the place and so he would pick up medals and ID tags and other bits and pieces and put them in an empty ammunition box, and then handed them over to the authorities to give back to the families of the dead. 'It was,' he says, 'the last thing I could do for my fallen comrades.'

THE LAST BATTLE

MAY — 1944

NORTH CAROLINA

ME

CARNERA

LEO

PERSONAL DIARY ★

HINGHAM MASS.

U.S. MARINE CORPS
Identification Card
William T. PIERCE
Name
William T. Pierce
Signature
Color Hair Brown Eyes Brown
Weight 124 Birth 1-16-25
Void after INDEFINITE
James G. Tales Capt. U.S.M.C.
Validating Officer

NAVAL AMMUNITION DEPOT
HINGHAM, MASS.

APRIL 1944

APRIL 1944

UNITED STATES MARINE CORPS
N. A. D., HINGHAM, MASS.

LIBERTY PASS

No. Rank PFC
Name PIERCE, William T.

The above named man has authorized liberty and is authorized
to return to station duty during any emergency.

By Order of the Commanding Officer.
L. L. GOVER.
Major, USMC
L. L. Gover

APRIL 1944

APRIL 1944

Bill Pierce

April 1, 1945 – April Fools' Day, Easter Sunday, and, as it happened, D-Day for the invasion of Okinawa.[7] In the deep blue waters around the island were over 1,457 ships and landing craft, crammed with more than half a million men, and including a joint US Army and Marine Corps landing force of around 182,000 troops.

As a beautiful, clear spring morning broke over the massive invasion fleet, twenty-year-old Bill Pierce, aboard the troopship APA *General Clymer*, was readying himself for his first-ever taste of combat action. From Queens Village, New York, Bill was a Marine, and proud of it too. Part of the US 6th Marine Division, he had waited nearly two years for this moment; two years of training, first in the United States, and then, for the past ten months, on the island of Guadalcanal in the Pacific. And he felt ready – if not a little apprehensive – for the task ahead.

One of a five-man 37mm gun crew, Bill was in the Weapons Company of the 29th Marine Regiment, and as such was not to be in the first wave of landings. Even so, he and his comrades were up early, roused from their bunks shortly after six in the morning. In the mess hall, the men were given a good breakfast of steak and eggs –

---

[7] Although actually, it was termed L-Day – 'Love' Day – to distinguish it from other D-Days.

what for many could be their last cooked meal. Some were too nervous to eat, but not Bill, who wolfed his down then went up on deck to attend Mass. Coming from a Catholic family, Bill had always gone to church every Sunday as a boy. Now, on this day of days, praying to God gave him comfort. Despite the vast armada surrounding him, the sea looked calm, and twinkled in the early morning sunlight as he received Holy Communion.

The service over, Bill went back down to his bunk to put on his combat gear and to wait for the call to board their landing craft. He and his comrades did not have long to wait. Over the speaker his Weapons Company was called to get ready to board their landing craft. Bill put on his helmet with its distinct Marines' camouflage, heaved his 60lb pack onto his back and slung his M1 rifle over his shoulder. No one spoke much. The jokes and normal banter had dried up. 'My throat was already dry,' Bill noted later, 'and all of us looked at each other with wide eyes.' Up on deck, there was a mass of activity. Cranes were hoisting up trucks, guns, tanks and jeeps from the lower decks. Bill and his gun crew watched their 37mm appear from the depths of the ship and then swing over the rail and down into the waiting landing craft below. Then it was the turn of the men themselves, who clambered awkwardly down the ropes, rifles clunking and their heavy packs slipping, and then jumped into the boat as it bobbed gently on the surface.

The noise and smell of the diesel engines was overpowering, and although Bill was never seasick, the stench of fumes made him feel nauseous as they circled round and round waiting for the order to head to the shore. It got to the point where no matter what horrors awaited them on the beaches, he just wanted to get off the landing craft and get onto dry land. By mid-morning, however, they were at last heading inland. Bill could not really tell what was going on. Overhead, naval shells whistled through the sky. He and his buddies stood up on the side of the boat, their arms on the railings so they could see where they were heading. The shoreline itself was shrouded in smoke from exploding shells, but along the landing beaches it seemed calmer, with hundreds of landing craft already moored at the water's edge. None of

. them had much idea what to expect, however. All Bill knew about Okinawa was what they'd been told in the briefing: that it was an island some sixty miles long, and that because of its relative proximity to mainland Japan itself, it would be an important staging post for the ongoing aerial assault on the last of the Axis powers.

Okinawa was, in fact, the largest of the Ryukyu Islands that made up the long, curling tail south of Kyushu. The island lay 320 miles south of mainland Japan, and although home to nearly 450,000 native Okinawans, it was also heaving with Japanese Imperial Army troops. Part of Japan's home territories, it was unthinkable for the Land of the Rising Sun to concede such a jewel. The Americans might have assembled a task force of astonishing fire-power – the largest of the entire war – but they would need it. On every island onto which the Americans had stepped during the Pacific War, the Japanese had shown what tenacious and determined troops they were: Guadalcanal, Saipan, Iwo Jima; these had become bywords for the savagery with which every one of these pinprick islands had to be prised from the Japanese forces that held them. No one expected Okinawa to be any different, least of all Bill – he'd heard the stories from the combat veterans amongst them; he'd even seen evidence of the fighting during his time on Guadalcanal. US Army and Navy planners reckoned it could take as much as a month to complete operations on Okinawa.

Their landing craft came to a halt some hundred yards from the shore, and the ramp lowered. Bill and his crew heaved their gun off the boat, but it immediately dropped several feet into the water – unbeknown to the coxswain, they had become grounded on a coral bar. Cursing, Bill and his crew hailed a Marine Alligator, a kind of tracked beach craft, which came to their rescue. Even so, cursing furiously and soaking wet, they had to heave the 900-pound gun up the Alligator's ramp themselves.

There seemed to be a fair amount of confusion on the beaches, but there was little sign of the enemy. Small-arms fire was only sporadic and so Bill and his crew were ordered to dig in for the night. 'No one was hit, killed, or wounded whatsoever in the area we were

in,' noted Bill. 'The units assigned to take the airfield at Yontan took
it in a matter of hours.' As dusk began to fall, the sky was lit up with
tracers fired without let-up from the vast naval armada sitting off-
shore. Shells screamed over, aeroplanes rumbled through the night
air, and the men now ashore looked up and watched a fireworks
display more spectacular than any 4 July celebration. At the end of
Day 1, the invasion was ahead of schedule.

But the attackers were to be cruelly deceived. The Japanese had
chosen not to contest the beaches, believing they would have suffered unsustainable casualties defending them against overwhelming American fire-power. As the sea lapped gently against the shore
on that warm spring evening, few could have guessed what lay in
store; for the next eighty-one days, Okinawa was to witness the
largest single land-air-sea battle of all time, a brutal campaign
whose savagery and brutality surpassed anything that had come
before in the Pacific War. At sea, naval casualties were higher than
at any point in the war, with Japan unleashing almost its entire
kamikaze effort against the joint American and British task force
around the islands. On land, the scale of killing was even worse.
Okinawa was to witness a bloodbath of barbaric savagery, where
American and Japanese regarded each other with both contempt
and hatred, and in which more than a quarter of a million people
were killed. Okinawa was to be the last, and most costly, battle of
the Second Word War.

Before I met up with Bill at his home near Charleston, South
Carolina, I spoke to him on the phone and even in that brief conversation he was unusually frank about his experiences. 'I tell you,
Jim,' he said, 'we went in with thirty-five hundred men and after
eighty-two days of combat, more than twenty-eight hundred were
gone. We had casualties of more than eighty per cent.' On Sugar
Loaf Hill, he told me, the 29th Marines lost 500 men killed in a week
of bitter and bloody battle. No Marine regiment in the history of the
Corps has ever suffered such high casualties in a single battle as the

29th Marines did on Okinawa. He also freely admitted that at the time he hated the Japanese with a vengeance. 'They were animals. They'd cut off guys' penises and stuff them in their mouths. They'd behead people, cut off arms, gouge eyes out. Put it this way,' he said, 'we didn't take many prisoners.'

When I suggested I'd like to visit him in Charleston, he assured me he would be happy to talk to me about it as much as I liked. Every third Wednesday in the month, he said, they had a 6th Marine Division Association reunion in Charleston – a small, informal lunch for members living in the area. I'd be more than welcome to come along and meet some of the other guys too. He sounded charming, good-humoured, and friendly; and I was immediately struck by the contrast between the man inviting me into his home and the young Marine he was describing from sixty years before.

When we finally met up at his home some months later, he quickly confirmed my earlier impressions. The hospitality extended by Bill and his wife was extraordinary. Both were tremendously good company – kindness itself – so that by the time Bill and I finally got round to talking about his wartime on a Wednesday morning in November, I felt I'd known both of them for years rather than just one day.

One of the interesting aspects of talking to veterans of the Second World War is hearing about their backgrounds and childhoods, and realizing that most lived perfectly normal ordinary lives before they had to head off to fight against people they knew little about in far-flung corners of the globe. Bill's childhood was refreshingly happy and carefree, and as we sat in his back porch, sun streaming through the glass roof and windows, he told me about growing up in the outer limits of New York City. In those days, he told me, Queens was quite countrified. 'There were huge potato fields and farmland galore,' he recalled. 'We had all the space we needed to play baseball and so on.' A keen sportsman, he loved baseball, basketball, football – anything with a ball. He was very keen on track and field as well. His physical fitness and the fact that he never smoked, he told me, made his life a lot easier when it came to his military training.

His parents were loving and kind and he adored them, while he also got on well with his siblings – an older brother, younger sister and much younger brother. His father ran a motor garage, and although Bill was never mechanically minded himself, he used to spend as much time as possible outdoors. He's still a fast eater, he said, stemming from when he was a boy: he'd eat as quickly as he could so he could go out and play ball with the other kids. 'I'd eat four mouthfuls,' he said, 'and I'd be out of there.' In the summer the whole family would head up to the mountains where they had a house by a lake. 'We swam like you can't imagine,' he grinned.

He knew something about the war from what he heard on the radio or saw on the newsreels when he went to the movies, but admitted that as a teenager, 'it wasn't predominant in your mind.' There were other more important things to think about: 'I was fifteen, sixteen, and still sporty and athletic, and I'd just found out what a girl was.' When he heard on the radio that the Japanese had attacked Pearl Harbor, he confessed that he'd had to get out his atlas and find out where Pearl Harbor was.

Even so, despite – or perhaps because of – this happy, sheltered, upbringing, he and a few of his buddies bunked off school and went downtown into New York City to enlist into the Navy. They queued most of the day before being told that all enlistments were being closed. Figuring it was too much hassle to bunk off school again, they decided to postpone their enrolment into the services.

In any case, Bill soon decided he wanted to be a Marine rather than join the Navy. His cousin had turned up at their house one day in his Marine uniform which impressed Bill greatly. 'He looked so neat,' said Bill. 'He had been in the 1st Marine Division on Guadalcanal and so as soon as I was out of school I went right to the Marine Corps enlistment.' Once again, he was told that enlistments were closed, but was sent home armed with a letter confirming that he had tried to volunteer for the Marines. 'So when I turned eighteen and was drafted, I had that letter.' He presented this to the Marines recruitment office, and it seemed to do the trick. Although initially told they had already accepted enough recruits for one day, he was not turned away, and after passing his medical, signed on the dotted line and was told he would soon be called up for duty. Two weeks later he was on a train heading south to Parris Island in South Carolina for boot camp and his induction into the United States Marine Corps.

His mother and father were naturally worried about him – Bill's older brother was already in the Army. 'But they were fantastically accepting,' said Bill. 'The patriotism ran so marvellously high that they realized their sons had to serve.' Nor was Bill put off when on his arrival at Parris Island other Marines yelled, 'You'll be sorry,' at the busload of recruits. Rather, he found his initial training rewarding: the parade-ground drill, stripping down and reassembling a rifle, the spit and polish, and the route marches and assault courses. 'I enjoyed that stuff,' he confessed.

After his initial training, he spent a further seven months in the US on guard duty at a naval ammunition depot before finally being transferred to Camp Lejeune, a Marine training base, prior to being shipped overseas. It was at Lejeune that Bill was assigned to a 37mm gun crew in a weapons company. 'I didn't care where they put me,' said Bill. 'I was just happy I was a Marine.'

Like so many before him, when Bill was shipped to the Pacific, it was his first time at sea. 'We had no idea where we were going,' he said. 'We were loaded on a ship with 4,000 other guys, I guess, then eventually we learnt we were heading to Saipan because the battle was still going on there.' But before they reached Saipan, the island was secured, so instead they were sent to Guadalcanal, where they would carry out further combat and training. 'There was nothing when we got there,' Bill told me. 'Not a tent up, not a road – nothing.' There were, however, plenty of remains from the fighting two years earlier. 'We found dead bodies all over the place,' said Bill. 'I was walking in a field one time and we thought they were coconuts and I looked down and I said, "Jesus, do you see what we're walking on? These are skulls."'

*   *   *

It was about this point in our conversation that Bill's friend Dick Whitaker turned up. Dick's wife had dropped him at the door, and he was going to catch a ride with Bill to the monthly 6th Marine Division Association lunch. Like Bill, he had fought throughout the Okinawa battle and had also been in the 29th Marine Regiment, although in a machinegun team in Fox Company. Dick was one of the lucky ones to survive the assault on Sugar Loaf Hill, despite getting a bullet through his hand for his trouble. Also like Bill, Dick was amusing, affable, and only too happy to talk about his experiences.

Sitting back down again, Bill began telling me about his gun crew. All were new to combat when they arrived on Okinawa, he said, but they all trusted one another and their abilities implicitly. 'There were five of us and one extra,' Bill explained. 'You all had to be adept at every role, so that if one was shot dead, the others could keep firing.' Weighing 900lbs, the 37mm had been originally designed as an anti-tank gun, but had proved ineffective in the European theatre, where it lacked the velocity to pierce armour plating. It was, however, ideal for the kind of close-range fighting experienced in the Pacific. 'I never saw a Jap tank once on Okinawa,' said Bill. 'At 500 yards the 37mm could put a round through a porthole – it was very accurate.' They would use different types of shells – mostly high explosive ('HE'), but also canister, which were full of ball-bearings.

'Were they the size of marbles or something?' Dick asked.

'No, much smaller,' said Bill. 'A little heavier than buckshot, like a small pea.' Bill then told me about his first action. The invasion force had landed roughly in the middle of the island on the west coast. From there, the Army units had headed south, while the Marines had been sent into the more mountainous north. They eventually ran into some Japanese dug in at the foot of the steep, rocky and wooded slopes of a series of hills known as Yae-dake on the Motobu Peninsula. But after taking some hits from sniper fire, the Marines spread out across the valley beneath the hills, their 37mm guns spaced out in a line. In front they also set up a number of trip flares. Sure enough, that night the flares were triggered, hissing into the night and lighting up the valley with an eerie phosphorescence. 'We could see about a hundred people advancing,' Bill recalled, 'so we asked what we should do. "Mow them down," came the reply. So we let go with the canister, and in the morning there were eighty women and children lying there and just a few Japs. The Japanese pushed the civilians out in front of them. They used them to try and get away.'

Dick said, 'It was the same with us,' and explained how the machine-gun teams would set up trip wires with telephone cable, and attach tin cans to them. 'At night,' he said, 'as soon as you heard those cans tinkle, you'd swing the gun back and forth. You couldn't afford to wait to properly identify what or who it was because otherwise you could have been dead. The next morning you'd have pigs, goats, people.'

'It was unfortunate,' Bill added, and then explained that later in the battle, in the south of the island where the Japanese became boxed in, a lot of Okinawans would take cover in the numerous caves there. 'If a baby cried, a Jap soldier would say, "Take that baby outside and don't come back with it," because they didn't want the baby to give the position away. But outside the cave the woman was exposed to artillery and mortars and she soon would be dead too. A day didn't go past when Dick and I didn't see a dead civilian, just lying there. A hundred and fifty thousand – Jesus.' *At least* that number of Okinawans were killed during the battle, more than a third of the indigenous population. It is a figure that exceeds the deaths caused by either of the atomic bombs that were to follow. As is so often the case in war, innocent civilians suffered the most. The battle brought a holocaust sweeping over Okinawa, a formerly peaceful island only absorbed into Japanese political control in 1867. Okinawa had been a beautiful island, a green and wooded place Bill likened to Connecticut. But in the south, especially, where most of the fighting took place, the landscape soon became more akin to the desolate and poisoned battlefields of the Western Front in the First World War.

Presumably, I suggested to Bill and Dick, they became hardened to seeing so much death and loss of innocent lives. 'Oh, absolutely,' said Dick. 'There's more agony that comes from reflection later, than at the moment.'

'We could be sitting there eating a C-ration can or a Hershey bar,' added Bill, 'and right there, there's a dead Jap, with an arm sticking up or a mangled leg. It didn't mean a thing. We'd become completely immune to it. You became hardened to it immediately.' To illustrate the point, Bill mentioned a time early on in the battle when the Marines were still clearing the north of the island. One night, Bill was huddled in a foxhole with a buddy of his, 'Big Ed' Graham. They too used to lay telephone wires with cans attached ahead of their positions, and suddenly he felt Big Ed's arm move and saw him aim his carbine. 'I looked down the carbine and there's a Jap crawling towards us on his hands and knees,' said Bill, 'and Big Ed shot with one hand. My buddy shot him and he dropped but he was still moaning.' Bill fired his carbine too. 'I must have fired that thing seven, eight or maybe nine times . . . Some kind of fear takes over. It was adrenalin racing.' The unfortunate Japanese soldier was still moaning, however, so Big Ed took out his pistol and shot him again. 'He said, "He won't moan now," and in the morning we saw that half this Jap's head was blown off.'

'We made no distinctions between civilians and Japanese soldiers,' continued Dick, 'because the Jap soldiers made no distinction. They demanded the Okinawan population retreated with them. They had nurses, and Korean labour – everybody retreated together. They would use those people for deception at night. They would dress up as civilians so you never knew who you were shooting at.' He paused, then said, 'You got to be killing somebody to win.'

Operations in the north of the island had been wrapped up by the third week of April 1945, and the 6th Marine Division were left to carry out mopping-up patrols and to pick up a few souvenirs of their twenty-day battle, silk kimonos being a favourite. But while operations had gone to plan in the north, the same could not be said of the fighting in the south. When the landings had not been contested, the

American commanders had wondered where all the Japanese were, and as the Army units pushed south, they soon found out. The majority of the 100,000-strong Japanese 32nd Army were dug in along a series of defensive lines that crossed the south end of the island and were linked in typical Japanese fashion by sixty miles of tunnels and carefully hidden gun and mortar positions. There were also a large number of caves in the south, ancient tombs that made effective dug-outs.

Although US Army units breached the outer Japanese lines of defence, they soon became bogged down in a highly costly battle of attrition, and so on 4 May, the 6th Marines were sent south, taking the place of the embattled and much-depleted 27th Army Division, along what had become known as the Shuri Line.

'We had actually been packing up to leave to go to Guam,' said Bill. 'Next thing we knew, the 27th Division were being pulled out of the line because they'd performed terribly and we were put there instead. They passed us on the road and we threw cans and pebbles at them.'

In command of the land campaign was General Simon Bolivar Buckner Jnr, and even during the battle, debate was raging as to why he didn't try a further landing in the south behind the Japanese positions. 'Buckner's approach sucked,' Bill told me. 'The 2nd Marine Division was sitting on Saipan, fully trained, fully equipped and ready to go, but Buckner wouldn't do it.'

Instead, the 6th Marine Division was thrown against Sugar Loaf Hill, the main western anchorage of the Shuri Line. While in Europe, and far across the Pacific in the United States, victory in the war against Germany was being celebrated by the Allied nations, on Okinawa the Marines were fighting just about the bloodiest battle of the entire war. Sugar Loaf was a tiny, insignificant landmark – three hundred yards long and no more than sixty feet high. 'You could run up it in no time at all,' Bill told me. Yet whole companies of the 22nd Marines and then the 29th – Bill's and Dick's regiment – were decimated as they repeatedly assaulted the feature.

With the Americans unable to bring their advantage in naval and air fire-power to bear on Sugar Loaf, it became a battle of guns, mortars, and small-arms – machineguns, grenades, carbines and rifles, what *Time* magazine called, 'the old-fashioned, inescapable way, one foot at a time against the kind of savage, rat-in-a-hole defence that only the Japanese can offer'.[8] The Japanese, Bill pointed out, had very good, rapid-fire machineguns. 'The bullet was smaller than ours. They'd be so rapid, a guy would get hit two, three, four times and survive. With ours, they had a slower rate of fire, but one hit would kill you.' It was, he suggested, a crucial difference, and then told me about his friend Dominic Spitale, who was shot through the temple by a Japanese machinegun bullet and lived to tell the tale. 'It went through his head and out the other side – no lasting damage. He was in hospital a year or more. Didn't know who he was then one day he said, "I know who I am! I'm Dominic Spitale and I'm a Marine!"'

The Japanese were also very skilled in the use of mortars. 'They killed a lot of Marines,' said Bill. 'If a mortar shell landed beside you, the guy was blown to bits and his body was nothing but a black hulk. His pants would go black instead of green from the scorching he took.' Bill was once ten yards away from a Marine who was blown up by a mortar. 'You look at it but you keep going,' he said. 'You don't stop because he's dead.' On the other hand, the wounded were always attended to, and extraordinary, often fatal, attempts were made to rescue them. 'You don't leave anyone behind,' said Dick, 'that's the rule.'

Adding to the misery was the rain, which fell annually on Okinawa throughout May, and usually in the form of a deluge of as much as ten inches a day. May 1945, however, was worse than usual, and combined with the massive amount of shell and mortar fire, soon turned the battlefield into a thick quagmire. 'Jeeps would sink up to the top of their wheels,' said Dick. 'They had to pull them out with tanks.'

---

8   *Time*, 21 May 1945.

'We were wet all the time,' added Bill. 'You never dried off. We landed with what we were wearing and one extra set of clothing, and if they were wet or worn out, it was tough shit. We were filthy.' They were also riddled with lice and fleas, irritants they were powerless to do anything about.

Dick then told me about the time he tried to put on new socks. They'd been relieved from the front line and had been given a helmet-full of water each with which to clean. 'I cleaned my feet and put on my last pair of socks, but slipped and fell down in the mud. Jesus, that was a bad moment.'

The rain and the close nature of the fighting meant that no fires could be lit at the front. There was no hot water for coffee, and no hot food. Bill told me he ate mainly C-rations, tins of pre-cooked food, usually bully beef. 'C-rations with an "A" at the end meant they were from Australia and were much worse than the others,' he said. 'Jesus, there were empty cans of C-ration tins with "A"s on them everywhere.'

'For about thirty days I existed on K-bars,' added Dick, 'hard chocolate bars. It was the only thing I could handle.' They shed large amounts of weight. 'I lost fifteen pounds, easy,' said Bill. 'We all had diarrhoea. We all had the shits.'

Dick nodded. 'If I laid on my back, I'd shit my pants,' he told me. 'If I laid on my stomach, I'd throw up. The only thing I could do was get out of my foxhole, walk with a tight arse to the nearest corpsman and get a shot of paregoric. It was an eighteenth-century "cure" that tasted horrible and rarely worked.'

'Loads of people shat in their pants, believe me,' added Bill, 'even if you didn't have diarrhoea.'

'Fright alone could cause you to shit or piss your pants.'

The stench that pervaded the battlefield was also overpowering. 'The whole island stank,' said Bill. 'The stench of death was all over. It stank no matter where you were. Horrible, horrible.' Bodies would be left where they had fallen. Dick had to walk over them as he attacked the hill yet again. There were also millions of flies and maggots, feeding on ever-mounting numbers of corpses strewn across the battlefield. Eating became a hazardous and difficult operation. 'When you ate, you opened a can and the flies would be all over it in seconds,' said Bill. 'You had to try and cover the can up.'

Unsurprisingly, in such conditions many soldiers went round the bend. Over 26,000 casualties were caused by battle fatigue, illness and non-battlefield injuries. One of Dick's pals went 'bonkers' after becoming isolated from the rest of the platoon. 'I knew him so well,' said Dick. 'He was a nice guy and I helped him back. He didn't say a word. He walked like an old man, bent over. He was just destroyed.'

'I've seen guys sitting there sobbing,' Bill told me. 'Others refused to go up the line.'

'The atmosphere becomes surrealistic,' said Dick. 'People start doing strange things. One guy's cutting off Jap ears and putting them on a string, another guy's picking up Jap teeth. One guy in our company – GP Lindsay – found a phonograph and cranked it up and began playing a Japanese record and singing along. Another guy, Jack McCrary, was trying to sleep and told him to knock it off, but Lindsay kept right on going.' Eventually Jack McCrary got up, marched over and without saying a word, put a bullet into the machine.

Neither Dick nor Bill suffered combat fatigue themselves, but they were certainly exhausted. 'You know what it feels like when two nights in a row you don't get good sleep?' Dick said. 'Put a hundred and one days of that back-to-back, and during that time you're sleeping in a hole every night and anything you do could get you killed, including absolutely nothing. That's what it felt like.'

We had been talking most of the morning and it was now time to go to the Association lunch. Bill drove us in to Charleston, to the Citadel, the Military College of South Carolina. A number of Marine cadet officers are schooled there and at the lunch there were not only veteran Marines but also cadets and those still on active service, many who had only recently returned from Iraq. On our table was a young, anxious-looking cadet from Connecticut. It was impossible not to be struck by how young he looked. It was boys like him that had been pitched into the carnage on Okinawa. Boys like Bill and Dick.

After the lunch, Dick had to head home – another of the members was giving him a lift – but later, back at the house, Bill told me about the day Mort Cooper was killed, a death that seemed to affect the men of the Weapons Company profoundly. Older than most, Mort was married and from Georgia. He was one of the Weapons Company truck drivers, and would bring up their ammunition, driving as close as he could to their gun positions. The gun crew would then carry the shells up to wherever their gun was dug in – and with a special kind of sack each man could carry forty-two 37mm shells at one time. One day, towards the end of the battle, Mort delivered the ammunition as normal, then backed up the truck so he could turn around – but as he did so, he drove over a mine. Bill and his gun crew were only forty-odd yards away, where their gun was positioned on the top of a hill, and they heard the explosion and turned to see the truck turning over and over and Mort's body flying into the air. They ran over and Bill reached him first. 'There wasn't a scratch on him,' said Bill. 'He was lying on his back but still moving, and I said, "Mort! Mort! You all right?" The corpsman next to me said, "He's dead, Bill. That's concussion making his body shake." We all broke down crying. It really hit us; we loved the guy. We really broke down over his loss.'

Incredibly, Bill's gun survived the entire battle. The protective apron was badly dented from shrapnel marks, but it never received a direct hit. Their technique was to fire a number of rounds then as soon as the Japanese began to get their range, Bill and his crew would clear out for half an hour or so, until the enemy mortars ceased. One time, the Japanese fired a field gun horizontally against an oncoming tank. The shell bounced off the ground and ricocheted end over end towards Bill and his crew. 'We dived into our foxholes as quick as we could and looked up just as it came over,' said Bill. 'It landed behind us and killed two Marines.'

But like the vast majority of those on Okinawa, Bill did not survive the battle unscathed. Sugar Loaf and the nearby Shuri Castle had finally been captured and the Americans were pressing south into the largest of the island's towns, the port of Naha. A reconnaissance team were going to the waterfront to reconnoitre the island in the middle of the harbour and wanted two 37mm guns to accompany them in case they ran into any Japanese. The city had been largely destroyed. It was, Bill remembered, 'a shambles'. The island in the harbour, they soon discovered, was still full of Japanese, so the Marines took cover in a blasted-out building while they directed shellfire onto the island.

'They shelled the shit out of that island,' Bill told me, but he and the two reconnaissance party were still camped out in the building the following morning when they saw Japanese troops trying to get off the island across a concrete causeway. Bill had a BAR light machinegun with him and firing from a window, let off a number of rounds. 'The adrenalin was pumping, but I should never have done it,' he admitted. 'I'd been in enough action to know better than to stand up in a window.' Suddenly, the BAR jammed, and just as he turned to try and clear the breech, he felt something smack his neck as though he had been belted with a baseball bat and a soldering iron. 'I just dropped to the floor,' he said. 'There was a lot of blood and a couple of the guys were sitting there and I'll never forget the look on their faces – they looked kind of wild and horrified.' Bullets were pinging all across the building and Bill saw a corpsman trying to reach him. 'No, stay there,' Bill told him, as he tried to pull a bandage from his own first-aid kit. 'I'm all right.' To cross the open doorway was inviting death.

Three other men were wounded, but all four were still able to walk and managed to get out the back of the building. They were then driven back to an aid station, but found themselves under attack again, this time from a US Navy fighter plane that had mistaken them for Japanese and opened fire on them. After being bandaged at the aid station, Bill was put in a truck and taken to the hospital. 'It was bad in that hospital,' Bill recalled. 'One guy had his back all torn apart. Another guy was holding his helmet. A bullet had gone through it and he had a scar right through the middle of his fore-head. He looked dazed, with glazed eyeballs.' The bullet that hit Bill had missed his spinal cord by an inch – a lucky escape indeed. Had he not moved to check his machinegun at that precise moment, he would almost certainly have been killed. Despite the pain and a stiff neck, after a couple of days, he simply walked out and went back to his gun crew.

By the end of June, the battle was, at long last, drawing to an end. 'We knew it was over,' said Bill, 'but guys were still getting killed.' Only 7,000 Japanese troops ever surrendered. The rest were killed or hid in caves. Bill was foolish enough – as he freely admits – to go into one of these caves along with three other men, hoping to get some souvenirs to sell to the 'Navy boys'. 'It was four levels deep,' he said, 'and on the second level we found some dead Japs. They'd killed themselves by lying on grenades. When we turned them over, their lungs sprung out of their chests. Oh God, it was horrible.' Further down, in the depths of the cave, they could see small flashes of light in the distance. The remaining Japanese troops down there were killing themselves. 'We then got out of there real fast!' says Bill.

On 22 June the American flag was raised on the southernmost tip of the island and ten days later, it was announced that the battle was officially over. For the exhausted survivors there was to be no imme-diate return home but with the war finally over, the remnants of the 29th Regiment were posted not to Japan, as they had been expecting, but to Tsingtao in China. There they spent six months doing very light duties and gradually recovering their strength. A few went off the rails – Bill's pal, Big Ed Graham for one – but most found that drink and a bit of time with some Chinese girls was as good a therapy as any.

They were shipped back to the USA in February 1946, and after a few days at Camp Pendleton, were sent to discharge centres and then home. Bill considered staying in the service, but his mother, relieved to finally have him back safe and sound, talked him out of it. Even so, he was, and remains to this day, extremely proud of his time in the US Marine Corps. Friends he made during those years are friends still to this day. 'One cannot describe "brotherhood" as the Marines use the word,' he wrote later. 'You have to be a Marine to know it.' Like so many others in the Second World War, it was the camaraderie, above all else, that helped Bill through those darkest of days on Okinawa.

Afterwards, he was a little wild for a while. 'I thought, "I'm twenty-one, I'm a Marine, and I want a bike,"' he told me, and so he bought an Indian Harley. 'I rode around the country, went to motorcycle races. Picked up girls. I enjoyed it. It was wind-down time. A guy needs that.' He was, he admits, a completely different person from the teenager who'd sailed off to war, but realized that he couldn't bum around on his bike for ever. Making the most of his life, he went to college. Two years later, he met and married his wife, Marie, and then settled down to get on with the rest of his life. Together they had five children, and prospered well. Bill spent most of his life working for a trucking company, before ending his career as Vice President of a large international shipping firm.

Bill was on Okinawa for all eighty-two days of the battle. Eighty-two days in a life of almost as many years, and yet it was clear from his study full of books and memorabilia, his connections to the 6th Division Association, and from the typed memoir of his wartime experiences, that the Battle of Okinawa was the defining experience in his life, one that has had a profound and lasting effect on him. And understandably so. He's even been back to Okinawa – twice – and was instrumental in helping to set up a museum to the battle on the island.

I wondered, though, whether the many terrible things he went through and witnessed in that most bitter of battles had ever come back to haunt him. 'Not now,' he told me. 'When I first got home I'd dream about combat, but it went away. My job became more important, and my family.' He has, however, always talked about his experiences, even to his parents and younger brother when he got back home. 'I've always been open about what I went through,' he told me. 'Those guys that bottle it all up are the ones who struggle later.' He was, he admits, very lucky to have survived Okinawa, but has made the most of the experience and has lived a full and happy life. Bill is one man who is at peace with the legacy of the war. Despite all that happened, there are no ghosts haunting him from the past. Fiercely proud of the part he played for his country, he nonetheless insists that he is no hero. 'The real heroes,' he noted on the sixtieth anniversary of the landings, 'died on that battlefield of hell called Okinawa.'

Acknowledgements

This book would not have been possible without the enormous help and support of the veterans themselves, who sat through hours of my questioning, and who were pestered and harassed repeatedly. They have been an inspiration and I am deeply grateful to them and to their families for giving me, freely, so much of their time. So to: Sir Ken Adam; Wing Commander Roland 'Bee' Beamont, CBE, DSO and Bar, DFC and Bar, DFC (USA), DL; Henry Bowles, Silver Star; Tom Bowles, Bronze Star and Bar; Bobby Brown; Bill Byers, DFC and Lil Byers; Captain Tubby Crawford, DSC and Bar; Warren and Frances Evans; Sir Tom Finney, CBE, OBE; Lise Graf, Légion d'Honneur, Médaille Militaire, Médaille de la Résistance, Croix de Guerre avec Palmes; Squadron Leader Jimmy James, DFM, AFC and Bar; The Right Honourable Sir George Jellicoe, 2nd Earl Jellicoe, KBE, DSO, MC, PC; Bill and Linda Laity; John and Jean Leaver; Bill and Marie Pierce; Heinz Puschmann; Gianni Rossi; Wladek and Teresa Rubnikowicz; Bill Morison; Dick Meredith and Dick Whitaker – my heartfelt thanks. I would also like to thank Tom Bowles's youngest son, Tim, who greatly helped me with pictures and also shared with me his own interviews with his father and uncle.

I am also particularly grateful to Sarah Helm for putting me in touch with Lise Graf, and to Dr Peter Liddle and Cathy Pugh of the

Second World War Experience Centre in Horsforth, Leeds, for all
their help, especially with Earl Jellicoe. I have drawn on their interviews with Earl Jellicoe – as well as my own – for my chapter on him.

I must also make special mention of the work Teresa Rubnikowicz
has done in writing her husband's memoirs. She allowed me to draw
on this extensively for my chapter about Wladek and although I have
not listed every direct quotation, I would not have been able to write
such a full account without her considerable help. Although English,
she works tirelessly for the Polish Veterans and has been instrumental in getting them greater recognition for the enormous part they
played in the war.

I do not propose to list the books and documents used in writing
this book, but I did draw on a large number and to the authors, my
grateful thanks. Enormous thanks go to Lalla Hitchings and Mark
Hitchings, who painstakingly transcribed all the interviews. Their
help was invaluable. My thanks, as ever, to my editor, Trevor Dolby,
whose friendship, encouragement and support has been enormous.
My heartfelt thanks also go to Patrick Walsh and to all at Conville &
Walsh. I would also like to thank the following: Roddy Bassett; Giles
Bourne; Lucie and Richard Dixon; Jane Bennett, Terence Caven,
Rachel Nicholson and all at HarperCollins; the photo archivists at
the Imperial War Museum; David Hindley; Guy Walters; and Julia
Whaley.

Finally, I would like to thank Ned and especially my wife Rachel,
who is always there for me and whom I am eternally grateful that I
have never had to leave in order to go off and fight in a war.

P.S.

Ideas,
interviews
& features ...

Led Down the Path of the Second World War

Sarah O'Reilly talks to James Holland

You've gone from working in the publishing industry to being a writer. Was that transition a planned one?

I never had any long-term game plan to write. I would say, however, that being in publishing broke down a myth. If you're an ordinary punter and you want to publish a book but don't know anything about how the industry works it seems impossible, but when you're working in that environment and watching hundreds of books going through the process it doesn't seem that way. In fact, I started writing because I didn't really want to be in London and I needed to find something that I could do which would enable me to live where I wanted! And though I'm almost too embarrassed to admit it now, I began by writing absolutely appalling chick-lit novels. Having said that, they did serve a purpose; it was just that having written two of them, I thought, 'Hang on, why am I writing stuff that I'm not really interested in? Why don't I write a book that really ticks all the boxes for me?' The remit I set myself was that if I picked up this book in a bookshop and read the blurb I'd just have to buy it. I decided to set my novel in the Second World War but I didn't know an awful lot about the period. So I took the research very seriously, and went off to interview a lot of Battle of Britain veterans, which I found thrilling. It was amazing to meet people who had been there, flying these planes; ordinary guys touched by one of the greatest events in history. They were like the soldiers that had taken part in Trafalgar and Waterloo – venerated by the people that came after them. Somehow, by circumstance, by misfortune almost, these men were touched; they became the few. They're very special people. So it was talking to them that I realized, 'This is what I want to do. What a great opportunity to travel around the world, interviewing people and visiting archives.' Because of course it's also thrilling to go to archives: you might read letters signed by Churchill or Roosevelt, or read a paper that Eisenhower has touched, in which case there's a tactile link; you might find top secret documents, or a diary which you can immediately see has been written by a man in a dug-out, and yet here it is, sixty years later, preserved for posterity in an archive in Johannesburg. To me that is amazing. So really, by setting my first novel against the backdrop of the Battle of Britain and swooping Spitfires, which was great fun, I was led down the path of the Second World War.

What's the most exciting thing you've discovered during your archival research?
Whilst I haven't come across anything in an archive that has made me stop and think, 'It's a national scandal that this hasn't been revealed,' it is absolutely amazing to ▶

⸺ Generally historians get the big points right. But it's the little things that might be incorrect, and what I've discovered is that because I come at a subject completely fresh, I have an advantage. ⸺

Author photograph by Emily Hohler

LIFE
at a Glance

BORN
27 June 1970

EDUCATED
Chafyn Grove School, Salisbury; King's School, Bruton, Somerset

CAREER TO DATE
Joined Random House Publicity & Marketing Department 1994; moved PR Department William Heinemann, Reed Books 1996; joined Penguin Books PR Department 1997; left to become full-time writer January 2002.

LIVES
Broad Chalke, near Salisbury, Wiltshire

FAMILY
Married to Rachel, has a son Ned and another baby on the way, plus dog and a number of chickens.

Led Down the Path of the Second World War *(continued)*

◄ discover how much historians can miss. Jimmy Jones's story is a case in point – to get to the truth of what happened there for the first time was exciting. Up until then every account was mistaken. I don't want to overstate it; generally historians get the big points right. But it's the little things that might be incorrect, and what I've discovered is that because I come at the subject completely fresh, I have an advantage. I haven't already been steered down one particular route, or already taken a particular view. What I have noticed, though less now than in the years that followed the war or even, in fact, right up until the 1980s, is that a certain approach to a subject matter is taken and then aped over and over again. For example in North Africa the view is that we should look at the battle from the ground, so no one bothers to write about what was happening in the air. To me that seems insane, because the two are inextricably linked – you can't separate them. Nonetheless it happens because the first person started writing about it in those terms, and others followed.

Reams of material have been written about the Second World War. How do you make sure that you look at it with fresh eyes?
For me, *Heroes* took a fresh approach because whilst a number of people have written oral histories that recount specific aspects of the war, or have given a general overview of it by taking little chunks and quotations from diaries, I wanted to keep my

account more focused: I wanted a tighter cross-section of people from all the different services and countries involved, and from all the people who'd fought in its different theatres. I wanted to give a snapshot, if you like. Secondly, although everyone's experience of war is different and highly personal, I would say that there are certain themes that are universal: the loss of friends, the horrors of what you're seeing, the fear of being in battle for the first time, your attitude to the enemy, et cetera, and these are themes that you can put to a full body of people, which speak for the millions involved. So that was the idea behind the book; to focus on the individual.

What really interests me is the experience of war. We live in a time of comparative peace. We're certainly not being called up and expected to leave our families to fight for years on end. The point is that most of the men and women who were called up were just ordinary people who would not have been in the armed forces were it not for a global war. When I was talking to them, I would find myself thinking about how when I was eighteen I was pretty immature and feckless, off at university getting drunk and having a good time. The idea that I might have been even a lowly infantryman seemed absolutely ridiculous. Impossible to imagine.

Many of the people you interview for your research have harrowing memories of the war which they might find difficult to ▶

> ❝ I wanted a cross-section of people from all the different services and countries involved, and from all the people who'd fought in its different theatres. I wanted to give a snapshot, if you like. ❞

Led Down the Path of the Second World War *(continued)*

◄ **talk about. How do you ensure that you gain their confidence?**
I don't go with a list of prepared questions. I never do any preparation at all, really, apart from going with a basic knowledge of the subject matter. For the interviewees, I think it's easier to confess all more openly to a total stranger than it is to a member of the family, and I always do the interviews face to face because people like to see the cut of your jib, as it were, and have eye contact. I start by talking about their childhood memories of growing up, sports, friends, first girlfriends and hobbies, which generally puts them at ease. Then I go through it chronologically. We talk about training and how they joined up, and then move on to what they felt when they were put on that troopship, for example, and so on.

I'm interested in the idea that it's easier for veterans to speak to strangers about their experiences than to members of their own family. Did you have grandparents who fought in the Second World War, and if so, did you ever speak to them about their experiences, or do you perhaps regret not doing so?
Actually I didn't, but that was because all my grandparents died before I was born, with the exception of my grandmother. My grandfather on my mother's side was old enough to escape the Second World War, though he fought in the First, at Passchendaele, where he was gassed, and survived. Apparently he did talk about it,

6 The ideal person to interview is someone whose memory is very good, who wrote letters, kept a diary or wrote a memoir after the war. They're the star players. 9

very occasionally, to my uncle rather than my mother, and when he was dying he started talking in his semi-conscious state about the war, telling his men to get down. In his delirium he was obviously back in the trenches. I'd have loved to talk to him about that period but unfortunately I never got the chance.

Many of your veterans could use the diaries they'd kept during the war to recall the detail of their experiences. Do you worry that in the future historians won't have the same amount of written source material to work from when covering, say, the war in Iraq or Afghanistan?
It depends. There are depositories of emails now, and there are film recordings and video diaries. Even so, I do think people keep written diaries when they're at war, even today, because they know they're taking part in something pretty special. Plus they have tons of time on their hands. Even if you're in the front line fighting the Taliban in Afghanistan you've got hours in the day when you're doing nothing but manning your machinegun or sitting in a sangar waiting for an attack. That is precisely why we have so many diaries from the Second World War, even though people weren't, in theory, allowed to keep them. For me the ideal person to interview is someone whose memory is very good, who wrote letters, kept a diary or wrote a memoir after the war, if only purely for their own family. They're the star players. ▶

A WRITING LIFE

When do you write?
All day, pretty much. I usually get to my office at about 8 a.m. and although I go for walks and get up and about throughout the day, I don't usually stop until some time between 6 p.m. and 7 p.m. Having said that, there's a lot of research so that takes me away quite a lot.

Where do you write?
In my office – which is attached to the house but can only be reached from the outside.

Why do you write?
Because it's enormously interesting and rewarding, and because it allows me to live in the country and see lots of my family.

Pen or computer?
Computer.

Silence or music?
Silence.

How do you start a book?
With a lot of research.

And finish?
I print the whole thing off, then go through it with a red pen and type up the changes. ▶

◄ Do you have any writing rituals or superstitions?
Not rituals but definitely routines.

Which living writer do you most admire?
My brother, Tom.

Which book do you wish you had written?
Brideshead Revisited.

What or who inspires you?
The people I write about – those who lived through the Second World War.

If you weren't a writer what job would you do?
It's something I worry about constantly…

What's your guilty reading pleasure or favourite trashy read?
They're far from trashy, but I love the Sharpe novels and anything by Bernard Cornwell.

Led Down the Path of the Second World War *(continued)*

◄ What has been your most memorable interview?
There have been some pretty harrowing ones, like an interview I did with an Italian civilian who had survived a massacre. But one of my best was with a man called Franz Maassen. He was an NCO, one of those incredibly tough sergeant figures. NCOs are the backbone of the army and he'd learnt every trick in the book: what he hadn't seen was not worth knowing. He'd been in Russia, twice, and in Italy, living through the most astonishing events. He'd been wounded three times and was clearly an incredibly brave, incredibly canny, fascinating man. He was the son of a baker from Düsseldorf – I think it's very interesting to hear from the men on the other side because you realize they're just like anyone else – and after the war he returned there to take over the family business. I also remember that interview because it was conducted just a few months after his wife had died. He had obviously adored her all his life, and he kept apologizing because he hadn't made us any cakes or tea – which of course he thought we would like, being English. Instead he'd gone out to a bakery and bought some, his own bakery having closed down years before. There were hundreds of cream cakes, and he was terribly concerned that we should eat them all.

You write fiction and non-fiction. Do they impact upon each other?
One of the things that writing fiction does is

help me concentrate on narrative drive, which gives my historical factual writing a bit of a lift, and conversely the knowledge I've acquired from writing history books helps with the novels. So yes, one helps the other. There is a kind of snobbery in the history world that you can't possibly be a 'serious' writer and write novels as well. Whilst I can understand that opinion, I've simply chosen to ignore it.

You must have spoken to hundreds of veterans in the course of your research – how do you track them all down?
Well some of them, like Jimmy James, I just found wandering around an airfield. I remember that we were chatting when he revealed that he was the pilot of General Gott's plane. Later we met up for a pub lunch and a discussion, and we were there until closing time. Bill Byers was another chance encounter: during the war there had been a bomber base in north Yorkshire, and a friend of mine was going to put up a plaque to honour the Canadians who had served there, which Bill had come over for. We got chatting and it so happened he'd been an identical twin. Others, like Jellicoe, I approached because I read that he'd been in the SAS and the desert. He was different from most people in that he thoroughly enjoyed the war from start to finish. He was atypical which is why I wanted to include him: a sort of stalwart, imperial Englishman that is caricatured, but who, in certain cases, actually exists. The war affected people in ▶

6 There is a kind of snobbery in the history world that you can't possibly be a "serious" writer and write novels as well. 9

Led Down the Path of the Second World War *(continued)*

◄ different ways. Some coped, others carried it around for years suffering nightmares and post-traumatic stress. But I think in the last ten to fifteen years there's been the growing realization that they are a passing generation. Many simply want to get their experiences off their chests before it's too late. ■

The Good German

By James Holland

IT WAS A PARTICULARLY cold February in
Germany. The air was sharp, and piles of
snow and compacted ice edged the road,
while a monochrome wash of white fields
and dark, skeletal woods shrouded the
countryside. All along the autobahn from
Berlin the landscape hardly changed at all,
but then, south of Leipzig, as I finally left the
motorway behind and wound my way
through the Thüringen forest, a different
countryside emerged – one of fairytale
woods, old-world houses and villages
seemingly less touched by the modern world.

I was in what, just fifteen years before,
had been part of Communist East Germany,
and the quiet little town of Ludwigsstadt,
although pretty enough, still seemed grey
and impoverished, as though time had
somehow stood still. The town had been
thriving a hundred years before, when it had
been the centre of the local slate trade. Most
of the male inhabitants worked in either the
nearby quarries or the factories in the town;
indeed, the man I had come to see had once
owned one of three factories there. In the
heyday of the business, before the First
World War, the Büchner family had been the
town's biggest employer.

Friedrich Büchner still lived in the family
home, a large, square wooden house that
stood in an imposing position overlooking
the main street that ran through the town
below. He had been born there eighty years
before and had, except for a few brief years
during and after the war, lived there all his ▶

11

The Good German *(continued)*

◄ life. Now just he and his wife remained; his children had long since grown up and flown the nest. Nor were they likely to ever come back. The quarries were empty and the factories closed. The industry that had brought prosperity to the town had died.

I was there because Herr Büchner had responded to an advert I had placed in a magazine for German veterans of the war. I was hoping to speak to people who had been involved in the Italian campaign for a book I was working on, and he was the first of a number of interviews I was conducting that week. From the outset, he was charming and courteous, and ushered me and my friend Sarah, my translator, into his living room and brought us coffee. However, it was clear that he was a little apprehensive; after all, we were complete strangers, and English too.

I began by asking him about his childhood. This brought a smile to his face. He had been too young to know about the hard times of the 1920s and instead remembered the contented and prosperous days of the thirties, when the town – and his father's business – had been thriving. The factory had specialized in manufacturing slates for schools – miniature blackboards for the children to write on. His childhood had been happy, he told me, very happy. He had plenty of friends, a younger brother, and parents who loved him. In Ludwigsstadt they had lived a sheltered life, largely cut off from the rest of the world.

Like nearly all teenagers during that time, he had joined the Hitler Youth, but had enjoyed it well enough. The camaraderie was good and the outdoor pursuits – hiking, camping, making things, and so on – were fun and interesting. But he knew little about what was going on. 'I was thirteen when the war began,' he explained. 'I didn't really know very much about it.'

Later, the war began to impact on his life more directly, as it did on every man, woman and child in Germany. There was less of everything: less food, less petrol, fewer clothes; and fewer men, as the war claimed them for duty. There was no more slate industry. The Büchner family business turned over to manufacturing wooden ammunition boxes. 'My father aged a lot,' Friedrich admitted. He himself would help his father whenever he could – at weekends and in school holidays.

So when did you join the Army? I asked. Were you called up? Friedrich shook his head, then confessed that he had volunteered when still only seventeen – not because he was itching to join the fight, but because he knew that if he volunteered he had a better chance of becoming an officer and was more likely to have some choice over which unit he eventually joined. Sure enough, after completing his basic training, he was sidelined to become an officer and then sent off to become an instructor – in part because they were so short of instructors by that time, but also because it was considered good experience for aspiring officers.

It was at this point that his wife appeared and told us lunch was ready – something I had not been expecting – and so we moved into the dining room and sat down to eat ▶

❝ It was a scene of utter carnage – burning vehicles and houses, dead men, slaughtered horses. ❞

The Good German *(continued)*

◄ a meal that had clearly been prepared with
great care. Afterwards, Friedrich suggested
we continue the interview upstairs, in his
study at the top of the house. I sensed that it
was only now, after several hours of talking
to us, and having decided we could be
trusted, that he felt comfortable about
leading us into this inner sanctum. The
room was full of books about the war, small
mementoes and objects of militaria.

We began talking about Italy. He had
been a gunner, an aspirant officer in charge
of a battery of anti-tank guns with the 98th
Infantry Division. When he arrived at the
front in March 1945, the division was
positioned along the River Senio, dug in and
waiting for the launch of the Allied spring
offensive that they knew would soon come.

His wife arrived with coffee, and I noticed
that as he then poured out the drink, his
hands had started to shake. As he passed us a
cup, the china rattled against the saucer. He
then began to tell us about those final
battles: the overwhelming Allied Air Forces,
the bombs and shells that rained down upon
them; the ignominious retreat to the River
Po. There, they had ditched their guns and
had been ordered to shoot their horses and
mules. Tears began to stream down his
cheeks as he confessed they had been unable
to carry out the order and so had instead let
the animals loose. Thousands of men had
drowned trying to swim across this wide
river, their screams carrying across the water.
It was a scene of utter carnage – burning
vehicles and houses, dead men, slaughtered
horses. Friedrich escaped by managing to get

14

on one of the ferries making the crossing. His voice was catching.

'Don't feel you have to tell me this,' I told him. 'Not if it's too painful.'

'No, no, I want to,' he replied, then apologized for his tears. The story, inevitably, grew worse. Eventually, in the foothills of the Alps, they were captured by Italian partisans, and taken to a mountain hut where there were a number of other captured troops. Among them were three Russians who had been fighting for the Germans. These were singled out and the Italians had shot them in turn. But they made a hash of the executions and failed to kill them cleanly, so the mortally wounded men had screamed out in pain and fear.

At this point, Friedrich broke down again. It had been his nineteenth birthday, and also the day they found out that Hitler had killed himself. 'These Russians – their screams,' he said. 'It was terrible.' Again, I told him that he did not need to tell me this if it was too difficult, but again, he insisted he wanted to. Two days later, he said, the war in Italy was over, and he became a prisoner of war. When he eventually returned home, in March 1947, his father was ill and worn out and so Friedrich took over the running of the family business. 'The war,' said Friedrich, 'it took its toll. It killed him really.'

He then made the most startling comment of all. He had never, he confessed, told anyone about his war experiences before. I then realized how different it must be for German veterans – after all, they were the losers of the war, tarnished by the evil ▶

❝ I realized how different it must be for German veterans – they were the losers of the war, tarnished by the evil of Nazism and the horrors of the Holocaust. There were no annual parades with banners flying for Friedrich and his fellows. ❞

The Good German *(continued)*

◄ of Nazism and the horrors of the Holocaust. There were no annual parades with banners flying for Friedrich and his fellows; no television documentaries, no films, no books exalting their bravery. Yet in so many respects, Friedrich's story was very similar to those of men I had interviewed on the Allied side – the childhood, the motivations, the fears, the sense of camaraderie he had experienced. He, like so many of that generation, had had his youth ripped away from him, yet for sixty years those experiences had been bottled away, never far from his thoughts, but secret and undisclosed all the same. Talking about it at long last on that cold February day had clearly been cathartic for him, however painful.

Friedrich had once been Britain's enemy, but he had also been a young man very much like our own young men – boys who had gone off to war not because they had wanted to, but because they had had to. And his experiences and his suffering were worthy of both respect and understanding. ■

Have You Read?
Other books by James Holland

NON-FICTION

Fortress Malta: An Island Under Siege
In March and April 1942, more explosives
were dropped on the tiny Mediterranean
island of Malta – an area smaller than the
Isle of Wight – than on the whole of Britain
during the first year of the Blitz. At the
outbreak of war it had become one of the
most strategically important places in the
world: from there, the Allies could attack
Axis supply lines to North Africa, and
without it, Rommel would be able to march
unchecked into Egypt, Suez and the Middle
East. The island had, in the words of
Winston Churchill, to be held 'at all costs'.

Fortress Malta follows the story through
the eyes of those who were there: submariner
Tubby Crawford – who served on the most
successful Allied submarine of the Second
World War; cabaret dancer turned RAF
plotter Christina Ratcliffe; and her lover, the
brilliant and irrepressible reconnaissance
pilot, Adrian Warburton. Their stories and
others provide extraordinary first-hand
accounts of heroism, resilience and loss,
highlighting one of the most remarkable
stories of World War II.

Together We Stand
By June 1942, Britain had reached her lowest
ebb. Her military command was in tatters,
her armies beaten, and in the Middle East it
seemed all might be lost. Her new ally,
America, had only fledgling armed forces ▶

Have You Read? *(continued)*

◀ and was severely under-trained. Yet it was
this alliance of the weary combatant and
naïve newcomer, coming together for the
first time in North Africa, that would
eventually bring about the defeat of Nazi
Germany.

In this new appraisal, James Holland
interweaves the personal stories of the men
and women who made up these polyglot
Allied forces: British and American, Nepalese
and Punjabi, South African and Australian,
Maori and Zulu, from all ranks and all
services. From the heat and dust of the
Western Desert to the mud and mountains
of northern Tunisia, this book charts the
extraordinary first days of an Alliance that
changed the course of history.

FICTION

The Burning Blue
Joss is a fighter pilot with more than his
share of problems on the ground. It's only
when he's up in the air that he can escape
the complexities of his life, and the shameful
secret about his origins. But when he falls in
love with Stella, the twin of an old friend,
Guy Liddell, it threatens an already faltering
bond between the two men, with tragic
consequences. As Joss continues to fly amid
the sand and heat of North Africa, his hopes
and dreams are seemingly shattered for
good.

'Holland has joined the few who can bring
history to life'   *Guardian*

A Pair of Silver Wings
At the school where Edward Enderby taught
for over forty years, there were few who
knew he'd once been a successful fighter
pilot during the war. It was not something
he ever talked about, not even to his family.
But fifty years on, he is alone, a widower,
with a strained relationship with his only
son, and a career behind him that has
brought him respect but little affection. In
1995, Britain is celebrating the anniversary
of the end of the war, and Edward finds
himself forced to confront the tragedy he
suffered during those years. Embarking on a
journey of self-discovery and personal
redemption, he travels from England to
Malta and then to Italy, and in doing so
comes face to face with the idealistic young
man he once was, and the devastated and
traumatized 23-year-old he was to become.
A Pair of Silver Wings is a story of friendship,
love and the terrible legacy of war, exploring
universal themes of grief and redemption,
and one man's quest to heal the scars of the
past.

'A remarkable story ... a loving enthusiastic
account'   *Daily Telegraph*

If You Loved This,
You Might Like...

The Imperial War Museum, Lambeth Road, London, SE1 6HZ Founded in 1917 to record the story of the Great War, the Imperial War Museum is now the national museum of twentieth-century conflict, covering all aspects of modern warfare up to the present day. With a remit that includes the individual's experience of war, whether Allied or enemy, service or civilian, military or political, the museum's collection is fascinating – and enormous. Its artefacts include over 15,000 paintings, drawings and sculptures; 30,000 posters; objects ranging from aircraft, armoured fighting vehicles and naval vessels to uniforms, badges, personal equipment, medals and decorations; 120 million feet of cine film and over 6,500 hours of video tape; 6 million photographs and photographic negatives and transparencies, and some 32,000 recorded hours of historical sound recordings.

Forgotten Voices of the Second World War
Max Arthur
With testimony gathered from the sound archive of the Imperial War Museum, Max Arthur's *Forgotten Voices* is a compelling oral history of the Second World War. Containing interviews with soldiers, sailors, airmen and civilians from Britain, the Commonwealth and Germany, plus first-hand accounts from British and US troops that fought the Japanese in the Far East, this is a unique and unforgettable testimony to one of the world's most dreadful conflicts, in the words of those who experienced it.

'The words of the soldiers are as fresh as if they were written yesterday... extraordinary'
Mail on Sunday

The People's War: Britain 1939–45
Angus Calder
Drawing on the Mass Observation archive at Sussex University, Calder's book describes the day-to-day lives of ordinary Britons in wartime, and uses the diaries and memoirs of soldiers from every theatre of war and from every nation involved in the conflict to give an enthralling and panoramic view of a world turned upside down.

'A tour de force of historical reconstruction'
Sunday Times

The Voice of War: The Second World War Told By Those Who Fought It
James Owen (ed.) and Guy Walters (ed.)
Season by season, *The Voice of War* charts the course of the war using the diaries, letters and memoirs of those who played leading roles in the conflict, and the famous men and women caught up in it, including Joseph Goebbels, Benito Mussolini, Christabel Bielenberg, Noël Coward, Robert Capa, Airey Neave, George Patton, Hermione Ranfurly, Arthur Koestler, James Lees-Milne, Martha Gellhorn, Sophia Loren and Primo Levi.

'An extraordinary anthology of first-hand accounts'   *Sunday Times*

....

Berlin: The Downfall 1945
Antony Beevor
Antony Beevor's gripping account of the bloody *Götterdämmerung* that brought the Second World War in Europe to an end combines sweeping historical narrative with a sense of the experiences of ordinary people caught in this nightmarish historical moment. He also gives an unforgettable portrait of the last, insane days of Hitler and his entourage in the bunker.

'Fascinating, extraordinary, gripping'
                    JEREMY PAXMAN ▶

Cabinet War Rooms, Clive Steps, King Charles St, London SW1A 2AQ
Shortly after becoming Prime Minister in May 1940, Winston Churchill visited the Cabinet War Rooms to see what preparations had been made to allow him and his Cabinet to continue working throughout the expected air raids on London. It was there, in the underground Cabinet Room, that he announced, 'This is the room from which I will direct the war.' In 1984 the Rooms were opened to the public for the first time. Later an adjoining Churchill Museum was added to explore both the private and the public life of the man who led Britain through the Second World War.

Imperial War Museum, Duxford, Cambridgeshire, England, CB22 4QR
During WWII Duxford was one of the most important air bases in Britain, and planes flying from here played a major role in the Battle of Britain. Today it houses the largest collection of ▶

◄ historic aircraft in Europe, ranging from WWI vintage biplanes to Spitfires, Concorde and Gulf War jets.

The Second World War Experience Centre, 5 Feast Field (off Town St), Horsforth, Leeds LS18 4TJ
Although you'll have to make an appointment if you wish to visit, the Second World War Experience Centre is an invaluable source of information on the various campaigns fought during the Second World War and the dates on which they took place, as well as biographies of the key individuals involved in the conflict, supported by photographic images.

SURF

http://www.secondworld warforum.com
James Holland's excellent Second World War Forum contains a treasure-trove of material. You can browse transcripts of his numerous interviews with veterans, check his blog for the latest information on what he's up to, and dip into his recommended reads.

If You Loved This... *(continued)*

◄ *Warriors: Extraordinary Tales from the Battlefield*
Max Hastings
An exhilarating account of the lives of sixteen 'warriors' from the last three centuries that includes a compelling portrait of Squadron Leader Guy Gibson, the 'dam buster' whose heroism in the skies of World War II earned him the nation's admiration but few friends. While celebrating feats of outstanding valour, Hastings explores our ever-adapting notions of heroism and casts a beady eye over why it is that so often the most successful warriors rarely make the grade as leaders of men.

'A damn good war story is always worth repeating, and few tell them better than Hastings'
                              Mail on Sunday